Advance Praise for *Agency*

"*Agency* is a book that people on both the left and the right should read. It is a guidebook for those who want to help lift up lower-income communities and struggling individuals. It is common sense reimagined."
—**Ayaan Hirsi Ali**, research fellow at the Hoover Institution and founder of the AHA Foundation

"This book is a gift to all those in the rising generation who are baffled by the ominous pessimism that our culture now projects at them from every direction and find themselves unable to envision a future that speaks to their highs longings. They deserve better from us. And Rowe offers them better by helping them see where a morally meaningful sense of direction might be found."
—**Yuval Levin**, director of social, cultural, and constitutional studies at the American Enterprise Institute and editor in chief of *National Affairs*

"This hope-filled, wise and spiritually enlightening book should be read—must be read—by every parent, teacher, legislator and community activist in America. With passion, clarity of thought and an abiding faith in the unlimited possibilities of this great nation, accomplished educator and entrepreneur Ian Rowe provides a road map for all of our children to realize their full human potential."
—**Glenn Loury**, Merton P. Stoltz Professor of the Social Sciences and professor of economics, Brown University

"What a strange world we live in, where the party of libertarians declares we are radically free, and the party of fate—the party that preaches the dogma of 'systemic racism'—declares that only the state can save us. Ian Rowe tells us there is a third, realistic alternative: we flourish and discover true liberty only in and through our mediating institutions, most notably, our families. In this fine-grained and deeply personal account, we discover a way forward for our entire country."

—**Joshua Mitchell**, professor of government and political theory, Georgetown University

"Ian Rowe offers a serious look at how we're failing our kids— and how we can course correct. This isn't hyped-up flimflam— Ian's impressive time in education, politics, media, and philanthropy help him offer a sober analysis of the challenges our kids face. Ian's not grumbling about kids or sitting on the sidelines—he puts forward a thought-provoking game plan that draws deeply from the American Idea. He's got the data, the stories, and the experience to make his argument well worth your time, regardless of your political leanings. We can't ignore these problems—our kids are counting on us."

—**Ben Sasse**, United States senator from Nebraska

"In *Agency*, Ian Rowe provides a thoughtful and nuanced analysis of the challenges facing struggling communities and offers a practical, data-driven framework to empower even those from the most difficult circumstances to overcome barriers and succeed. Rowe's FREE framework centers on the importance of faith, family, education, and personal responsibility, and he recognizes that a vibrant civil society with strong local institutions is a key ingredient for human flourishing. Rowe's message is a compassionate, inspiring, and refreshing alternative to the divisive, disempowering rhetoric we so often hear today."

—**Elise Westhoff**, president and CEO, Philanthropy Roundtable

AGENCY

Agency

THE FOUR POINT PLAN (F.R.E.E.)
for CHILDREN *to* OVERCOME *the*
VICTIMHOOD NARRATIVE
and DISCOVER THEIR PATHWAY
to POWER

Ian V. Rowe

TEMPLETON PRESS

TEMPLETON PRESS
300 Conshohocken State Road, Suite 500
West Conshohocken, PA 19428
www.templetonpress.org

Set in Miller Display and Warnock Pro by Westchester Publishing Services

This paper meets the requirements of ANSI/NISO Z39.48-1992
(Permanence of Paper).

ISBN: 978-1-59947-583-7 (cloth)
ISBN: 978-1-59947-584-4 (ebook)

Library of Congress Control Number: 2022931534

A catalogue record for this book is available from the Library of Congress.

Printed in the United States of America.

22 23 24 25 26   10 9 8 7 6 5 4 3 2 1

To my parents,
Eula and Vincent,
and my family,
Sylvia,
Camille, and Oscar

INVICTUS

Out of the night that covers me,
Black as the pit from pole to pole,
I thank whatever gods may be
For my unconquerable soul.

In the fell clutch of circumstance
I have not winced nor cried aloud.
Under the bludgeonings of chance
My head is bloody, but unbowed.

Beyond this place of wrath and tears
Looms but the Horror of the shade,
And yet the menace of the years
Finds and shall find me unafraid.

It matters not how strait the gate,
How charged with punishments the scroll,
I am the master of my fate,
I am the captain of my soul.

—William Earnest Henley

CONTENTS

PART 3 How FREE Can Usher in a New "Age of Agency"
for Young Americans

FOREWORD

Yuval Levin

If Ian Rowe did not exist, America would have to invent him. As the book before you demonstrates, and as Rowe's extraordinary career has shown, he is moved by an unwavering commitment to put a flourishing life within the reach of young Americans who start out lacking the opportunities they deserve. That dogged commitment somehow renders Rowe immune to both the rigid orthodoxies and the ephemeral fads that so often disfigure our social-policy debates. It lets him cut through the culture-war rhetoric that can easily make our problems seem insoluble and chart a path forward that takes seriously the insights of assorted partisans who think they have nothing in common.

That may be what stands out most about this book. It has been written in a moment when every old consensus around the challenge of mobility appears to have fractured and our debates break down along a stark disagreement about how change can happen. But it persuasively demonstrates that we have more than just those two familiar and simplistic options before us.

Some people, mostly on the right, argue that only personal change can make a change of circumstances possible, which means that young Americans who start out at the economic bottom can rise only by virtue of their own effort, discipline, and energy. Young Americans looking to improve their prospects need somehow to hold themselves apart from the breakdown that too often surrounds them and to act on their own to make the sorts of decisions that can help them achieve an ordered and successful life.

Other people, mostly on the left, suggest that social change must always precede personal change, so that no one can really transform his or her own life. Instead, all we can do is wait for others to effect broad systemic change or seek somehow to make ourselves part of such change through political action.

Each side of this dispute views the other as unrealistic and cynical. And indeed, each side's view has increasingly come to be mostly a reaction to the other rather than a response to the real circumstances of young Americans who need a better shot at success. But because Rowe is focused on those young people and not on one side or the other of our bifurcated politics, he can see that both are partially right but also that being partially right is not enough. He offers another path that takes the best of both.

"Pure self-reliance is a myth," he tells us. But systemic change without personal change is hollow and dispiriting, and ultimately cannot work. It's true that people need to act on their own behalf. But "individuals do not develop such dogged self-determination until someone or some institution *first* helps them grasp that their effort is integral to achieving that goal. It is this core conviction that allows them to endure as they encounter barriers along the way. This precondition is agency."

In other words, there is a vast space between the individual alone and the society as a whole. That space is where we actually live our lives—and it is where positive change can happen. It is a space filled with institutions—from the family to the school, church, work, civic associations, charitable groups, the private economy, and the sphere of local political action. And those institutions need to be filled with people who want to help form young Americans for success in life.

The work of these institutions can give those young Americans a sense that their fate is in their own hands and yet that they are not alone. We might call that recognition a sense of agency. And as Rowe so powerfully shows, agency is not a synonym for independence or for energy. It is more than that. "Just as velocity is not just speed but rather speed and direction, agency is more than free will: it is free will guided by a moral sense of right and wrong," he writes.

That sense, developed through the combination of family, religion, education, and entrepreneurship—the FREE framework that Rowe introduces in this book—is the missing ingredient in the lives of countless Americans, and not just those enduring economic hardship.

A shortage of agency is a defining fact of contemporary American life. It afflicts the young in particular, as Rowe puts it, "from kids in low-income communities to those in the wealthiest of neighborhoods who nevertheless find themselves leading lonely, rudderless lives." In that sense, this book almost sells itself short. It is about more than a path to opportunity, and it is a gift to more than just young Americans afflicted by narratives of victimhood and paralysis.

This book is a gift to all those in the rising generation who are baffled by the ominous pessimism that our culture now projects at them from every direction and find themselves unable to envision a future that speaks to their highest longings. They deserve better from us. And Rowe offers them better by helping them see where a morally meaningful sense of direction might be found.

In the end, Rowe's framework is a call for commitment. People don't thrive by getting what they want. We thrive by being what others need. Only by living our lives embedded in commitments to family, religion, schooling, work, community, and country can we really become what we are capable of being. Narratives of narcissism and narratives of victimhood both seek to distract us from the possibility of such flourishing and persuade us that there is nothing we can do. A recovery of agency would show us that there is not only something we can do but something we *should* do, and which is worth throwing ourselves into.

This exceptional book charts the path to that recovery. And our guide, Ian Rowe, knows that it is possible to travel that path, because he has seen it in his own life and has made it possible for countless children through his work.

Your sense of what's possible will be changed by the book you've picked up. And when you've read it, you'll want to make sure that others do too.

AGENCY

INTRODUCTION

Man does not simply exist but always decides what his existence will be, what he will become the next moment. By the same token, every human being has the freedom to change at any instant.

—Victor Frankl

It was a late September night in 2015, and my wife, Sylvia, and I were at the Richard Rodgers Theatre in New York City. The smash hit *Hamilton* was weeks into a Broadway run that continues to the time of this writing. That night's performance was a fundraiser for the tenth anniversary of Public Prep, a network of public charter elementary and middle schools primarily located in the South Bronx.

As Public Prep's CEO at the time, I was, of course, filled with gratitude that the *Hamilton* family was helping to raise funds for our schools—schools for largely low-income and black or Hispanic kids who live a short subway ride but a world away from Manhattan's bright lights. But that evening's *Hamilton* performance hit home for me in other ways. Like Alexander Hamilton, who is celebrated in the musical, my parents, Vincent and Eula, had come to America from the Caribbean (Jamaica) to start a new life and seize the opportunities their new land offered. Like Alexander

Hamilton, they had succeeded beyond their wildest dreams and built a great life—an American life—for me and my brother. We, the sons of two black Jamaican immigrants, are Alexander Hamilton's children—America's children—no less than Vincent and Eula's.

And here's the other realization that washed over me that September night: the musical may celebrate the incandescent Alexander Hamilton, but it also celebrates our nation, despite all its sometimes-grotesque imperfections—this "unfinished symphony"—which allowed a young émigré from the Caribbean to rise. Individual drive and determination to make a difference in your life ("I am not throwin' away my shot") only works in "a place where even orphan immigrants can leave their fingerprints and rise up." More precisely, it only works in a place where everyone, including orphaned immigrants, *believes* they "can leave their fingerprints and rise up." Take away that belief and you take away agency. If you tell young people the system is irremediably rigged against them—pound it into them that they are victims of "systemic racism" or large economic forces and that they have no opportunity and there is nothing they can do to make a difference—then do not be surprised if they act, or fail to act, accordingly. That is not what we did at Public Prep. And that is not what we will do at Vertex Partnership Academies, the new network of public charter high schools I am currently developing to open in the Bronx in 2022.

I think the seeds of the book you have before you were planted that night. What is agency? I'll flesh out the concept in Chapter 1, but my short definition is that it is the force of your free will guided by moral discernment. It is the force that closes the delta between "isness" and "oughtness" in our lives—what *is* and what *ought to be*. It is the conviction that we are active players in our own story and, as Martin Luther King, Jr., once said, not simply "flotsam and jetsam in the river of life."[1] Agency is learning to see ourselves not as victims of our circumstance, but rather as architects of our own better futures, and to do so even in the face of real obstacles.

Agency is a concept, a character force, a mind-set, and an outlook that is threatened in our young people today. In October 2021, the Archbridge Institute think tank released an eye-catching report on existential agency showing that only 39 percent of American adults under age twenty-five think they have the power to live a meaningful life.[2] Compare this to the 63 percent of all American adults who think so. This is despite the fact that young people are traditionally more idealistic and energetic than their elders and have their whole life ahead of them. This is also despite the fact that social, scientific, and technological progress has given the rising generation greater access to knowledge and more opportunities. Moreover, Archbridge Institute's senior research fellow Clay Routledge, who authored the study, points out that these findings align with other research showing that young adults are increasingly anxious and afraid.

Indeed, a global UNICEF study of twenty-one countries released in November 2021 showed that 56 percent of Americans aged fifteen to twenty-four said that children today would be worse off economically than their parents.[3] That prediction by young Americans was a worse forecast than all but five of the remaining countries studied. According to Routledge, "This [pessimism] is a barrier to agency and ultimately human progress because people are less inclined to take risks, explore unfamiliar ideas, be tolerant of those who are different, and have the confidence and optimistic mind-set needed to take on big challenges when they are anxious and afraid."[4]

In Chapter 2, I describe two visions that currently compete for dominance. One, which is by far the more popular (especially in educational circles), is the "blame-the-system" mind-set: impediments to young people achieving the American Dream are primarily, if not solely, due to insurmountable institutional and systemic barriers—racism, classism, and the like. The other is the "blame-the-victim" mind-set: roadblocks to realizing the American Dream are primarily, if not solely, due to an individual's bad choices or lack of effort.

Both visions are wrong, each in their own way.

I will make the case that a "blame-the-system" perspective not only fails to stand up to analytical scrutiny but also harms and disempowers the kids who most need our help—like the students in my charter schools. It robs them of agency. On the other hand, a "blame-the-victim" perspective that simply calls on individuals to make better choices or work harder is insufficient, as it does not acknowledge the necessity of local, character-forming institutions to help young people build agency.

Yes, Horatio Alger rags-to-riches stories make for compelling reading.[5] Exceptional individuals from humble beginnings who, by pluck and determination, pull themselves up by their bootstraps and achieve their dreams—what is not to like about these uniquely American stories? And there are so many of them. But pure self-reliance is a myth. Individuals do not develop such dogged self-determination until someone or some institution *first* helps them grasp that their effort is integral to achieving that goal. It is this core conviction that allows them to endure as they encounter barriers along the way. This precondition is agency.

Simply put, behavior follows belief. As necessity is the mother of invention, so agency gives rise to determination. Somewhere prior to what Carol Dweck calls the growth mind-set (the confidence in one's ability to achieve a goal) and what Angela Duckworth calls grit (dedication to mastering that goal in the long run) is what I call agency.[6] A moral dimension distinguishes agency from a growth mind-set and grit. Just as velocity is not just speed but rather speed and direction, agency is more than free will: it is free will guided by a moral sense of right and wrong. Reverend Martin Luther King, Jr., once argued that education that stops at efficiency might prove to be the greatest menace to society. He said that "the most dangerous criminal may be the man gifted with reason, but with no morals," underscoring that a growth mind-set and grit *alone* could produce the next despot, someone without healthy character formation.[7] No, agency is the character-based strength that young people can tap into as a source of morally directed power, and our kids do not achieve this by this themselves. Young people do not typically find success or meaning in isolation; they need social support from vibrant, well-functioning mediating structures. They need the help of our families, schools, houses of worship, nonprofit organizations, and community groups to build agency. In Chapter 3, I set out my third way.

Fundamental to my thinking is Urie Bronfenbrenner's "bio-ecological" theory. This groundbreaking psychologist and father of Head Start established the vital factors that drive human development, for good or ill. The most influential? The immediate "microsystem" a child lives in and the deeply personal connection with "the one institution that bears primary responsibility for socialization in our society—the American family."[8]

Family matters. More specifically, the structure and stability of the family within which a child is raised matters monumentally in the acquisition of agency. I will make the case over several chapters that the breakdown in the two-parent family in the United States—particularly the explosion of households headed by single mothers in their early twenties—explains national woes that are too often, and too easily, attributed to race or other, increasingly less relevant factors. As Isabel Sawhill of the Brookings Institution says, "Social policy faces an uphill battle as long as families continue to fragment and children are deprived of the resources of two parents."[9]

To usher in a new era of American agency in which the rising generation becomes the master of their own fate, we must simultaneously launch a movement that encourages young people of all races to adopt a new cultural norm concerning education, entrepreneurship, hard work, faith, responsible parenthood, and the timing of strong family formation.

Shifting cultural norms may seem daunting, but we as a nation have done this before. In Chapters 8 and 9, I will describe how in the early 1990s, during a time of deep political divide, a small coalition of normally warring factions came together to forge a consensus to address the crisis of skyrocketing teen pregnancy rates, and over the ensuing thirty years achieved one of the greatest public health achievements on record. The past can be prologue.

There is a way—a third way—which I call FREE. FREE is a framework based on *F*amily, *R*eligion, *E*ducation, and *E*ntrepreneurship that is designed to build agency in all our children, from kids in low-income communities to those in the wealthiest of neighborhoods who nevertheless can find themselves leading lonely, rudderless lives. FREE is built upon four pillars designed to unleash a morally informed free will—agency—in our children so they are not bound by a challenging past nor present and can envision a better future.

One key component of FREE that is particularly important in the formation of strong families across generations is the Success Sequence, a series of life decisions that involves first graduating from high school, then securing full-time work, then getting married, and then having children. Among millennials, evidence shows that following this series of decisions creates a 97 percent chance of avoiding poverty.[10] Despite concerns that imparting this information to young people might be viewed as condescending, overwhelmingly large majorities of all Americans (77 percent) and

American parents (76 percent) support "teaching students that young people who get at least a high school degree, have a job, and get married—before having children—are more likely to be financially secure and to avoid poverty in later life."

But just teaching this information in schools is not enough. The other key component of FREE is the enlistment of society's mediating structures—schools, churches, civic associations, neighborhoods, and, most importantly, the family—in helping our kids to achieve agency.

We must offer a hopeful path forward, a strategy to defeat the debilitating narrative that many kids—who are too often kids of color or from low-income neighborhoods—have no power to exercise their individual agency nor achieve better outcomes in their own lives. I believe we have a moral imperative to help our young people understand the series of life decisions within their control that create the greatest likelihood of success.

In short, my third way recognizes that young people do not have to be trapped between the heavy burden of having to pull themselves up by their own bootstraps alone and the immobilizing delay of having to wait for someone else to effect massive "systemic" change. That is a false choice when, in fact, we can be FREE.

As a child of stable, married parents, a proud product of the New York City public school system K–12, and a long-time leader running high-performing schools in low-income communities, I know what is possible to achieve when we refuse to lump kids into preordained social or racial categories. I know what is possible when adults resist practicing the "soft bigotry of low expectations" at the expense of the children in their care.[11] From the time I completed my education, I chose a professional road less traveled in order to help kids of all races find their inner greatness. I have had remarkable opportunities at premier institutions involved in education, media, government, and philanthropy to shape the attitudes and behaviors of the rising generation, especially the most economically disadvantaged.

At each step along the way, whether at my own entrepreneurial startups or at top-flight organizations in the for-profit, non-profit, and public sectors, including Teach for America, Third Millennium Media, the White House, MTV, the Bill & Melinda Gates Foundation, Public Prep, and now Vertex Partnership Academies, I learned the key individual and institutional factors that positioned young people to control their own destiny—or not to control it. Little did I know that this lifelong journey would be an extended research project on how to empower the rising generation to overcome a victimhood narrative and carve out their own pathway to power. I have seen what works and what does not work from inside those mediating institutions that, as sociologist Peter L. Berger and Rev. Richard Neuhaus wrote, "stand between the individual in his private sphere and the large institutions of the public sphere."[12]

I believe we all must abandon the poisonous notion that any disparity we see between certain groups must be due to discrimination of that group as opposed to other factors that transcend that group designation, which are far more determinative (most notably, family structure).

My hope here is to help young people learn the ways in which they can bridge the gap between what "is" in their life and what they want it "to be." This is unrelated to a specific goal that requires thousands of hours of dedicated practice—say, playing the piano or perfecting a basketball jump shot. Instead, it is a general belief about controlling your own destiny, being resilient when the unexpected occurs and resolute even in the face of daunting resistance. That is agency. That is "not throwin' away your shot."

Positive psychologist Martin Seligman has spoken of the "Age of Agency" that awaits us. It will be an age that holds the promise to move human endeavors "from the relief of suffering to the building of [well-being itself]."[13] It will also be an age in which generations of Americans—today's and tomorrow's Hamiltons—can leave their fingerprints and rise up.

What Is Agency and Why Do We Need It Today?

1

What Is Agency and Why Is It So Crucial to Human Flourishing?

There is something vital, practical, and urgent about becoming reacquainted with agency. Something apart from individualism. It is the vital life force that flows through us through divinities' will. To be an agent, to possess agency is to be in touch with that creative force that shapes us all.

—Prabjhot Singh

On a Sunday evening in early September 1977, I did the unthinkable. I was twelve years old and standing in our living room. My dad sat in his brown recliner; my mum was next to him. I remember locking eyes with her as I spoke.

In the late 1960s, my parents, my brother, and I had emigrated to New York from Jamaica, West Indies. After a stint in Brooklyn, we "moved on up" and ultimately settled in Laurelton, which at the time was a predominantly white, middle-class community in

Queens. However, Laurelton was changing from a Jewish enclave to what is now a neighborhood of mostly African American and Caribbean residents. In 1977 I was attending I.S. 231, a junior high school that had historically been mostly white. Like the surround-ing area, however, I.S. 231 was rapidly becoming integrated. Racial tensions were growing and the increasingly bitter daily disputes were driving the school leadership to seek solutions.

Citing "overcrowding," the local school board had voted to open an annex, a separate academic building located two miles away in Rosedale, a small, Irish American and Italian American community on the border of Nassau County, Long Island. That decision led almost every white family in my junior high school to transfer their children to the Rosedale annex, which made I.S. 231 a segregated, virtually all-black school.

My Jamaican immigrant parents, who were determined that their two sons would get their shot at the American Dream, were ready to transfer me as well. Wherever the white kids go, so goes high-quality education—that was their theory. My nineteen-year-old brother had already started college, so their decision was entirely about my education, and my parents knew best (full stop).

Dad and Mum would have crawled over broken glass if they thought it would help my brother and me to have a better life. They were my rock growing up. At the root of everything that I have ever accomplished are the sacrifices they made for me. But some-thing was not right here. I did not want to leave my school. I loved my friends. I loved my teachers. I loved my school. And I did not accept the reasons my parents gave for transferring me.

I had never before questioned my parents about anything that really mattered. Why would I? They had repeatedly demonstrated that they had only my best interests at heart, even if that some-times meant tough love. Surely this decision about school was simply another moment in which my parents' wisdom and long-term thinking should outweigh my immature posturing.

But something inside me said no, so here we were facing off in our Laurelton living room. That is when I did the unthinkable. That Sunday night, the night before my parents had to file the transfer documents, I found a voice I had not known existed. I stood in our living room pleading with my mum and dad. I begged my parents to reconsider and let me stay in I.S. 231. "Why should the other school be better?" I asked. "Why should the education suddenly be worse in my school just because most of the kids who are going to be left are black?" I didn't see why my education would have to suffer just because I refused to go to the school with all the white kids. I told my parents that if they let me stay in I.S. 231, I would work even harder. They would never regret their decision, I promised. They could believe in me because I believed in myself.

Perhaps at that moment my parents realized that my pushback was evidence of a strength of character that they themselves had helped to cultivate in me. Perhaps they hearkened back to a time in their own lives when they had had difficult conversations with their own parents about leaving Jamaica in pursuit of a better life. Whatever the reason, an amazing thing happened: my parents relented and said I could stay at I.S. 231. I think of this now as my coming-of-agency moment.

I often wonder what would have happened if I had not spoken up to my parents that Sunday night. What if my parents had not acquiesced and instead insisted that I attend the nearly all-white annex? Would I have exhibited the same ownership over my learning as I did when I convinced them to grant my wish to stay? (Sadly, my parents' fears regarding I.S. 231 materialized. It became one of New York City's most dangerous schools and closed in 2013 after consistently being on the state's list of the lowest-achieving schools.)[1]

Yet in allowing me to forge a path contrary to their better judgment, my parents taught me a valuable lesson: my own effort would influence my outcomes. At the time, I felt an enormous, added responsibility to make my parents' decision worth the trust they had placed in me. I was "on the hook."

Something changed for me that Sunday night. Something had awakened in me to give my twelve-year-old self the confidence to respectfully challenge my parents. I had now become an active player in my own education as I took ownership of my own destiny. This self-belief was the precursor to the ensuing actions that were necessary for me to fulfill the commitment I had made to my parents and, most important, to myself. The faith I placed in myself was what I now understand to be my sense of personal agency. I had become an agent of my own uplift; I had exercised agency.

But exactly what is agency? The word *agency* is a linking of two Latin roots: *ag*—to "do, act or drive"—and *ent*—"that which does something." Deriving from the medieval Latin word *agentia*, the word *agent* refers to one who does something in the "mode of exerting power or producing effect."[2] Thus it is small wonder that the word *agency* and the words *agenda*, *agile*, and *agitate* share the same Latin root concerning action. All four involve the tasks, movement, and drive we need to get things done. For me, however, the essence of agency goes beyond one's capacity simply to achieve. The concept also encompasses one's ability to persevere despite adverse conditions or hostile environments while simultaneously following a North Star of righteous behaviors.

The three pioneers who have most shaped my thinking about agency and self-determination are Reverend Martin Luther King, Jr., the religious and civil rights leader; Martin Seligman, the "father of positive psychology," which is the scientific study of what makes life most worth living; and Albert Bandura, a psychologist who developed a theory of social cognition grounded in self-efficacy.

The practical wisdom of these three men holds that each of us has the capacity for conscious volition, which is the ability to make informed choices that determine our own fate. However—and this is the key—no human being acts alone. Agency is individually practiced, yet socially empowered. Unique to our species is the way in which early character development determines how those choices are shaped to achieve good or ill. All three men stress that social forces from a range of morally formative institutions can create the conditions under which young people exercise free will and build the mental muscle of agency.

Reverend King was awarded the 1964 Nobel Peace Prize "for his non-violent struggle for civil rights for the Afro-American population."[3] He had inspired a movement of largely young people (as he said in his acceptance speech in Stockholm) who were eager to move forward with "a majestic scorn for risk and danger, to establish a reign of freedom and a rule of justice." But precisely how these freedom fighters demonstrated that "majestic scorn" would decide whether the larger objectives of the movement were achieved. King was keenly aware that black Americans were being victimized by subhuman treatment based on racial animus, but he believed that being victimized did not mean taking on a victim mind-set; nor did it mean that his followers had to respond in kind. King knew that if black Americans adopted and internalized an identity defined by victimhood or resorted to the vicious tactics they were condemning, they would sacrifice their moral authority and undermine the goal of self-determination. Instead, they must choose a path that achieved moral ends through moral means. "I refuse to accept the idea that the 'isness' of man's present nature makes him morally incapable of reaching up for the eternal 'oughtness' that forever confronts him," he said. "I refuse to accept the idea that man is mere flotsam and jetsam in the river of life, unable to influence the unfolding events which surround him."[4]

King rejected powerlessness and passivity; but he firmly believed that substituting revenge for powerlessness was not the way for humans to achieve true freedom and flourish. By advocating for individual and collective self-restraint—a key component of agency—King felt that humanity would be much more likely to bend toward justice. In the end, he believed that while circumstances do impact and shape a person, they are not the sole determining factor in their life. Each person is responsible for their own choices and can choose to grow from mistakes and hardships. In short, Reverend King advocated agency.

Similarly, the theme of Marty Seligman's fifty-year career as a psychologist has been the study of agency, which he sees as "the controlling engine of human progress."[5] Seligman defines agency as one's belief that she or he can change the world *for the better,* which is the component of Seligman's definition that I find most compelling. Free will exists for all humans. You can indeed change the world—but toward what end? Is it a world in which free will drives inspiring advances in human well-being or one marked by dark periods of terror and subjugation?

In short, agency is not free will alone. Rather, agency is the force of free will when it is governed by morally discerned choices that dictate its eventual impact. Efficacy, optimism, and imagination give free will a direction. They create the vector of agency. The philosopher William James seemed to understand that something preceded free will—something more important—as suggested in a diary entry, where he wrote, "My first act of free will, shall be to believe in free will."[6]

Albert Bandura was one of the first psychologists to argue that a sense of personal efficacy forms the foundation of self-determination. "Among the mechanisms of agency, none is more central or pervasive than people's beliefs about their capabilities to exercise control over events that affect their lives," he wrote.[7]

"Unless people believe they can produce desired effects by their actions, they have little incentive to act, or to persevere in the face of difficulties. Whatever other factors serve as guides and motivators, they are rooted in the core belief that one has the power to effect changes by one's actions."[8]

Herein lies the paradox of agency, both its true promise and its peril. Its presence creates the conditions for unprecedented human advancement. It allows us to surmount previously insurmountable obstacles and endure the seemingly unendurable—while on a self-determined path to achieve widespread improvements in our social well-being. But the absence of agency is not a neutral, no-fault state of benign existence. An individual or society immersed in self-disbelief, pessimism, and closed-mindedness is like a planet in retrograde: it moves backward. According to Bandura, "people who perceive themselves as highly efficacious act, think, and feel differently from those who perceive themselves as inefficacious. They produce their own future, rather than simply foretell it."[9]

To return for a moment to my own birth of agency, I stayed on at I.S. 231 and, with the support of my parents and teachers, I received a public education that made me believe anything was possible. I studied hard and ultimately entered Brooklyn Technical High School as a sophomore. From there I graduated with a BS in computer science engineering at Cornell University and an MBA from Harvard Business School. All this prepared me for leadership roles at Teach for America, MTV, the Bill & Melinda Gates Foundation, and the White House. Moreover, it brought me full circle by preparing me for the work I have done over the last decade: running New York City public charter schools that are dedicated to inspiring more young people to understand the pathways by which they can master their own fate.

I run high-performing public charter schools in the heart of the South Bronx in New York City because I believe agency is not some abstract concept to be debated in the ivory towers of academia, think tanks, or newsrooms. Each weekday morning, our principals and teachers greeted nearly 2,000 elementary and middle school students by name and talked with their parents and guardians at drop-offs and pickups. On issues large and small, from homework challenges to family conflicts and trauma to preventing deportation to financial concerns, our faculty tapped into the hopes and fears that our parents have for their children. Those daily interactions are a constant reminder of just how much parents entrust our schools with the responsibility to instill in their children the notion that they can create a better future for themselves. This experience has bolstered my view that agency plays a pivotal role in human flourishing for the next generation, driving it when present and resulting in its suppression when absent. Fundamental to my view is the idea that agency metaphorically serves as a shield and a sword to combat helplessness. It is a power that can be conferred on young people that allows them to shape their individual response to a challenging environment or circumstance.

I decided to form my own working definition of agency, as the belief and ability to overcome the divide between what "is" and what "can be" and become an active player in one's own life. Then I began to develop strategies to build agency within young people from all backgrounds. Defining agency is, of course, far easier than cultivating it in practice. For many children, closing the chasm between "isness" and "oughtness" in their lives is a daunting task. How do we get kids to develop a positive future orientation and to realize how agency can become a not-so-secret weapon to improve their condition? How can we help them be informed, but not constrained, by seemingly daunting surroundings on their way to a more prosperous life?

Critical to the goal of defining agency is helping young people develop a sense of meaning. According to the Archbridge Institute, meaning is the moral component of agency that "helps people flourish in many areas of life, in part, because it is a self-regulatory and motivational resource. The more people believe that they have a meaningful role to play in the world, the more motivated they are to *direct* their behavior in ways that [help] keep them alive and thriving" (italics added).[10]

Not helping students develop a sense of meaning can make them vulnerable to defeatist thinking that becomes a self-fulfilling prophecy, or more to the point, a self-*un*fulfilling prophecy. Unlike today's harbingers of doom, the "victim mongers," who stress the futility of individual action in the face of systemic forces, we need to offer an empowering, evidence-based alternative centered on agency. Our kids need to know that, as the quote oft attributed to renowned psychoanalyst Carl Jung says, "I am not what happened to me; I am what I choose to become."[11]

Agency is accessible to everyone. But too often young people's efforts to develop agency are thwarted, sometimes tragically, by the very people and institutions with the power and moral responsibility to propel their lives forward. Let's look now at two widespread mind-sets that, each in their own way, are robbing America's children of their agency—and their future.

CHAPTER

2

Two Competing Visions of What Impedes the American Dream and the Effort to Build Agency

What happened to the American Dream? Is it alive today for most young Americans? Was it ever a reality for all but a select subset of Americans?

Today there seem to be two prevailing answers to these questions, two visions that are at war with one another for the soul of our nation and its rising generations. One is a bleak vision of individual powerlessness against insurmountable historic and systemic forces. The other is a brighter but still wanting vision of determined individuals of all colors pulling themselves up by their bootstraps and triumphing over any and all adversities. Both, I'm sorry to say, are unequal to the task of making the American Dream more accessible to a rising generation.

One vision posits that the impediments to young people achieving the American Dream are primarily, if not solely, due to insurmountable institutional barriers. This blame-the-system ideology rests on the assumption that structural discrimination based on race, class, gender, and other identity markers forms a fortress of intersectionality that is too imposing for individuals to scale. America's past and present racism, sexism, classism, and other "-isms" (even capitalism) simply rob young people of the ability to be *masters of their own fate.* These vast forces render them powerless as adults to become agents of their own uplift.

An example of how this ideology plays out is the color-bound (versus color-blind) "analysis" of the Federal Reserve Board's Survey of Consumer Finances, a cross-sectional survey of U.S. families that is undertaken every three years.[1] The survey data include families' balance sheets, pensions, income, and demographics. Wealth is defined as the difference between families' gross assets and their liabilities.[2] The Fed's 2019 survey found that the median black household was worth $24,100, while the median white household was worth $188,200.[3] Thus, there was a black-white wealth gap of $164,100.

For some, this great gap is proof enough of America's ugly and insurmountable legacy of racial oppression. It is also irrefutable evidence of the present-day, systemic assault on black Americans. Individual action is deemed futile in the face of this overwhelming systemic oppression. The American Dream has been an American Nightmare for African Americans. The argument goes that unless institutional barriers are demolished, black Americans will remain trapped in a perpetual cycle of economic victimhood. According to the Institute for Policy Studies in Washington, D.C., "Changes in individual behavior will not close the racial wealth divide, only structural systemic policy change can do that."[4] In *What We Get Wrong about Closing the Racial Wealth Gap*, William Darity, Jr., and colleagues assert that "there are no actions that black Americans can take unilaterally that will have much of an effect on reducing the racial wealth gap."[5] Noelle Hurd, assistant professor of psychology at the University of Virginia, cautions that "it is a mistake to think that there is any one thing a person can do at the individual level to sidestep the consequences of living in a racist society."[6]

Since individual effort is useless, "blame-the-system" advocates—today's enemies of agency—often claim that the only solution is a massive government redistribution scheme. In making her case that African Americans have no other option but to be paid back trillions of dollars in cash reparations for generational theft, *New York Times* reporter Nikole Hannah-Jones put forth the defeatist position that "none of the actions we are told black people must take if they want to 'lift themselves' out of poverty and gain financial stability—not marrying, not getting educated, not saving more, not owning a home—can mitigate 400 years of racialized plundering."[7] Even Oprah Winfrey—whose own story of escaping poverty and abuse has been an inspiration to millions—describes an American "caste system" in which "white people . . . no matter where they are on the rung, or the ladder of success, they still have their whiteness . . . which [creates] an advantage, no matter what."[8]

There are many problems with today's "blame-the-system" narrative of individual powerlessness. One is the power it gives to others to somehow rescue black Americans. Glenn Loury, a Brown University economist, made this point at a 2019 Manhattan Institute event entitled "Barriers to Black Progress: Structural, Cultural or Both?" Loury was asked whether we need to tackle white people's supremacist attitudes before black people address the factors within their control—factors like high levels of single parenthood—that create a greater likelihood of child poverty. Loury's response could not have been clearer—or a better explanation of the need for agency: "You just made white people, the ones who we say are the implacable, racist, indifferent, don't-care oppressors, into the sole agents of your own delivery. Really?"[9]

But there are other—and perhaps larger—problems with the fashionable blame-the-system vision or powerlessness narrative. One is that it does not stand up to scrutiny. It's a false narrative that often masks the hypocrisy of its most vocal advocates. Take that $164,100 wealth gap between black and white Americans in the Federal Reserve survey. When factors other than race are considered, the picture changes dramatically for both blacks and whites. According to the 2019 Survey of Consumer Finances, the median net worth of a two-parent, college-educated black family is $219,600. For a white, single-parent household, the median net worth is $60,730. While the racial wealth gap is $164,100 for whites over blacks when race is considered alone, when family structure and education are included, it is $158,870 *in favor of blacks over whites*. Individual choices do make a difference.[10] It is worthy of mention that Nikole Hannah-Jones, who emphasized the futility of black people marrying, purchasing a home, and so forth, rarely acknowledges that her own biography reveals that she has done *all* these things in order to achieve economic success for her family.

Not only are blame-the-system advocates often hypocrites in preaching futility while practicing behaviors in their own lives that lead to prosperity, their rhetoric hurts the very kids they claim to want to help. As an educator, when I hear the collective messages that emphasize grievance and dependency, I think of their corrosive impact on the primarily low-income, black and brown children who attend the schools I lead. This negative worldview can convince otherwise able kids that they are trapped in a lower caste of society and there's simply nothing they can do—they are powerless—in the face of this rigid, discriminatory systemic structure. It can turn them into victims. Whether intentional or not, this debilitating ideology will have a psychological impact on kids. It resurrects a long-gone period of physical enslavement in a

modern-day form of mental enslavement. Worse still, their liberation relies on their "enslaver."

The danger in all this victim-mongering is that the next
generation of young Americans—black and white—might grow
up believing that the entire destiny of one race or class rests in
the hands of another that is so powerful that it must first renounce
its "privilege," or evil intent, before any progress can be made. It
is a kind of grand theft; it robs people of personal agency and the
belief that they can control their own destiny.

Imagine, for example, that you are a twelve-year-old black boy
living in the South Bronx. You aspire to work hard to achieve the
American Dream. Yet you are repeatedly told there is nothing you
can do individually to achieve that goal. Imagine further that this
message comes from adults who claim to advocate on your behalf,
but they are really telling that you it is pointless to even try. This is
an emotionally crippling message. You are being told that you are at
a disadvantage because of your skin color, no matter what you do.

How deeply has this ideology infected the K–12 world? In 2019,
Education Week, which bills itself as "America's most trusted
resource for K–12 education news and information" and which
many educators see as a kind of Bible, asked Bettina Love to write
a series of essays on race in America. Love is a University of Georgia education professor and widely published writer. In her lead
essay, Love argued that schools "never acknowledge how racism
is systemic, institutionalized, and structural, or how racism breeds
and is maintained by violence." Sadly, she was just getting started:
"Physical and psychological attacks on black and brown children's
bodies and culture are more than just racist acts by misguided
school educators; they are the spirit murdering of black and brown
children. . . . What I am talking about is a slow death, a death of
the spirit, a death that is built on racism and intended to reduce,
humiliate, and destroy people of color."[11]

Linger on these words for a moment. Would you want to send your child to a school that practices Love's "physical and psychological attacks"? Imagine you are a parent of color. How would you respond to being told your child's teacher is "spirit murdering" and deliberately intending to "reduce, humiliate and destroy" your son or daughter rather than opening up new learning possibilities. This dark and cankered pessimism is the exact opposite of the optimism that Martin Seligman correctly identifies as a precondition for young people to have the agency to thrive. It's small wonder that parents, especially those in disadvantaged communities, are desperate for empowering educational alternatives.

Ben Wilterdink of the Archbridge Institute think tank correctly decries what he calls the "narrative of identity-based soft determinism" in which human beings are no longer seen as individuals with unique hopes and capabilities. Rather, they're seen as little more than stand-ins of some gender, race, or ethnic identity. "There is a growing danger that simply by convincing people that claims of soft determinism are true now, could be the thing that makes them true in the future," he writes. "In other words, this kind of rhetoric could be the ultimate self-fulfilling prophecy."[12]

As someone who has run public charter schools in low-income communities in the Bronx, I know how debilitating such a narrative can be for a student's hopes and aspirations. If a teacher were to espouse such a philosophy in our classrooms, it would be grounds for termination. Rather than helping young students develop personal agency and an understanding of the behaviors most likely to propel them into success, this message will only teach what psychologists term *learned helplessness.*

What's more, this depressing message is demonstrably wrong. There *are* decisions within the control of black kids—and children of all races—that increase their likelihood of improving their economic outcomes within one generation and thus their ability to transfer wealth across generations. Imagine that instead of the message that "no matter what, you are disadvantaged," young people of all races understood that nothing is predetermined in their lives and that they themselves have the greatest level of influence over their own futures.

If we did so, more young people would begin to think like Makeila Ward, age sixteen, from Nevada, who was taking classes at community college while attending high school and planned to become a flight nurse in the Air Force. Makeila told the *New York Times* that "people who start off with a better life than others have higher chances of getting more successful more easily," she said. "But even with a hard background, if you put the work in and save up the money, most of the time you get what you deserve."[13] More on how we can counteract the blame-the-system vision of individual impotence will be covered in Chapter 10.

The other school of thought—blame-the-victim—posits that the roadblocks to realizing the American Dream are primarily, if not solely, due to an individual's bad choices or lack of effort. It essentially accuses unsuccessful young people of being the architects of their own shortcomings—never mind the fact that they likely never received the kind of support that would have equipped them to succeed. If only they had exercised more grit or exhibited more mental toughness, they, too, could have succeeded. The exhortations are all too familiar: *"Have fewer babies outside marriage and you won't live in poverty." "Commit fewer crimes and you won't be abused by the criminal justice system." "Study harder so you won't be so far behind academically."* These exhortations are familiar because they are true at a surface level. They encourage behavior we want to propagate and discourage behavior we want to lessen, because the end result should be happier, more prosperous human beings.

The problem is that in government parlance, these directives are the equivalent of unfunded mandates—orders without the means to achieve them. In each scenario they can place the full burden of success or failure on individuals—young individuals, at that—who, through no fault of their own, have only known a reality where the ideal of self-responsibility is never taught, encouraged, or reinforced by local institutions.

Perhaps one way to understand how even well-meaning ideas to advance human progress can fall prey to accusations of being guilty of the blame-the-victim ideology is to consider the work of Carol Dweck and Angela Duckworth, both research psychologists and authors of bestselling books on growth mind-set and grit. As an educator who has seen a slew of fads—each billed as the "next big idea" that will transform outcomes for kids—I cannot overstate how much Dweck's *Mindset: The New Psychology of Success* and Duckworth's *Grit, the Power of Passion and Perseverance* have gained traction in the world of education reform and beyond. Since its 2007 publication, Dweck's *New York Times* best seller *Mindset* has sold more than 800,000 copies and been translated into twenty-six[14] languages.[15] Likewise, Duckworth's *Grit* has sold more than a million copies since 2016 and has also been a *New York Times* best seller.[16] The TED Talks that Dweck and Duckworth gave about their best sellers have been viewed more than 38 million times.[17]

Both Dweck and Duckworth set out to debunk what they believe to be harmful myths regarding youth success. For Dweck, it was the fallacy of the importance of self-esteem and of the notion that each person is born with a certain maximum level of intelligence. For Duckworth, the conventional wisdom to be undone was the belief that successful people were endowed with raw, "natural" talent at birth, an innate ability that wasn't learned but simply received as a gift.

Instead of artificially propping up a young person's positive *feelings* about their capabilities, Dweck's research showed that "what students believe about their brains—whether they see their intelligence as something that's fixed or something that can grow and change—has a profound effect on their motivation, learning and school achievement. These different beliefs or mind-sets create different psychological worlds: one in which students are afraid of challenges and devastated by setbacks or one in which students relish challenges and are resilient in the face of setbacks."[18]

Duckworth, for her part, builds on Dweck's work by situating a growth mind-set as the cornerstone of what a person must first possess in order to achieve her definition of grit. She describes grit as the sustained application of effort toward a long-term goal. This, she argues, is the biggest predictor of lifelong achievement. In *Grit*, Duckworth analyzes the "never-give-up" attitudes and "hang-in-there" behaviors of West Point cadets, spelling bee champions, and urban teachers who were completely committed to ensuring their students succeed. Her central finding was that talent, while a necessary ingredient, is no guarantee of either grit or achievement: "Talent is how quickly your skills improve when you invest effort. Achievement is what happens when you take your acquired skills and use them."[19]

Duckworth uses two simple equations to show that one's effort actually counts twice toward achieving one's goal:

$$\text{Talent} \times \text{Effort} = \text{Skill}$$
$$\text{Skill} \times \text{Effort} = \text{Achievement}$$

"Without effort," Duckworth argues, "your talent is nothing more than your unmet potential . . . and your skill is nothing more than what you could have done but didn't."[20] According to Duckworth's unified formula:

$$(Talent \times Effort) \times Effort = Achievement$$

Thus, effort is twice as important as talent.

The combination of Dweck's concept of growth mind-set and Duckworth's concept of grit is powerful because something special occurs when individuals have confidence in their ability to achieve a goal (growth mind-set) and then dedicate themselves to do whatever is necessary to master that goal in the long run (grit). There is a lot to like in Dweck and Duckworth's complementary visions of a growth mindset and grit. This is clearly a sunnier outlook than the "blame-the-system" ideology, and it incorporates an element of agency. But, as the saying goes, no good deed goes unpunished. Not everyone agrees that grit is good. One of the detractors who has a problem with the emphasis on grit is Jal Mehta, a professor at the Harvard Graduate School of Education, who wrote in *Education Week* that "the most prominent critique is that an emphasis on grit is a way of 'blaming the victim'—rather than take up larger questions of social, economic, and racial justice, if only the most disadvantaged kids were a little 'grittier' they could make it in life."[21]

Indeed, Dweck and Duckworth's messages of self-empowerment have been found wanting by those who believe that *any* reference to the importance of individual responsibility—rather than wholly focusing on systemic barriers—is inherently implicating the very people suffering a problem as the source of the problem itself. For example, noted education historian Diane Ravitch wrote a blog post entitled, "'Grit' and 'Resilience' Are Buzzwords That Blame the Victim for Not Pulling Him/Herself by Bootstraps." Ravitch cites a youth advocate at a community-based organization who rejects the idea of resilience, because "when 'resilience' is applied to at-risk kids, it implies 'the solutions reside within an individual and not their context.' . . . The assumption is that having 'character' will help traumatized people flourish—and if they don't flourish, there is an implied lack of character." Ravitch concludes that one has to "call *grit* and *resilience* what they are: a substitute for the structural and financial changes that give people genuine opportunity to get ahead."[22]

I do not believe Dweck and Duckworth are blaming the victim. In my view these are unfair criticisms, but they highlight the minefield you enter if you offer a proposition of human progress that does not fully conform to either blame-the-victim or blame-the-system ideology. In my experience, growth mindset and grit are both necessary, but they are not sufficient to help individuals to truly fulfill their potential. Somewhere along the continuum from the adoption of a growth mind-set to the exercise of grit lies the overcoming concept of agency. One can simultaneously call for personal responsibility and grit while also acknowledging the shortfall of blame-the-victim thinking, which often fails to recognize that young people may be living in environments in which weakened local institutions focused on family, faith, education, and employment have not fully equipped young people with the knowledge, skills, and moral code necessary to embark on a self-sufficient life.

Both blame-the-system and blame-the-victim approaches offer superficial, reductionist arguments. Neither supposition offers a full explanation to illuminate the complex factors that drive success or failure for any one individual—much less whole groups of people—and especially not whole groups of young people. Moreover, the problem with the two dominant theories of causality is that they crowd out any other possible explanations for why kids of *all* races do not flourish in life. As a result, they limit the

universe of potential solutions that could spur the rising generation to achieve increased prosperity as they enter young adulthood. If you believe causality is systemic, you will be obsessed
with strategies that dismantle systemic bias. If you are a blame-
the-victim devotee, you will champion self-reliance efforts that
exclusively help individuals pull themselves up by their proverbial
bootstraps.

But is there another way? In his introduction of *To Empower
the People*, Michael Novak, a George Frederick Jewett Scholar in
Religion, Philosophy, and Public Policy at the American Enterprise
Institute, described how public policy solutions in the United States
tend to be pulled toward one of two polar notions: the *individual*
or the *state*:

> Pose a social problem to an American conservative, and the
> chances were high he would appeal to everything the individual
> could do for himself, if only the collectivist state would get out of
> the way. Pose a social problem to an American liberal, and the
> chances were he would try to invent a new federal program, pol-
> icy initiative, or agency to tackle it. American conservatives
> expressed their ideals in terms of "the individual." American lib-
> erals liked to describe themselves as "the party of compassion,"
> bringing "an activist government" to the support of the needy.[23]

I believe there is, at least, one additional way—a way that keeps
the individual at its center but relies on social institutions, families, churches, schools, and work—all of which shape and demand
expectations—to help our young people to build agency and make
the decisions that will lead to successful lives.

Onward.

The Third Way

Revitalizing Mediating Institutions to
Strengthen Civil Society and Spark
Individual Agency

One of the most vital insights of modern social thought is
the importance of mediating institutions–churches, schools,
fraternal organizations, professional associations, and even
clubs–for a free society . . . for they are a bulwark of freedom
against the encroaching power of the state.

—William Klimon

"God helps those who help themselves." These were the six words my father invariably uttered whenever he wanted to remind me of my responsibility to show some effort before I could expect assistance. Typically, this admonition came in response to my prematurely asking him for help on a school assignment or before I had even attempted to finish a really hard chore. He would not let me off the hook. First, I had to try. As my dad said, I had to give in order to get.

Now my dad certainly wasn't comparing *himself* to God when he said this. And he didn't always mean God in the sense of "God Almighty." For him, "God" was a proxy for the universe of nearby individuals and institutions that had the daily responsibility to hold me to high expectations *and themselves* to the solemn obligation to shape my character if I held up my end of the bargain. In short, I was responsible for doing the right thing—doing the work—but I wasn't in this alone.

My parents formed the nucleus of the support system dedicated to my success. From there, that cocoon of love and guidance radiated out. It included extended family members who provided me a sense of belonging; our church, which cultivated my faith; the schools that built my knowledge of the words and world around me; the neighbors and neighborhood that nurtured me; the police who protected us; the doctors and hospitals that cared for me; and the voluntary associations spontaneously formed for the good of our community. Each one of these institutions helped me, provided I also helped myself. Little did I know then that I was in the care of society's mediating structures.

Sociologist Peter Berger and pastor Richard Neuhaus coined the phrase *mediating structures* in their landmark 1977 book, *To Empower People: From State to Civil Society*. They believed these "mediating structures"—stable families, houses of worship, neighborhoods, and community-based organizations—were vital to the ongoing enterprise to revitalize America by shaping the character of the rising generation. They were the institutions that "stand between the private world of individuals and the large, impersonal structures of modern society."[1]

These mediating structures facilitate in-person, human connections that are moderated by agreed-on standards of conduct. They form the immediate environment in which an individual child lives and in which they learn the norms, values, and behaviors expected in the environment. Due to the close and ongoing nature of these interactions, family members, fellow parishioners, and neighbors, who are more likely to know one another, empathize with their peers. They are invested in each other's mutual success and best interest. They hold each other accountable to preserve a certain way of life. They are the messengers and preservers of "the way we do things around here."

The large institutions of the public sphere, by contrast, are those organizations that can influence our lives but are far more removed. They are governed by values largely outside our control as individuals. They include the media, which broadcast the images and stories that become the fodder for water cooler and playground discussions or perpetuate stereotypes. They include large, sometimes faraway philanthropic and nonprofit institutions that exist (or should exist) to promote the welfare of others and fill the space between the private and public sectors. And they include the legislative, executive, and judicial branches of government, whose elected officials set, administer, or enforce the laws and policies that provide the guardrails of our society. The weaker the people-centered mediating structures, the less defense there is against the politics and frequently conflicting values of these distant forces infiltrating the lives of our children and local communities.

What does this mean in practical terms? In his landmark study of the intergenerational mobility of 40 million children and parents, Harvard University economist Raj Chetty and colleagues described the United States as a "collection of societies."[2] Some are "lands of opportunity" with high rates of economic mobility across generations. Others are wastelands in which "few children escape poverty." A major conclusion was that the makeup of a neighborhood had a huge effect on intergenerational mobility. Chetty and his team found that "the strongest predictors of upward mobility are measures of family structure such as the fraction of single parents in the area," and that "high upward mobility areas tend to have higher fractions of religious individuals and greater participation in local civic organizations."[3]

In his 2009 review of the twentieth-anniversary edition of *To Empower People*, historian Wilfred McClay highlights Neuhaus and Berger's contention that local "mediating structures were essential to democratic society . . . because they are 'the value-generating and value-maintaining agencies in society.'"[4]

Urie Bronfenbrenner, a behavioral scientist specializing in human development and, not coincidentally, the father of the Head Start program, spent a distinguished career explaining how all this worked on the individual level. His particular area of interest was, he told Congress in 1969, "the processes through which the new-born infant is gradually transformed into an effective member of society."[5]

In forging a new model of interdisciplinary analysis that studied children in their real-world environments, Bronfenbrenner found that children did not function as independent actors in a vacuum. Rather, they acted within a layered system of immediate to distant relationships in the family, school, church, community, parental workplace, government, media, and larger society. An individual's experience from childhood to adulthood proceeded within "a set of nested structures, each inside the next, like a set of Russian dolls."[6] This was a metaphor that came naturally to Bronfenbrenner, who had immigrated with his parents from Moscow to the United States as a child.

Bronfenbrenner defined his ecology of human development as "the scientific study of the progressive, mutual accommodation, throughout the lifespan, between a growing human organism and the changing immediate environments in which it lives."[7] With the child and their unique genetic and personality traits at the center, Bronfenbrenner's ecological environment includes the microsystem, the mesosystem, the exosystem, the macrosystem, and the chronosystem to reflect how human development occurs over time. He defined each system as shown in Figure 3.1.

The most influential system, the microsystem, is the immediate environment in which the child lives and maintains deeply personal connections with parents, siblings, and caregiving relatives, which typically includes the nuclear family, as well as neighbors, teachers, and clergy. The quality and stability of these relationships determines the child's level of influence—or vice versa—over the other layers of the ecosystem.

Why have our country's academic outcomes been so poor for so long and for so many, despite expenditures of hundreds of billions of dollars and the heartfelt commitment of exceptionally talented people? Bronfenbrenner's human development framework explains why some children predictably fail and others more reliably succeed.

Those of us who have worked in low-income communities know that kids suffer—and sustain long-lasting damage—if they come of age in a fractured microsystem. The 30-million-word gap research documents the daunting vocabulary deficits that result when a child grows up in a home without quality verbal interaction with parents.[8] And the antisocial behaviors some children exhibit entering prekindergarten or kindergarten are likely a direct result of having been raised in a chaotic microsystem.[9]

Bronfenbrenner saw this coming. As he testified to Congress in 1969,

> There is a growing body of scientific evidence that the process of making human beings human is breaking down in American society. . . . And the indications from the evidence are that these trends will be continuing at an increasing rate. The causes of this breakdown are, of course, manifold, but they all converge in their

FIGURE 3.1 Author's adaptation of Urie Bronfenbrenner's bioecological model of child development.

SOURCE: AEI graphic design team.

disruptive impact on the one institution that bears primary
responsibility for socialization in our society—the American
family.[10]

A step removed from the family in Bronfenbrenner's microsystem is the neighborhood. It's there that young people most frequently experience the face-to-face interactions of everyday life.
As the National Commission on Neighborhoods declared in its
1979 final report, neighborhoods are quintessential mediating
structures, "Since their scale is manageable, they nurture confidence and a sense of control over the environment. Neighborhoods
have built-in 'coping mechanisms' in the form of churches, voluntary associations, formal and informal networks. The neighborhood is a place where one's physical surroundings become a focus
for community and a sense of belonging."[11]

Families, neighborhoods, religious institutions, and all the
other mediating structures within a child's microsystem weave
together to shape the civil society that can produce generations
of individual citizens capable of self-governance and cognizant of
the life-long habits and virtues necessary to lead an independent,
fulfilling life.

What's the bottom line? We must pursue both individual
responsibility *and* institutional support. We cannot confine
ourselves—and, ultimately, our children—to the false binary choice
of "blame the system" or "blame the victim." We can help young
people as individuals learn the paths to success taken by millions
of their predecessors who have overcome hurdles of their own. To
reiterate, young people do not typically find success in isolation.
They need social support from vibrant, well-functioning mediating structures—most importantly, as Bronfenbrenner saw decades
ago—from the family. In short, there is a third way.

In many ways, what I have come to understand tracks with the conclusion of the British government's recent Commission on Race and Ethnic Disparities. Launched in the summer of 2020, the panel was asked to examine why racial disparities there persisted. As explained in the report's opening statement,

> As we met with people in round table discussions . . . we were taken by the distinctions being drawn between causes that were external to the individual and those that could be influenced by the actions of the individual himself or herself. As our investigations proceeded, we increasingly felt that an unexplored approach to closing disparity gaps was to examine the extent individuals and their communities could help themselves through their own agency, rather than wait for invisible external forces to assemble to do the job.[12]

In the ensuing pages of this book, I will share how my own coming-of-age experiences, as well as my work leading some of the nation's premier youth-serving institutions, shaped my view of what is possible for the next generation. I will debunk the notion that impediments to success are found solely in institutions or individuals and flesh out a set of interventions to help young people learn the virtues that will lead to a fulfilling life and give them the tools to vault over life's inevitable hurdles. But first I want to tell a story.

As a young adult, I tried to pay my own good fortune forward by mentoring at my alma mater, P.S. 156, and other New York City elementary schools. On weekends, I tutored students in math and reading in predominantly low-income, black neighborhoods. I relished meeting kids who were inquisitive and hopeful about their future, no matter their circumstance.

Some of my pupils seized every opportunity. Their families helped them to see obstacles not as stumbling blocks but as stepping stones to a better future. Often these were children of first-generation immigrants, similar to my parents. Or they might be nieces and nephews of exacting aunts and uncles who had assumed the responsibilities of parenthood, or grandsons and granddaughters of older native-born blacks, many of whom had experienced state-sanctioned segregation firsthand. All these families hoped their young charges would live the American Dream. All knew that their children could take on life on their *own* terms, even in the face of structural barriers. But there was a price for admission. They placed enormous emphasis on strong family ties, usually practiced a religious faith, and instilled in their children a work ethic. Whether they liked it or not, they believed their black children had to outwork, outstudy, and outhustle the competition.

These children did—or, more likely, their elders saw that they did—several hours of nightly homework. By putting in the work, these students grew more confident in their ability to read and, as a result, more confident in math, science, history, and other subjects. Little victories begat more little victories. Mastery in one area tended to inform a willingness to try hard in other areas. I remember one parent's oft-repeated words when his struggling student was reluctant to even attempt a difficult math problem: "It's better to fail than to procrastinate. Just try." With that kind of pushing, that student and his mates usually did more than just try. They learned the value of hard work and persistence. Most importantly, these persistent kids saw a direct connection between their individual effort and their individual accomplishment.

But there were other kids who were no less talented yet were falling behind. By happenstance, these kids had been born into an economically struggling region or a chaotic family environment.

Often they were children of twenty-something, never-married single mothers valiantly trying to hold it together. At the time when I was volunteering, in the early 1990s, New York did not have charter school laws to spur the creation of high-quality education alternatives. Catholic schools were providing a values-based religious education, but parental demand far outpaced supply. As a result, these low-income parents usually had little choice but to send their child to a neighborhood public school that had been academically failing students for generations. These kids were largely alone on a pathway to receiving the kind of poor education that led to the kind of dire statistics that had marked their community for generations.

I remember thinking, there but for the grace of God go I. I had no more raw gifts at that age than my tutees. But I had received a golden ticket: faith-driven parents in a long-term, stable marriage who ensured that I studied hard every night and built the habits to take advantage of a good education. I had the same support—the essential mediating structures—as some of my tutees who had cultivated a learned tenacity, principally because of their demanding parental guardians. And that made all the difference.

Addressing this dichotomy between the differing realities of these young people has become the animating obsession of my life. I now run public charter schools because I want kids to know that they can do hard things, that success is within their grasp, and that there are caring adults ready to show them the pathways to the life they want to lead. I want them to know there are values concerning hard work, entrepreneurship, family and faith—the building blocks of agency—that can carry them toward their dreams.

4

How Believing You Live in a Good, If Not Great, Country Helps Build Agency

My parents, Vincent and Eula, came to the United States in 1968. They were black immigrants who arrived during the tumultuous year in which both Robert F. Kennedy and Martin Luther King, Jr., were assassinated and the country suffered through a wave of civil disturbance and race riots. Yet while they had both left their homes and families in Jamaica, my parents were not running *from* a tyrannical regime or impossible economic conditions. Rather, they were running *toward* a brighter future in the United States. Although they were fully cognizant of the nation's struggle with racial discrimination and its legacy of slavery, nevertheless, they wanted to live and raise their children in a "land of opportunity" where anything was possible.

My parents' focus on family, religion, education, and entrepreneurship (a framework I call FREE and will lay out in Chapter 12), their model of hard work and marriage over forty-eight years—and, yes, their decision to come to this exceptional country with its many opportunities and possibilities—all contributed to what

I have become today. I like to think that my mother and father see me now as the embodiment of what they envisioned so many years ago.

My parents, like so many before them, saw the United States as a beacon of hope for billions of people around the world. They believed our founding principles—liberty, equality, personal responsibility—were central to the realization of the American Dream. It strikes me that one building block of agency in young people is they must believe that they live in a good country, if not a great one; a country that is not hostile to their dreams and that, however flawed, is still full of possibilities that will reward them with great works in return for their great work. This symbiosis of possibility between individual and country is artistically exemplified in the song introducing Alexander Hamilton in Lin Manuel Miranda's Broadway smash musical *Hamilton*:[1]

> *Hey yo, I'm just like my country,*
> *I'm young, scrappy and hungry,*
> *And I'm not throwin' away my shot!*
> *I prob'ly shouldn't brag, but dag, I amaze and astonish.*
> *The problem is I got a lot of brains but no polish*
> *I gotta holler just to be heard.*
> *With every word, I drop knowledge!*
> *I'm a diamond in the rough, a shiny piece of coal*
> *Tryin' to reach my goal.*
> *Ev'ry burden, ev'ry disadvantage*
> *I have learned to manage . . .*

The lyrics of "My Shot" make plain the critical linkage between the sense of possibility in one's country and the sense of possibility in one's own life. You cannot say you are not "throwin' away your shot" if you think your country doesn't give people like you—"a shiny piece of coal"—an opportunity to succeed. Learning to manage "ev'ry burden, ev'ry disadvantage" and "tryin' to reach my goal" will have no meaning if the system is stacked against you.

Building agency in the next generation will depend partly on teaching our young people to appreciate and embrace America's founding principles rather than teaching them to denigrate and reject those ideas as somehow illegitimate because they have been too often violated in practice. Those principles have been a pathway to success for legions of marginalized groups who have shouldered "ev'ry burden, ev'ry disadvantage." That is why we must oppose distorted histories that paint America as an irredeemably racist or inherently unjust nation. Meta-narratives of a permanent American malignancy of oppression such as those promoted in the *New York Times*'s 1619 Project or Howard Zinn's *The People's History of the United States* (1980) are not just fraudulent as history, they also hurt kids. They rob our children of agency and turn them into disempowered victims. Again, why worry about not throwing away your shot if the game is rigged anyway?

Consider the 1619 Project. "The 1619 project is a major initiative from the *New York Times* observing the 400th anniversary of the beginning of American slavery," the paper said in introducing a special interactive version of the project on its website. "It aims to reframe the country's history, *understanding 1619 as our true founding*, and placing the consequences of slavery and the contributions of black Americans at the very center of our national narrative" (italics added).

The 1619 Project made a series of specious claims: the introduction of slaves in 1619, and not the Declaration of Independence in 1776, marks America's true founding. The practice of American slavery, and not the principles of the declaration ("all men are created equal"), define the American project to this day. The nation's founding ideals were "false when they were written," and our "nation was founded on a lie." Moreover, the project asserts that "anti-black racism runs in the very DNA of the country."[2]

Dozens of the nation's most well-respected historians discredited the project's history, particularly its claim that the American Revolution was fought to defend slavery. In particular, Brown University religious studies professor Michael Satlow drew a bead on the project's use of the DNA metaphor in a dead-on letter to the *Times*. "The metaphor is misleading and perhaps pernicious, as it obscures *agency*," he wrote. "Every generation receives traditions, found in laws, customs and institutions, but every person in every generation has significant leeway in how to understand and live those traditions. Traditions—perhaps the meaning of 'DNA' in this metaphor—make racism easier, but ultimately it is the quotidian choices that we have and continue to make that cause racism, as they will [cause] its eradication."[3] He is exactly right.

Regrettably, the *New York Times* was not satisfied with simply putting out a special edition of its publication. It also partnered with the Pulitzer Center to create a curriculum that has now been adopted in thousands of classrooms. School districts in Chicago, Washington, D.C., and Buffalo, New York—interestingly enough, some of the country's poorest academically performing districts—incorporated the project into their K–12 course materials in early 2020. Sadly, the 1619 Project's messaging is not an anomaly. Young people of all races and ages are being taught to see racism and oppression everywhere. In one enrichment block at Hanover High School in New Hampshire, students were asked to complete a "Race Literacy Quiz." The quiz included the following question: "The rise of the idea of white supremacy was tied most directly to: A. Indian removal[,] B. Slavery[,] C. The Declaration of Independence[,] D. The U.S. Constitution[,] E. Ancient Greece." Astonishingly, the "correct" response was C, the Declaration of Independence. The answer key explained that "it was freedom, not slavery, that gave rise to modern theories of race."[4]

This defamation of the nation's founding document so disturbed New Hampshire Board of Education commissioner Frank Edelblut that he asked me to testify before the state Board in March 2021. Inspired by my colleagues at the Foundation Against Intolerance and Racism, here is part of my testimony:

> Increasingly, American institutions—colleges and universities, businesses, government, the media and even our children's schools—are enforcing a cynical and intolerant orthodoxy. This orthodoxy requires us to view each other based on immutable characteristics like skin color, gender and sexual orientation. It pits us against one another, and diminishes what it means to be human. In many instances, we see faculty forced into professional development or students in their classrooms divided by race, and forced to confess their status as oppressor or oppressed.[5]

Yes, our nation has a flawed and tragic history and we have not always lived up to our founding ideals. Moreover, our schools should address this dark history. But our nation also has a beautiful and an inspiring past. It is a story—a uniquely American story—that chronicles the struggle to live up to those no-less-great principles in practice. Our students should be taught this part of the American story, too. (It is worth noting that in 2019, only 15 percent of all eighth grade students scored as "Proficient" on the National Assessment of Progress U.S. History assessment, which examined students' understanding of historical chronology and differing perspectives across time and their grasp of historical facts and contexts.)[6]

In the middle of his work to overcome the legacy of slavery and reality of that day's Jim Crow racism, Dr. Martin Luther

King, Jr., spoke at the New York Civil War Centennial Commission's Emancipation Proclamation Observance on September 12, 1962. An excerpt of what he said that day highlights the importance of our founding principles in our nation's history:

> If our nation had done nothing more in its whole history than to create just two documents, its contribution to civilization would be imperishable. The first of these documents is the Declaration of Independence and the other is that which we are here to honor tonight, the Emancipation Proclamation. *All tyrants, past, present and future, are powerless to bury the truths in these declarations, no matter how extensive their legions, how vast their power and how malignant their evil* [italics added].[7]

In his 1835 classic, *Democracy in America*, French writer and sociologist Alexis de Tocqueville explored the norms and culture that made America so unique—observations from his tour of the United States that have stood the test of time. "The greatness of America lies not in being more enlightened than any other nation," he wrote, "but rather in her ability to repair her faults."[8] I have always found this statement compelling because it accords with the notion that America is always in pursuit of becoming "a more perfect union." Our founding principles—principles beautifully set down in the Declaration of Independence—are the measure of perfection, as Martin Luther King, Jr., would come to understand.

While America's founders laid out inspiring ideals that they themselves did not always fulfill as individuals, the legacy they left is a country constantly working to fully live up to those ideals. America's founding and governing documents—the Declaration of Independence, the Constitution, the Bill of Rights and the other constitutional amendments—are the tools of national betterment, the mechanisms for national repair and renewal.

We cannot escape the fact that America's history will forever be scarred by the horrific stories of chattel enslavement. But today's revisionist history projects ignore the peculiar duality of America. As Hendrik Hertzberg and Henry Louis Gates, Jr., wrote in their comment on the 1996 *New Yorker* special edition, "Black in America," "For African-Americans, the country of oppression and the country of liberation are the same country."[9]

The peculiar duality can be seen in the fact that this is the country in which enslaved people with a certain skin color at one time were once considered only three-fifths of a human being. Yet it is the same country that has now twice elected Barack Obama, someone of that same skin color, to the presidency. It is the same country that, in 2020, elected Kamala Harris, a woman of Jamaican and Indian descent, as vice president. That's the duality. The question is this: What are we going to lead young people to believe they can achieve? Are we going to teach them a narrative of oppression, tyranny, and victimization? Or are we going to provide them with the character and tools to thrive? Are we going to promote a mind-set of victimization? Or are our schools, families, and faith communities going to encourage our young people to prepare themselves to seize the opportunities that are out there and not to throw away their shot?

On March 18, 2008, then-presidential candidate Barack Obama spoke at the National Constitution Center in Philadelphia. It was an important speech, one that's even more relevant amid today's fierce debates over what to teach young Americans about the nation's origin story and true birthdate. Obama argued that, despite America's original sin, the abomination of slavery, he was optimistic that future generations would continue to make progress toward "a more perfect union." Why did he think so? Because our nation was founded on the principles embedded in the Constitution. In closing, Obama described the path toward a more perfect union:

For the African American community, that path means embracing the burdens of our past without becoming victims of our past. It means continuing to insist on a full measure of justice in every aspect of American life. But it also means binding our particular grievances, for better healthcare and better schools and better jobs, to the larger aspirations of all Americans. . . . And it means taking full responsibility for our own lives—by demanding more from our fathers, and spending more time with our children, and reading to them, and teaching them that, while they may face challenges and discrimination in their own lives, they must never succumb to despair or cynicism. They must always believe that they can write their own destiny.[10]

Just as our founding ideals have allowed America to continue to become a better nation, they also help us as individuals to better ourselves. That is what we need to tell our children—that they also have an inner strength and can learn the tools of self-betterment and self-repair and renewal. That is the mindset and skills that the mediating institutions of family, religion and education need to celebrate and cultivate.

Of course, as it relates to the United States and its young people, our future is still to be written. Here again, the writer Lin Manuel Miranda captures the linkage between the promise of America and its people in the closing song that marks Hamilton's death:

> *Legacy. What is a legacy?*
> *It's planting seeds in a garden you never get to see.*
> *I wrote some notes at the beginning of a song someone will*
>   *sing for me.*
> *America, you great unfinished symphony,*
> *You sent for me.*
> *You let me make a difference.*

*A place where even orphan immigrants can leave their
fingerprints and rise up.*

Our young people have the power to shape their legacy. As
adults, it is our responsibility to prepare them to write the next
stanza in their own and their country's unfinished symphony.
Rather than teaching them to lament what was or might have been,
we need to teach them that they can make a difference in what is
to come. We need to show them that they themselves have the
capacity—the agency—to wise up, rise up, and leave their fingerprints on what is to be.

CHAPTER

5

How the Hard Bigotry of "Antiracist" Expectations and the Pursuit of "Equity" Erode Agency for All

In the education world, few Internet memes are better known than the equality-versus-equity cartoon showing what happens when people of varying heights receive two different types of support (see Figure 5.1).[1]

Millions of educators have used this image to explain why equality is not enough and why we must pursue equity if our goal is a truly just society. For many, it is the end of the story. But is it? No.

Equality is based on the idea that all humans are equal in fundamental worth and individual dignity. Equality means equal treatment. Each individual should have equal access to the same opportunities, no matter their race, creed, sex, or color and no matter their *immutable* characteristics (in this case, height). In the cartoon, equality means providing each of the three individuals with the same-sized box to stand on. But because not all three fans in the left frame can see over the fence, the question becomes what

FIGURE 5.1   Viral meme mapping out equality versus equity.

EQUALITY   EQUITY

SOURCE: Medium.com.

action should be taken so each has a real opportunity to see the baseball game. What steps should we take—how should we distribute resources—to ensure that everyone can see the playing field?

When these challenges—not in heights, but rather in learning needs—arise in a classroom, the answer would typically involve what is called "differentiated instruction." Every student—every human being—possesses a unique mix of strengths and weaknesses that influence their attitudes and ability to learn. Good teachers recognize this and customize their teaching approach or assignments. Students receive differentiated instruction (in some sense, *unequal* treatment) so they have an equal opportunity to achieve or even surpass the same learning objectives. On a larger scale, leveling the playing field of opportunity might mean ensuring universal wi-fi access to all students, providing a laptop per child, or offering school choice so all parents, regardless of race, income level, or zip code, have the power to choose a great school for their child.

Equity—more precisely, the pursuit of equity—is where things get tricky. While the equity fix presented in the cartoon's right panel seems fairly benign at first glance, it is a far cry from using differentiated instruction to provide equal access to learning. Rather, it masks a frontal assault on the ideals of self-determination and agency that empower young people to reach their full potential. It promotes an outcomes-oriented "equity" that "recognizes that each person has different circumstances and allocates the exact resources and opportunities needed to reach an *equal outcome*." This is equity as defined by the Milken Institute of Public Health at George Washington University.[2] Sadly, this definition— equity as equality of *outcome* rather than equality of *opportunity*— has become the unspoken *real* meaning for many of today's educators, especially in the ever-lucrative industry of diversity, equity, and inclusion consulting. Darnisa Amante-Jackson, for example, is an educational and racial equity strategist and lecturer at Harvard's Graduate School of Education. She's currently also CEO of the Disruptive Equity Education Project, which holds that "equity exists when disparities in the outcomes experienced by historically under-represented populations have been eliminated."[3] In other words, equity will only exist when group outcomes are equal.

The problem is that guaranteeing this type of equity requires a process that ignores the individuals. *It makes assumptions about group ability and artificially suppresses differences in outcomes that organically emerge from individual differences in attitudes and behaviors.* To achieve equity, some authority must necessarily determine what resources a group should receive and who should receive them. The equity cartoon illustrates this point perfectly. In order to ensure that all three individuals can see over the fence, some entity has overseen the allocation or reallocation of resources. The shortest character's boxes have been doubled while the tallest character's one box is taken away entirely. And all this because of the difference between equality and equity. Addition is achieved through a perverse form of subtraction. As Karl Marx said, "From each according to their ability. To each according to their need."[4] This zero-sum thinking grants some entity the power to unilaterally and subjectively determine a reapportionment of boxes so that everyone's vision of the field is unblocked.

The cartoon also calls to mind the legendary fictional figure John Galt in Ayn Rand's *Atlas Shrugged*. Rand's 1957 novel described a dystopian American future suffering under the weight of a coercive government that forcibly allocates or denies resources to achieve leveled outcomes. Galt revolted against the state-planned economy and tried to call attention to the dangers of a socialist practice that would suffocate human imagination and stifle innovation in the name of equity. John Galt's dystopian America is now in our nation's schools when it comes to the misguided pursuit of equity. And it is disempowering children of all colors by robbing them of the agency they need to build flourishing futures.

Consider this data on reading proficiency from the 2013 National Assessment for Educational Progress as a way to understand the implications of today's overemphasis on equity. On the 2013 National Assessment of Educational Progress (NAEP) exam in West Virginia, according to the Schott Foundation's *Black Boys Report*, the percentage of black male eighth graders reading at NAEP proficient levels was 18.7 percent. Meanwhile, the white male eighth graders' rate was 19.7 percent.[5] What kind of Pyrrhic victory would it be if we closed that whopping one percentage point achievement gap? Yes, equity would be achieved—but a tragedy would remain. Less than one in five black *and* white eighth-grade boys would be reading at proficiency. White and black young men would be tied in a race to the bottom. Would this be cause for celebration?

What makes the "equality-versus-equity" meme so disturbing is not simply its graphic representation of a dangerous ideology. It is the trendy cartoon's application of that ideology in the real world—in the tough neighborhoods where the schools I lead are located—and how this latest educational fad erodes the personal agency of our children. Proponents of equity over equality see the image as a metaphor for the struggle between the inherently advantaged and the inherently disadvantaged, the "privileged" and the "nonprivileged," the victimizers and their victims. There are no individuals in their world and no need for personal agency. There are only groups to count and sort.

While the meme portrays equity for people of differing heights, its most frequent and damaging implementation occurs when social justice is sought in pursuit of *racial* equity. Imagine if all three figures were the same height. In fact, visualize three young people who are the same in every possible way except one. Then, in the name of racial equity, ignore every aspect of an individual— attitudes, behavior, family structure, senses of humor, resiliency, agency, education level, and so on. In short, disregard every dimension of what makes an individual an individual and elevate one other factor above all others. Then conjure up a single variation based on nothing but skin color. One individual is white, one is black, and the third is Hispanic. That's how proponents of racial equity view the world and its inhabitants. They never see the person. Through their "racial equity lens," they see each of the three figures as a flattened representative of a group. Worse still, they see the black individual as a stand-in for an inherently victimized, structurally oppressed group and the white person as a stunt double for their inherent victimizer or structural oppressor.

Although these caricatures of racial hierarchy seem to have been adopted with warp speed in both higher education and K–12 classrooms, advocates of racial equity have been at it for years. Estela Mara Bensimon is a former professor of educational equity at the University of Southern California's Rossier School of Education and director of the Center for Urban Education. She is one of America's better known educational scholars. She has written extensively about the need for explicit color-consciousness to achieve racial equity and improve outcomes for "racially minoritized students" and has described racial equity as a "focus on 'dismantling whiteness.'"

And what is "whiteness"? For Bensimon, it's "a culture of values that favor white people at the expense of others. In education, it prevents historically marginalized students from reaching their potential, and professionals from advancing in their career."[6] The National Museum of African American History and Culture fleshed out "whiteness" in a July 2020 chart on "Aspects and Assumptions of Whiteness" in its website's "Talking about Racism" section. Self-reliance, individualism, hard work, rational thinking, delayed gratification, objectivity, and the nuclear family— all were identified as hallmarks of "whiteness."[7]

It is hard to capture how repugnant, wrong-headed, and racist this so-called "antiracist thinking" is. For Bensimon and others, however, an all-powerful "whiteness" itself is the culprit. It is the sole force preventing "marginalized" students from excelling, or adults from being promoted. To achieve racial equity, their remedy is to "dismantle whiteness" and to fight racism with "antiracism."

"The 'antiracism' narrative has tremendous momentum in modern educational institutions," notes journalist Christopher

Rufo. "It reduces complex phenomena to a simple explanation of white racism—and lets teachers of all racial backgrounds shift blame for failing schools to the abstract forces of 'systemic oppression.'"[8]

The problem with so-called "antiracism"—with the real-world actions now being taken in its pursuit—is this: it hurts kids of all races, but especially its intended beneficiaries. The San Diego Unified School District typifies this dysfunction. On June 23, 2020, the district's school board adopted a resolution to "focus on eliminating those barriers that prevent our students of color from receiving an equitable education." The district had conducted a grading review and discovered that 20 percent of all its black students had received a D or F grade in the first semester of the 2019–2020 school year. By contrast, only 7 percent of white students had received those grades.[9]

Such a discovery might have prompted the district to ask just what contributed to the success of the 80 percent of black students or 93 percent of white students who received passing grades. Were there particular teachers whose students demonstrated gains? Did the passing students study more? Did they submit homework on time? Did they take advantage of tutoring hours? Were their parents more engaged? The answers might help teachers and students across the district. If "students of color" had to be the focus, the district might have addressed the fact that only 6 percent of its Asian students received Ds or Fs.[10] Why were they doing so well? Why were they doing better than the district's white students? Could it possibly be related to American Time Use Study data showing that, on average, Asian students spend nearly three hours per night on homework? (See Figure 5.2.)[11]

If excellence, not equity, were the goal, wouldn't the district want to highlight the likely role that nightly study and homework played in these results—for *all* students? The short answer is no,

FIGURE 5.2   Average time spent on homework, high school students by race (2015–2019).

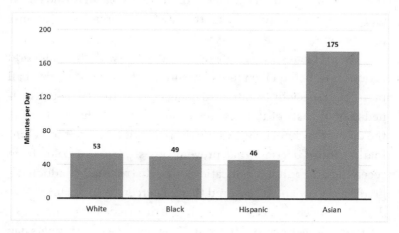

SOURCE: American Time Use Survey, 2015–2019, queried through the Integrated Public Use Microdata System. https://www.atusdata.org/atus/.

this was not the goal for equity-obsessed educators and their enablers.

The district focused exclusively on racial inequity in failure rates, the difference in the percentage of black (20 percent) and white (7 percent) students receiving Ds and Fs. School officials decided that the 13 percent disparity between blacks and whites was wholly a function of systemic racism. In their "honest reckoning as a school district," the San Diego district determined that the "removal of non-academic factors from academic grades was critical in addressing the discriminatory grading practice harming our students."[12] And what qualified as a "non-academic factor"? One was asking students to hand homework in on time.

Imagine telling a child that submitting a completed assignment by the teacher's due date is "discriminatory" and "harming you," even though this most basic requirement prepares students to meet the greater expectations of timeliness later on in college, work, and life. It is educational malpractice and typifies the "soft bigotry of low expectations."

Surely it is possible to have both high expectations *and* deep empathy for students who live in poverty or face chaotic, if not traumatic, situations that can make handing in homework on time a challenge. I run schools in low-income communities so that students facing such challenges can be equipped to *defy* diminished expectations. Some of our students are already disadvantaged by home factors. They shouldn't be doubly disadvantaged by "compassionate" adults who condescend to them because of those circumstances.

We do our kids no favors by robbing them of the opportunity to learn the very habits (punctuality, accountability) and behaviors that are most likely to lift them out of poverty and put them on a path to prosperity. In addition, subject mastery requires frequent checks of understanding—interim assessments and homework along the way—so teachers can know what students have learned and, if necessary, provide differentiated instruction.

Despite the fact that many San Diego students of all races were, in fact, demonstrating habits of excellence, the board voted unanimously to "interrupt" these "discriminatory" grading practices.[13] In its quest to "be an anti-racist school district," it dumbed down the grading system for everyone.[14] In the name of equity, now none of the 106,000 San Diego students are required to hand in their homework on time. And teachers are now prohibited from factoring in a student's classroom behavior when formulating an academic grade.

It is not hard to imagine how students and faculty of all races will internalize the lower standard's not-so-subtle message. After the board decision to eliminate on-time homework submission, a local TV station interviewed a white eleventh grader and student board member who had voted for these changes. As he explained, "We are seeing that the inequities in our communities are so strong and it is not fair of us to put forth policies that only cater to the students that are *able to meet these requirements*."[15] Yes, there is soft bigotry in low expectations. And it is all the more maddening when practiced by people who most likely hold themselves or their own children to high expectations.

Evanston, Illinois, is another school district that's moved to full "blame-the-system" victimization. This is what it meant for one of the African American families there. According to one parent,

> My children have always been so proud of who they are. Then all of a sudden they started to question themselves because of what they were taught after arriving here. My son has wanted to be a lawyer since he was 11. Then one day he came home and told me, "But Mommy, there are these systems put in place that prevent black people from accomplishing anything." That's what they're teaching black kids: that all of this time for the past 400 years, this is what [white people have] done to you and your people. The narrative is, "You can't get ahead."[16]

This is educational malpractice at best and child abuse at worst.

In April 1983, President Ronald Reagan released a landmark report about America's public education system entitled "A Nation at Risk: The Imperative for Educational Reform." Its opening statement was timeless: "Our nation is at risk. Our once unchallenged preeminence in commerce, industry, science, and technological innovation is being overtaken by competitors throughout the world. . . . We report to the American people that . . . the educational foundations of our society are presently being eroded by a rising tide of mediocrity that threatens our very future as a Nation and a people."[17]

In the ensuing decades, the nation has pursued various strategies to raise the academic outcomes for all students, but with mixed results. The NAEP—the "Nation's Report Card"—is the largest continuing biennial assessment of what America's students know and can do in mathematics, reading, science, and writing. How far have we and our students come over the last half-century? In 1992, 29 percent of all eighth graders scored as "NAEP Proficient" in reading. In 2019 (the last year the assessment was given), *only 34 percent of all 8th grade students achieved proficiency in reading*.[18] A staggering thirty-one states plus Washington, DC, reported declines from the 2017 exam. The ability to read, collect knowledge, and develop arguments is, of course, foundational to the goal of building agency in all kids.

But read the mission statement of virtually any educational organization today. You will likely find earnest language about achieving "equity" by "closing the racial achievement gap." Instead of seeking educational excellence for all, school reformers are now fixated on erasing disparities. They focus most often on the underperformance of black children relative to their white classmates and ignore the performance of Asian students, who are also "people of color." The problem with such color-bound thinking is this: achieving "racial equity" would merely allow a black student to reach an average white peer's potential. It has nothing to do with that black student achieving their own (or even higher) potential.

In fact, in every Nation's Report Card since 1992, *fewer than half* of the nation's white students in the fourth, eighth, and twelfth grades achieved NAEP proficiency in reading.[19] The sad irony is that closing the black-white achievement gap would simply mean black student outcomes would move from worse than mediocre to full mediocrity in reading levels. Why, in the name of racial equity, should the goal for black students be achieving the results of white students, the majority of whom have consistently failed to achieve NAEP proficiency levels in reading? I understand the desire to address racial disparities, but we must ensure that the primary gap we are addressing is the gap between current outcomes and 100 percent proficiency. We should be much more interested in achieving excellence for all rather than "racial equity" for groups arranged by skin color. As a *Nation at Risk* warned in 1983: "Our society and its educational institutions seem to have lost sight of the basic purposes of schooling, and of the high expectations and disciplined effort needed to attain them."[20]

Despite this important warning, school districts in San Diego and across the country are adopting the narrative that racial disparities in academic outcomes pose today's greatest educational challenge. In doing so, these educators are reinforcing the flawed belief that "white privilege" and "systemic racism" explain every racial disparity—never mind other factors such as decreases in stable families, insufficient hours spent studying, and a lack of school choice for low-income families. These factors play a far more powerful role in impeding the development of children of all races. Think about it. "White privilege" and "systemic racism" do not cause the perennially abysmal poor performance of white students. But rather than confronting all the factors that drive the development (or not) of flourishing human beings, "antiracist" and "racial equity" policies incorporate the soft bigotry of low expectations. They are soul-killing and skill-killing for all students, and especially our nation's economically disadvantaged students.

Public charter schools can sometimes provide one avenue of escape from such race-bound madness for children in low-income communities, and many have done just this with marked success. Charter schools are tuition-free public schools open to all students, regardless of their zip code. They are independently operated public schools that have the freedom to design classrooms that meet their students' needs. I have spent more than a decade running charter schools in the Bronx. I have seen the good they can do and the difference these in-demand schools can make in the lives of children in challenging communities. And yet it grieves me to say that even some historically successful charter schools are hopping on the antiracist, race-equity, and low-expectations bandwagon. It is a development that, I fear, has the potential to undermine both the legacy and future of charter schools.

Take, for example, the Knowledge Is Power Program, better known as KIPP public charter schools. Founded in 1994 by teachers Mike Feinberg and Dave Levin, KIPP grew out of a fifth grade program in a Houston public elementary school. KIPP's slogan from the outset was "Work Hard. Be Nice." It was not an empty catchphrase. "Work Hard. Be Nice." made clear that a student's effort is essential and that character matters if they want a real opportunity to control their destiny.

With that sustained focus on excellence, KIPP has grown from 47 fifth graders in 1994 to 112,000 students in grades Pre-K through 12, in 255 educationally underserved communities across the country today.[21] Eighty-eight percent of all "KIPPsters" come from households living below the federal government's poverty threshold and are eligible for federal free or reduced-price lunch.

KIPP distinguished itself because of the strong work ethic it cultivated in its students. At the start of each year, each student, teacher, and parent or guardian must sign the KIPP "Commitment to Excellence" contract. Students pledge to "always work, think, and behave in the best way I know how" and "do whatever it takes for me and my fellow students to learn." This includes a commitment to "complete all my homework every night," call their teachers if there's "a problem with the homework or a problem with coming to school," and "raise my hand and ask questions in class if I do not understand something."[22] Among other things, teachers commit to working Saturdays and summers and "doing whatever it takes for our students to learn." For their part, parents and guardians pledge to get their kids to school on time for days that run from 7:25 A.M. to 5:00 P.M. (4:00 P.M. on Fridays) and certain Saturdays (9:15 A.M. to 1:05 P.M.). Parents also promise to check their child's homework every night and read to them every night.

The results of this team effort have been staggering. Some 33,000 alumni have graduated from KIPP schools, going on to earn bachelor's degrees at rates four times higher than the 11 percent rate for a low-income student population. *Work Hard. Be Nice.* is the title of *Washington Post* reporter Jay Mathews's 2009 bestseller on "How Two Inspired Teachers Created the Most Promising Schools in America."[23]

Then, in June 2020, came KIPP founder Dave Levin's—in his words—"long overdue" letter to KIPP alumni. He wrote that over twenty-five years, he, "as a white man, did not do enough as we built KIPP to fully understand how systemic and interpersonal racism, and specifically anti-Blackness, impacts you and your families—both inside of KIPP and beyond." The letter went on, practicing the latest empty ritual of performative white guilt, capitalizing the "B" in black, while leaving the "w" in white lowercase: "It is clear that I, and others, came up short in fully acknowledging the ways in which the [KIPP] school and organizational culture we built and how some of our practices perpetuated white supremacy and anti-Blackness." A month later, the KIPP Foundation's CEO announced that the organization was retiring the "Work hard. Be nice." slogan because "it ignores the significant effort required to dismantle systemic racism, places value on being compliant and submissive, supports the illusion of meritocracy . . . and does not align with our vision of students being free to create the future they want."[24]

This was a stunning retreat from the core principles that undergirded decades of KIPP's success in helping primarily low-income students of color acquire the knowledge and behaviors to overcome the very practices the school's leader said they perpetuated. This about-face is so disheartening about this about-face is that KIPP literally helped tens of thousands of kids create the future they wanted. Many of these kids for much of their lives had been told they were incapable of beating the odds against them. Consider the words of a KIPP eighth grader who wrote a 2012 blog post about her experience at a KIPP school in Arkansas. It is worth quoting at length:

> A phrase that is constantly referred to within KIPP is: "Work hard. Be nice." Not only do our teachers constantly push us to work hard and to be nice, but they also model for us how this looks in everyday life. This is what I think makes KIPP different from any school I have gone to in the past and why KIPP has had a major impact on my life.
>
> I no longer fear new challenges, because, during my experience at KIPP, I have learned that hard work can overcome any obstacle. Teachers at KIPP constantly reiterate these beliefs and they are something that I have learned to live by:
>
> • Hard work is necessary to accomplish a goal.
> • Anything worth having or doing is going to be hard.
> • There are no shortcuts in life. You cannot take the easy way out.
> • If you want to be successful, you need to know how to work hard to get what you want.
>
> KIPP has not only taught me the importance of hard work, but also to be nice. We are expected to be nice to our teammates

and be a support system for one another. Each day a student wakes up, they have a Team and Family behind them rooting them on to be the best they can be. I have never experienced the type of support I am given within KIPP. It's immeasurable.

"Work hard. Be nice." is a phrase that gives you a sense of determination. These four words may not seem very meaningful, but they have had a major impact on my life. It is because of these words that I plan on going out into the world and making a difference. I know I am going to need to work hard and be nice to others in order to make the world a better place. Thanks, KIPP DCPS, for teaching me this life lesson![25]

As of 2022, I will be in the process of launching Vertex Partnership Academies, a network of public charter high schools based on the concepts of equality of opportunity, individual dignity, and our common humanity, as well as the cardinal virtues of courage, justice, temperance, and wisdom. (I will say more about Vertex in Chapter 15.) Among my greatest wishes is that someday Vertex alumni will describe the impact of our schools as "immeasurable," and say that we helped them develop a "sense of determination."

Despite the exhortations from some of their own students about the "immeasurable" impact of "Work Hard. Be Nice.," KIPP held firm to retire the slogan. In a letter in response to a *Wall Street Journal* op-ed criticizing the decision, KIPP's founder Dave Levin wrote that even though the slogan was to be retired, he affirmed that KIPP still believed that "hard work is essential. Character matters. But neither is enough."[26] Fair point. In life, there are no guarantees for anyone, even if you put your nose to the grindstone. But the attempt to set the record straight did not clarify if KIPP still believes meritocracy is an illusion. Instead, it went on to underscore the obstacle of systemic barriers and not the ability of children to overcome them through character and hard work: "In a world where our students confront anti-blackness and systemic racism at every turn, KIPP's slogan needs to reflect the importance of identity, excellence and the boldness needed to create a more just world."[27]

The phrase "students confront anti-blackness and systemic racism *at every turn*" suggests that there is an omnipresent white supremacist lurking on each street corner, or designing each aptitude test, or reviewing each college application, or hiring for each job opening. That kind of thinking will lead children to fall into a rabbit hole of hopelessness and cynicism. I have run schools in the heart of the South Bronx for a decade. I do not see, nor do I want my students to believe, that their current reality is so bereft of opportunity. The whole reason to run schools, especially in disadvantaged communities, is to equip students with the tools to move from victimhood to victory, from poverty to prosperity.

In the end, about a year later, KIPP announced its new slogan, moving from the action-oriented and inspiring words of "Work Hard. Be Nice." to the verbless, milquetoast tagline: "Together, A Future Without Limits."

While every organization preserves the right to decide its own marketing mantras, it is disappointing that KIPP chose to erase the language that empowers young people to play a role in crafting their own future and replaced it with a nebulous statement romanticizing about the future.

Through my own personal interactions, I know that the leaders of KIPP and other education organizations confessing the sins of their pasts care deeply about their students. Yet it is unclear to me what these tortured statements of regret and admissions of racism and privilege portend. How can practices that have yielded unbelievable gains for low-income, black and brown children facilitate the perpetuation of white supremacy?

Unfortunately, well-meaning school leaders across the country are taking steps that have the unintended consequence of subverting excellence and fracturing communities—all in the name of racial equity or antiracism. As a result, some districts are mandating so-called equity trainings, in which teachers are forced to locate themselves on an "Oppression Matrix" to identify their status as "oppressor" or "oppressed."[28] Others are requiring kids to line up for "Privilege Walks" in which participants are instructed to take two steps backward if they are black and three steps forward if they are white.[29] Still others are requiring professional development sessions in which teachers are separated by race and the white faculty are labeled enslavers.[30]

Parents across America need to fully understand what is at stake when the contagion of antiracism or racial equity infects their school and what it means for their child's pursuit of agency. The pursuit of racial equity is far more likely to result in lowered standards, division, and mediocrity and worse for kids of all races. Achieving racial equity typically means one of two outcomes: (1) black students must equal the performance of white students, or (2) black success equals the percent representation in the population. *Either formulation places a ceiling on possibilities for black students.* Why would we do that? Why would we adopt purportedly antiracist agendas that actually plant the seeds of white superiority and black inferiority instead of eliminating them?

Yes, when racist acts and discrimination occur, let's confront that bigotry. But let's not fight bigotry with further bigotry. Let's not demonize each other by reducing faculty and students to nothing more than their race or gender identities. For every blame-the-system advocate who insists on the presence of systemic racism, institutional racism, or structural racism, we must empower young people with the belief in the far greater reality of *surmountable* racism! The antidote to racism is not antiracism. It is a philosophy of humanism that celebrates the inherent dignity of each individual. The antidote to racial inequity is not diminished expectations for all. It's equal opportunity for all and a belief in each individual's capacity for upward mobility—their sense of personal agency—no matter their skin color, class, or sex.

How My Story of Discovering the Importance of Family Structure Opened the Door for Me to View Agency as the Path Forward for Young Americans

"Who's Your Daddy?"

The Moment I Realized Schools Were Not Enough to Build Agency

Once upon a time, there was a small village on the edge of a river. The people there were good, and life in the village was good. One day a villager noticed a baby floating down the river. The villager quickly swam out to save the baby from drowning. The next day this same villager noticed two babies in the river. He called for help, and both babies were rescued from the swift waters. And the following day four babies were seen caught in the turbulent current. And then eight, then more, and then still more!

The villagers organized themselves quickly, setting up watch-towers and training teams of swimmers who could resist the swift waters and rescue babies. Rescue squads were soon working 24 hours a day. And each day the number of helpless babies float-ing down the river increased. The villagers organized themselves efficiently. The rescue squads were now snatching many children each day.

Though not all the babies, now very numerous, could be saved, the villagers felt they were doing well to save as many as they could each day. Indeed, the village priest blessed them in their good work. And life in the village continued on that basis.

> *Then, one day the villagers noticed a young man running*
> *northward along the bank. They shouted, "Where are you going?*
> *We need you to help with the rescue." He responded, "I am going*
> *upstream to find the son of a gun who is throwing these kids into*
> *the river!"*[1]

At around 4 P.M. on July 11, 2016, near Third Avenue and 149th Street in the heart of the South Bronx, I experienced a turning point that challenged me to be brutally honest about what was required to empower kids to successfully navigate the swift waters of life and become masters of their own fate.

I was six years into my ten-year stint as CEO of Public Prep. Public Prep is the nation's first and oldest nonprofit organization established to develop exceptional, tuition-free Pre-K and single-sex elementary and middle-grade charter schools. Like other public charter schools, it was founded on the simple but powerful vision that every parent—regardless of race, family structure, income level, or zip code—should have the power to choose a great, tuition-free public school for their child.

In response to overwhelming interest from parents, Public Prep was in the middle of strategic growth discussions about where to open our future schools. Earlier that year, the Citizens' Committee for Children (CCC) had issued its annual report on child well-being in New York City. The nonprofit, nonpartisan child advocacy organization ranks the city's fifty-nine community districts from highest to lowest risk. It provides an excellent framework for determining where to direct social investments to improve the lives of the city's most vulnerable children. In 2015, the five districts showing the highest risk to child well-being were *all in the South Bronx.*[2] Figure 6.1 illustrates the startling disparity between the highest-risk district, Hunts Point in the Bronx, and—less than two miles away across the East River as the

FIGURE 6.1   Selected education outcomes compared in the highest- and lowest-risk community districts in New York City, 2015.

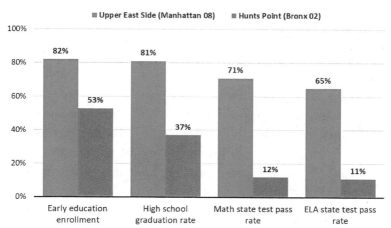

■ Upper East Side (Manhattan 08)   ■ Hunts Point (Bronx 02)

SOURCE: 2015 Citizen's Committee for Children Community Risk Ranking: Child Wellbeing in New York City's 59 Community Districts. https://cccnewyork.org/keeping-track-2015-our-newest-databook-on-child-well-being-in-nyc/.

crow flies—the lowest-risk district, on Manhattan's Upper East Side.

It is unconscionable that only 12 percent of the Hunts Point students were able to pass a math exam, especially when you consider that nearly six times that many children just two miles away were able to pass the same exam. And this had been the case for decades. A little earlier, a student advocacy group had released a study showing that at ninety New York City public schools, not a single black or Hispanic student had passed the 2014 state tests—not one.[3] And many of these schools were in the South Bronx.

Public Prep's elementary and middle schools were in high demand, especially in the Bronx. Each year thousands of Bronx families were entering our random lottery for fewer than two hundred open seats. Each year our student recruitment team heard shrieks of joy when we called the lucky families who had won the golden lottery ticket for a seat for their child. But the team also had to inform the nearly 5,000 Bronx families entering our lottery that the best we could do was put their child on a long wait list.

Given this situation, we decided to concentrate future school openings in the South Bronx. I also decided to move Public Prep's headquarters from Manhattan to the South Bronx so we could better understand and respond to our students' academic and social-emotional needs. Thus, Public Prep moved to a storefront location in the heart of the South Bronx in early July 2016, right next to St. Ann's Corner of Harm Reduction, a mental health counseling center that ran a free syringe program for drug users.

To get to know the area, my team took a walking tour of the neighborhood on that hot July afternoon to find a local deli, FedEx store, bodega, and place to score the best chili relleno. Along the way, we encountered a baby-blue Winnebago twenty-seven-foot truck that, judging by the cheery people standing nearby, was a familiar and welcome neighborhood fixture. This was my turning point. There comes a moment in the life of every education reformer when they confront the limits of education, and this was mine.

On the side of the Winnebago, in vivid graffiti lettering, was the phrase, "Who's Your Daddy?" The truck turned out to be a mobile DNA testing center that charges $350 to $500 to answer questions such as "Is she my sister?" or "Are you my father?" (see Figure 6.2).[4]

I was surprised that such a truck even existed, much less its on-demand services. Even more surprising, however, was the ho-hum acceptance of its existence. Who's Your Daddy? clearly met a strong demand in the community. "I realized that many of [my clients] were carrying around a huge burden—sometimes for decades," owner Jared Rosenthal wrote on his company's blog. "They live daily without the assurances that most people take for

FIGURE 6.2   "Who's Your Daddy?" DNA testing truck.

CREDIT: Barcroft Media/Barcroft Media Collection via Getty Images.

granted, such as: Who is my mother? Who is my brother? Am I really who I think I am?"[5]

The Who's Your Daddy? truck proved so popular that VH1, the New York-based cable television network, ultimately created a reality documentary series to tell "the stories behind some serious family drama and be right there when the truth is revealed." *Swab Stories* featured Rosenthal and his assistant medical technician, Ana Lopez (the "Swabinator"), who used a swab to collect saliva from their clients' mouths.[6]

Swab Stories was but one example of the media telling how family structure impacted the lives of young people. In November 2016, just three months after I saw the Who's Your Daddy? truck, the Lifetime Network premiered *30 Something Grandma*, a reality series chronicling the adventures of Chantal, Patricia, and Prudence, three single women in their early thirties.[7] Each had a teenage daughter who was about to have a child outside marriage, making them young, single grandmothers. *30 Something Grandma, 16 and Pregnant,* and *Teen Mom* all captured the dysfunctional cycle of single young women who get pregnant, become parents too early and unprepared, typically are abandoned or under-supported by their equally unready male counterparts, and then witness their young children repeat the same behavior less than twenty years later.[8] What was amazing about these shows was the racial diversity. Black, Hispanic, and white girls were all repre-sented, underscoring the fact that fatherlessness and nonmarital births among young women have become an equal opportunity tsunami, leaving children of black, brown, and, increasingly, white single mothers in its destructive wake.

My "Who's Your Daddy?" encounter and these shows prompted me to wonder whether the educational disparities between Hunts Point and the Upper East Side were due to more than geography, economics, and race. Could they result from some of these family dynamics? I looked back at the CCC data to explore additional cat-egories related to children and youth. Figure 6.3 displays some of what I found in comparing Hunts Point with the Upper East Side.[9]

The huge differences in family structure—yawning gaps in the percentage of children raised in single-parent households and teen birthrates—suggested that they could explain why education out-comes in the South Bronx and many urban and rural areas across the country had been so poor for so long.

Pursuing these questions put me on a path of no return. It turned out that the importance of family structure in academic success was not a radical nor novel concept. In 1966, the U.S. Office of Education commissioned the landmark Equality of Educational Opportunity survey to study the "lack of availability of equal educa-tional opportunities" for minority children.[10] James Coleman, the

FIGURE 6.3   Selected data related to children and youth compared in the highest- and lowest-risk community districts in New York City, 2015.

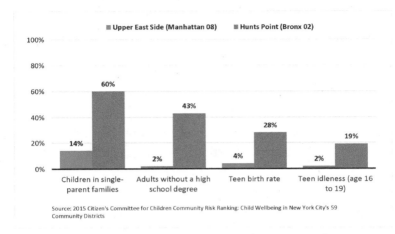

Source: 2015 Citizen's Committee for Children Community Risk Ranking: Child Wellbeing in New York City's 59 Community Districts

SOURCE: Citizen's Committee for Children of New York. https://cccnewyork.org /keeping-track-2015-our-newest-databook-on-child-well-being-in-nyc/.

noted sociologist and civil rights advocate who in 1963 had been arrested along with his family for demonstrating outside an amusement park that refused to admit African Americans, led the study.

The 700-page Coleman Report drew on data from more than 645,000 students and teachers in 4,000 U.S. public schools. One of its most controversial findings was that family background, not schools or race, explained most of the achievement gap between America's white and black students. As the report stated, "One implication stands out above all: That schools bring little influence to bear on a child's achievement that is independent of his background and general social context; and that this very lack of an independent effect means that the inequalities imposed on children by their home, neighborhood, and peer environment are carried along to become the inequalities with which they confront adult life at the end of school."[11]

Remarkably, the Coleman findings have stood up for more than fifty years.[12] In fact, a group of academics organized at Harvard even tried to disprove the report but their collective re-analyses reaffirmed Coleman's fundamental thesis: "Schools appeared to exert relatively little pull—explaining only 10 to 20 percent of the variability in student outcomes—while family background, peers, and students' own academic self-concept explained a much larger amount."[13]

I felt like a detective unearthing startling new clues in an ongoing case. I turned to state health data related to all births and nonmarital births in the Bronx.[14] I found that the nonmarital birthrate was 63 percent for all women and almost 80 percent for women under age twenty-five. The latter produced 4,133 newborns in the Bronx in 2016. These were the "floating babies" in the parable of the river that opens this chapter. They would likely grow up in economically impoverished, single-parent households with unstable family structures. And they would likely suffer the same consequences witnessed in the CCC's highest-risk category. Continuing on, I discovered that the Bronx in 2016 was simply a microcosm of the United States over decades.

As seen in figure 6.4, the last five decades have seen an explosion in nonmarital birthrates among women of all races. The share of all babies born outside marriage has risen from about 5 percent in the 1960s to today's "new normal" of 40 percent. It was becoming clear that these staggeringly high nonmarital birthrates—and the large numbers of children raised in single-parent families—impacted child well-being not just in the Bronx but also across New York and the nation.[15]

The macro-trends of nonmarital births across all ages masked even steeper increases among younger generations of all races.

FIGURE 6.4   Nonmarital birth share by race and ethnicity, 1960–2019.

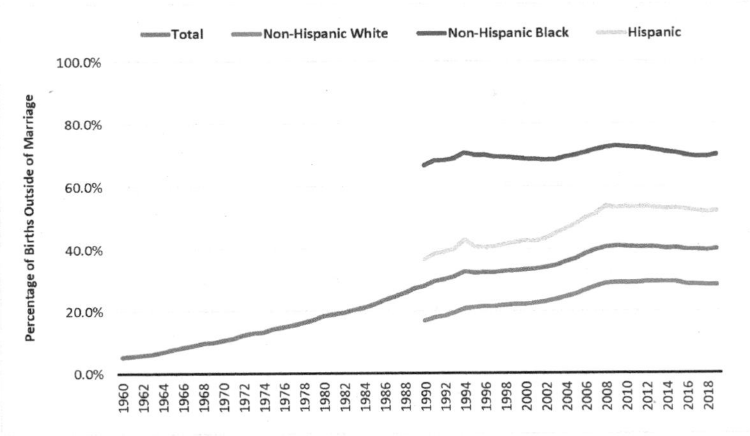

SOURCE: Centers for Disease Control and Prevention, National Vital Statistics Reports. https://www.cdc.gov/nchs/data/nvsr/nvsr48/nvs48_16.pdf; https://wonder.cdc.gov/natality-expanded-current.html.

Indeed, the youngest members of the Millennials (born 1979 through 1995) and Gen Z (born 1996 through 2010) are taking divergent paths into young adulthood. While today's teens forgo early births, and the birthrate of this cohort had fallen over the last two decades, another issue has cropped up among young twenty-somethings. Many young adults appear to believe that they simply have to wait until age twenty to have a child *on their own*. There is a high and growing nonmarital birth rate among twenty- to twenty-four-year-old women. They are waiting until they are out of their teen years to have a child, but they are not waiting until being married.

Figure 6.5 traces the nonmarital share of births for women of all races aged twenty through twenty-four versus the reduction in the teen birth rate over that same period. But it is also useful to

FIGURE 6.5   Nonmarital births to women aged 20–24 versus teenage births to girls aged 15–19, 1990–2019.

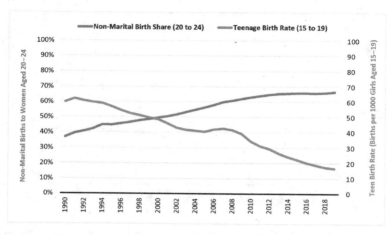

SOURCE: Centers for Disease Control and Prevention, National Vital Statistics Reports. https://wonder.cdc.gov/natality-expanded-current.html.

look at how this statistic breaks down across races (see Figure 6.6). In 2019, 91 percent of all babies born to black women under age twenty-five were outside marriage and 61 percent of babies born to white women under age twenty-five were outside marriage. Furthermore, approximately 40 percent of these babies in both groups were to a mother who already had at least one child. And that is a recipe more likely for negative outcomes—at the very least, for their children.

The research is clear and widely accepted: single parenthood among young adults is one of the strongest predictors of child poverty, school suspensions, incarceration, and educational disadvantage. Unmarried young mothers are far more likely to experience high levels of partnership instability and family complexity, and each of these is associated with poorer child well-being and inter-generational transmission of disadvantage.[16]

FIGURE 6.6   Nonmarital births to women aged 24 and under by race.

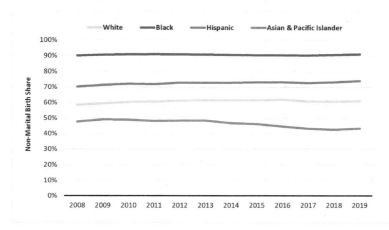

SOURCE: Centers for Disease Control and Prevention, National Vital Statistics Reports. https://wonder.cdc.gov/natality-expanded-current.html.

A colleague often tells me that rather than call our work to improve K–12 outcomes "education reform," a more appropriate term would be "education repair." The fact of the matter is that many of our schools do not do enough to support children who have grown up in non-intact families, especially when it comes to offering them effective strategies to move beyond the unique challenges that may come with a background of family disadvantage as they journey through adolescence and into adulthood. It is the rescue operation in the parable of the river. Although the parable analogizes the perpetual and often unwinnable game of academic catch-up for under-resourced children who enter kindergarten already far behind, the story's final passage commands us to seek out the cause of all those "floating babies"—and do something about it.

Yes, my life began to change the day when I happened upon that "Who's Your Daddy?" truck and began my trek upstream.

What I have learned since that day has convinced me that our schools are necessary, but not sufficient, to fully empower kids to reach their potential. If we truly want our students to break the cycle of poverty, we need to do more. In addition to educating our students in science, math, history, literature, and the arts, it is equally important to educate our middle- and high-school students in the proper timing, sequencing, and effects of key life events during the transition to adulthood.

There is a way to accomplish this. I call it FREE (more on that in Chapters 12–16), and it's based on what we know works. On the front end, we know that effective early interventions like home visiting can improve school readiness and reduce chronic exposure to toxic stress that inhibits brain development. On the back end, we can help teenagers entering adulthood reframe how they think about the timing of their own family formation to give them—and their future children—the best chance of success.

See you upstream.

Robbing Our Young People of Agency

Silence or Denial about the Importance of Family Structure

The day was February 15, 2013. President Barack Obama was back in his old stomping grounds, the Woodlawn neighborhood of Chicago's South Side, less than a mile from the home in which he and his wife, Michelle, had raised their two daughters. Cries of "We love you" came from the nearly 700 adoring students and faculty assembled at Hyde Park Academy High School. "I love you too," said Obama, but then the celebratory mood soon shifted to the somber purpose of his visit. Three weeks earlier the school's majorette team had performed at Obama's second presidential inaugural in Washington, DC. A week later, one of the squad's members, fifteen-year-old sophomore Hadiya Pendleton, had been shot in the back and killed. Hadiya (a name that means "gift from God" in Arabic) had been standing with friends and fellow students in a nearby park. An eighteen-year-old man drove by and, mistaking Hadiya's group for a rival gang, opened fire.

In the Hyde Park Academy gym, Obama lamented that Hadiya's killing was not unique to Chicago or the country—"Too many of our children are being taken away from us"—before calling on Congress to enact "some common-sense proposals to make it harder for criminals to get their hands on a gun." The president could have lingered on this theme. Many of his predecessors had done so at similar moments of national outrage and mourning. He could have called for new legislation restricting access to bullets and firearms or requiring more extensive background checks. Instead, Obama turned his attention toward forces *beyond* the reach of policy. "No law or set of laws can prevent every senseless act of violence in this country," he continued. "When a child opens fire on another child, there's a hole in that child's heart that [the] government can't fill—only the community and parents and teachers and clergy can fill that hole."

The hole Obama referred to is the lack of moral discernment that is so crucial to free will. It is at the heart of my definition of agency. Without naming them, Obama also identified the local mediating institutions in Chapter 3, and the indispensable role that these structures play in forming the character of whole and wholesome human beings.

Obama continued as the once-exuberant audience fell silent: "We all share a responsibility to move this country closer to our founding vision that no matter who you are, or where you come from, here in America, you can decide your own destiny. You can succeed if you work hard and fulfill your responsibilities. Now, that starts at home. There's no more important ingredient for success, nothing that would be more important for us reducing violence than strong, stable families—which means we should do more to promote marriage and encourage fatherhood."[1]

In this moment of tragedy, Obama had the audacity to look beyond the short-term factors that may have led this young man to commit his heinous crime. The president was bold enough to link the dysfunctional behavior to a few fundamental tenets whose absence or presence matter monumentally to human development and the acquisition of personal agency: marriage, family, religion, and education. It wasn't the first time he had struck these themes. As a presidential candidate in 2008, Obama had said in a Father's Day speech at Chicago's Apostolic Church of God:

> Of all the rocks upon which we build our lives, we are reminded today that family is the most important. And we are called to recognize and honor how critical every father is to that foundation. . . . We need fathers to realize that responsibility does not end at conception. We need them to realize that what makes you a man is not the ability to have a child—*any fool can have a child*—it's the courage to raise one.[2]

Obama knew Chicago was already in the midst of a multiyear crime wave. (Someone would be shot every other hour in the Windy City in 2017, pushing the rate there to the highest point in nearly twenty years.)[3] Obama also knew that Kenneth Williams, the teenager who randomly shot Hadiya, was not born with a gun in his hand or a predisposition to kill others. Yet, at the time of the shooting, this eighteen-year-old had not only been sentenced to two years of probation for aggravated unlawful use of a weapon. He had also been arrested three other times in the prior twelve months. The question is whether there had been leading indicators that could help us prevent such bloodshed in the future.

In that regard, it is revealing to look back a generation in Chicago, to 2000, around the time when the young people caught up in that day's violence were born. The Epidemiology Unit of the Cook County Department of Public Health produces a detailed yearly analysis of women who give birth by age and race. According to the unit's "Birth 2000" report, 62 percent of the 8,700-plus babies born to women of all races aged twenty-four and under were born out of wedlock. Of the 2,500-plus black babies born to women aged twenty-four and under, a staggering 89 percent had mothers who were unmarried at the time of delivery. Even more disturbing, 42 percent of these black babies had records that were "missing information for father," a far higher percentage than any other racial cohort.[4]

Unsurprisingly, children who grow up in these environments are much more likely to experience the kinds of toxic stress that have lifelong, adverse consequences on their development, which can lead to a generational treadmill of poverty, antisocial behavior at school, and a greater propensity for criminal activity. Given what we know about the adverse impact on boys and girls of growing up without a father, the rise in out-of-wedlock births might well explain the epidemic of gun violence in Chicago that ended Hadiya's life a generation later.[5] Consider also the findings of the powerful longitudinal study, "Father Absence and Youth Incarceration." It followed a cohort of more than 6,400 young men for more than twenty years, from birth through adolescence. This study found that teenagers who grew up in nonintact families committed more crimes and were 250 percent more likely to be imprisoned than those in married, two-parent families, regardless of race.[6]

The 2015 Closing the Opportunity Gap initiative, organized by the Saguaro Seminar at Harvard University, explored why this was happening. A dozen of the country's leading experts in education, family, and parenting drew on the findings of Harvard professor Robert Putnam's five-year effort to research the growing inequality gaps in America and determine why fewer Americans of all races today are upwardly mobile. The group identified a tangle of causal factors: the unraveling of the social fabric and safety nets in working-class communities, segregation along class lines, and economic insecurity. But here was the key takeaway:

Growing up with two parents is now unusual in the white (as well as non-white) working class, while two-parent families are normal and becoming more common among the upper middle class (both white and non-white). Most Americans are unaware that the white working class family is today more fragile than the black family was at the time of the famous alarm-sounding 1965 report, "The Negro Family: The Case for National Action," by Daniel Patrick Moynihan.[7]

As Moynihan had himself written at the time,

From the wild Irish slums of the 19th century eastern seaboard to the riot-torn suburbs of Los Angeles, there is one unmistakable lesson in American history: a community that allows a large number of young men to grow up in broken families, dominated by women, never acquiring any set of rational expectations about the future—that community asks for and gets chaos. Crime, violence, unrest, disorder—most particularly the furious, unrestrained lashing out at the whole social structure—that is not only to be expected; it is very near to inevitable. And it is richly deserved.[8]

Yet even stating these truths has become increasingly taboo. G. K. Chesterton, the English writer and philosopher, famously wrote, "Every high civilization decays by forgetting obvious things."[9] Obama was hammered for *not* "forgetting obvious things" and affirming the plain commonsense truth about the importance of marriage and fatherhood.

After Obama's Father's Day speech, civil rights activist Rev. Jesse Jackson had been caught on a live Fox News microphone telling another black guest, "See, Barack been, um, talking down to black people on this faith-based—I wanna cut his nuts out. . . .

Barack—he's talking down to black people—telling niggers how to behave."[10]

Jackson's metaphorical gelding operation picked up again after Obama's Hyde Park Academy remarks. Detractors pounced. They accused him of blaming age-old stereotypes about black families for gun violence and criticized him for not focusing *exclusively* on structural inequalities like the lack of jobs, decrepit public housing, and failing schools that plague the black underclass. Obama, of course, had acknowledged these forces. But he had to be punished for straying from the blame-the-system orthodoxy and, as a distraction, be accused of blaming the victim.

Noted author Ta-Nehisi Coates—who had himself previously written movingly about the importance of his own wedded mother and father in his childhood—railed against the president's embrace of marriage and fatherhood: "From the White House on down, the myth holds that fatherhood is the great antidote to all that ails black people. . . . The thread is as old as black politics itself. It is also wrong. The kind of trenchant racism to which black people have persistently been subjected can never be defeated by making its victims more respectable."[11]

It is extraordinary to reflect that one of America's premier black writers accused America's first black president of perpetuating a racist myth about fatherhood as the president tried to make sense of a black teenager's wanton killing of an innocent black teenager. It's also worth noting the hypocrisy of Coates and so many others who criticize a focus on marriage and fatherhood when it comes to the lives of others while they practice, or even celebrate, the importance of marriage and fatherhood *in their own lives.*

The public backlash against a sitting (black) president who had the temerity to say that family matters has had a chilling effect. It is small wonder that so few Americans of any race have the courage to speak honestly about how the decline in family stability has eroded lives and communities and interrupted young people's quest for agency and self-determination. Today, the nation's civil rights leaders and prison reform champions (the heroic human rights lawyer and activist Bryan Stevenson, for example) suffer the same affliction as leaders, researchers, and funders in the education reform community: an inability or unwillingness to acknowledge that when widespread numbers of men in a community—regardless of race—impregnate women but *shirk their responsibility* to be solid husbands and fathers, there are nearly irreversible emotional, behavioral, and academic consequences for the kids who live in those fragmented families.[12]

Indeed, organizations like Black Lives Matter seek to "disrupt the Western-prescribed nuclear family structure requirement" and attribute mass incarceration to virulent "anti-Black racism."[13] Rarely, however, do its leaders acknowledge that there is a predictive link between higher crime rates—and resulting imprisonment rates—and the staggering decline in family stability that now leaves 71 percent of all black babies born out of wedlock. It is a stunning collapse of family structure that is only surpassed by an 1100 percent increase in the nonmarital birth share among white women over the last six decades.[14]

Yes, black lives matter—period. I am one of them. But the data raise the question: to whom? Each black life, and each life of any race, must matter most to the two people who chose to create it. Moreover, each black life, and each life of any race, has to matter all the time. There has been a national response to several cases of police violence in which unarmed, but not necessarily completely innocent, black men were killed. But no amount of angry protest, liberal guilt, or "impact philanthropy" focused on symptoms versus underlying causes will ever completely fill the hole in a child's heart that President Obama identified. Nor will it replace

FIGURE 7.1   Number of children born to unmarried mothers, by age of mother and year of birth.

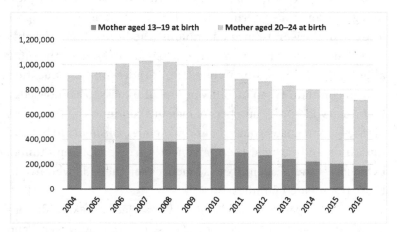

SOURCE: Centers for Disease Control and Prevention, National Vital Statistics Reports. https://wonder.cdc.gov/natality-expanded-current.html.

the fundamental love of two, married, indispensable parents who are ready to raise a child.

Those of us who are committed to achieving better outcomes for the next generation cannot succeed unless we confront the decline in family stability—a decline that is an equal opportunity social tsunami. To estimate the number of children in kindergarten through twelfth grade who were not born into a two-parent, married structure, I compiled the longitudinal birth data in Figure 7.1 from thirteen "National Vital Statistics Reports" produced by the Centers for Disease Control and Prevention. From 2004 to 2016, nearly 4 million babies were born to unwed teenage mothers, and about 12 million babies were born out of wedlock to women of all races aged 24 and under.[15] According to the National Campaign to Prevent Teen and Unplanned Pregnancy, an estimated 70 to 90 percent of these pregnancies were unplanned by these unmarried young people, many of whom already were or became poor.[16]

These staggering numbers of children born outside marriage—and the increased likelihood of negative consequences—are precisely why the education reform community must construct a curriculum and culture that teaches the next generation about family formation and the sequence of personal choices that gives students (and their children) the best shot at life fulfillment. These 12 million boys and girls are in our K–12 schools today, five days a week. They are at great risk of repeating the same cycle of family instability they have likely experienced, despite the best efforts of their young single parent or their guardian.[17]

Granted, there are no guarantees in life. Being born into a stable, two-parent home does not assure success, and being raised in a low-income, single-parent household does not lock in failure. Some troubled children come from the most well-resourced, married households. Other children thrive despite chaotic homes. I know this firsthand. Every day I work with extraordinary women and men who have defied the odds. They have overcome the challenge of having a child out of wedlock early in their lives and excel at being a single parent to wonderful, college-bound children. It is never too late to get your life back on track. We know, however, that having children while young and unprepared is a far more challenging path, especially when it comes to achieving the best outcomes for children.

No one should understand this better than principals and teachers who work in communities where children depend heavily on schooling to escape poverty. Yet rarely do my fellow education leaders openly admit that a primary cause of the challenges our students face is the wholesale collapse of the families in which they are being raised. Rather, the dominant blame-the-system narrative holds that structural barriers are far more decisive in determining life education outcomes for kids or in breaking the cycle of poverty.

I had come to believe that our collective silence was collective capitulation. My fellow educators seemed to feel that rampant out-of-wedlock birthrates are simply inevitable in the neighborhoods we serve, or that we can't talk about this because it would further stereotype already marginalized populations or risk "blaming the victim." I wasn't buying this ostrich-like approach. Burying our heads in the sand or being silenced into submission would not lift a rising generation when nearly 800,000 babies are born each year to unwed, unprepared, and usually poorly educated young women under the age of twenty-four. It's time for a new conversation and call to action.

I began writing a series of essays on this silent tsunami for the Thomas B. Fordham Institute.[18] These pieces outlined the impact that family structure and stability had on children of all races and the role public education leaders should play in meeting the challenge. Suffice it to say, my views were not always popular. For example, I heard from Nicole Sussner Rodgers of Family Story, an organization that advocates for "embracing the dignity and value of a wider range of family arrangements and models" and "works to address and dismantle family privilege in America" and "to expose the ways family privilege causes harm."[19] After reading one of my essays, she wrote to me, "Focusing on the family structure of low-income people and people of color implies that there is some sort of cultural pathology at play, and that strikes me as a deeply dangerous idea that progressives must reject." She wrote that she believes poverty is an issue of "systemic inequality, not personal failing" or bad relationship choices. "Endorsing marriage has become a dog whistle," she argued, "used to prime racist, debunked stereotypes about so-called absentee black fathers, to invalidate non-nuclear family arrangements, and to treat those within them as failures."[20]

In a follow up interview for this book, Ms. Rodgers shared with me her belief that focusing on marriage with young people is the wrong starting point and misdiagnoses the problem. She believes we should address the lack of financial stability and the socio-economic issues that get to the core of what makes people's lives unstable to begin with, and stop treating marriage as a silver bullet. In her words, "People are not poor because they marry less. People marry less because they are poor."[21]

Others who read my essays feared that bringing up the decline in family structure would mean "shaming" students whose parents were young single mothers. Or it would mean insulting grandparents, aunts, uncles, or other adult caregivers who had been thrust into the role of guardianship because the child's biological parents had abrogated their responsibilities. But I had determined that *not* talking about the realities of family instability and its impact on our students and their loss of agency would not make the problem go away. Nor would it give young people the tools to change the course of their lives. If the stability and structure of the family within which a child is raised is fundamental to that student's life outcomes, then why isn't addressing these factors at the center of our efforts to end this intergenerational disadvantage?

As one colleague wrote to me,

"I read your piece and in the spirit of candor, I thought it was missing the inclusion of the systemic and institutional barriers that have played a major role in eroding the black family (majority of the kids you and I work with). The absence of those variables results in an incomplete narrative of what has led us to this point—personal responsibility is critical coupled with the acknowledgement of systemic and institutional systems/policies that have

birthed these outcomes. In my opinion, we must give equal voice
to the intersectionality of policy, poverty and fatherlessness if we
are to dismantle and not circumvent these truths.[22]

In a sense, my colleague accused me of having a blame-the-
victim mentality. It became clear that I needed to have the moral
courage to talk about the importance of family structure and the
power of agency, as well as the need to revitalize the key institutions that cultivate agency. I also had to leverage my position as
an immigrant black American who, despite individual success, still
faces racial discrimination—yet still raise my own black children
to believe the American Dream is within their grasp. And, as someone actually running schools, I had to provide a tangible example
of the role schools can play in strengthening families and thereby
improving outcomes for kids so they can avoid these issues in the
first place.

I empathize with fellow leaders in education who are hesitant
to talk about these issues. I understand that they fear the type of
backlash from teachers and families that Obama received. And I
understand that they worry about being accused of judging—
shaming—the very people we are seeking to serve. Yet we can
ignore the data no longer. Great schools must confront the importance of family stability. We cannot control the decisions made by
the parents of our students. But it is within our control to influence the family structure of the next generation because we decide
what we teach children today about family formation and the likely
paths toward life fulfillment.[23] Phrases like "Who's your daddy? "
need not be commonplace in the disadvantaged communities,
whether they be in Chicago, Appalachia, the Rio Grande Valley,
or the South Bronx. It does not have to be this way.[24]

Princeton University sociologist Kathy Edin studies poverty
through ethnographic observations and in-depth interviews with

hundreds of unmarried, low-income mothers and fathers. Edin's unorthodox "embedding" approach led her, her husband, and their three-year-old daughter to move into a studio apartment in Camden, New Jersey, one of the nation's poorest cities, for two years of intensive fieldwork. Her must-read books—*Promises I Can Keep: Why Poor Women Put Motherhood before Marriage* (2005) and *Doing the Best I Can: Fathering in the Inner City* (2013)—reveal something critical. Poor young women and men of all races share a common set of human desires to get a good education, secure a decent job, fall in love, marry, raise children in a stable home, and earn a salary that provides dignity and supports their family. But an array of structural barriers—neighborhood effects, family history, and dysfunctional social norms—simply derail them. These factors lead to choices that unwittingly perpetuate their poverty and virtually guarantee the same outcomes for their children. Despite the regretful choices these parents may have made, Edin's work also reveals their deep commitment to helping their children build different and better lives than their own. It's why many poor parents enter lotteries for public charter schools, fighting to get their children an excellent education. They want their boys and girls to learn math, science, humanities, and the arts, and they also want them to be around empathetic adults who will teach children the most reliable paths to life success and the habits needed to overcome the obstacles they faced as parents.

In my own work in low-income communities, I started to see the disconnect between those who claim to advocate for people in challenging situations and those in the situations themselves. My conversations with single parents in the community revealed that, far from being insulted, these parents welcomed the idea that schools would have the courage to speak to their children about better life-course decisions. Indeed, in a study conducted in 2021 by the American Enterprise Institute, seven in ten respondents who had not graduated high school, were unmarried parents, or were currently not working—supported teaching students that young people who get at least a high school degree, have a job, and get married before having children are more likely to be financially secure and avoid poverty in later life. As Mona Davids, an African American single mom who now runs her own firm, Social Impact Strategies, to strengthen communities, wrote to me in a personal email:

> We want our kids to succeed. We don't want our kids making the same mistakes we did. . . . Let's be real. Ed reformers instill into kids: study, work hard and go to college. How about: don't get pregnant, study, work hard and go to college? Why can't we say that to kids and ask their parents to do so as well? Let's have this much needed conversation about what folks seem to think we, single mothers with kids, will feel offended about—when we're not offended.[25]

Yes, let's be real. Let's be unintimidated and unsilenced. We know what's best for all kids and, as we will see in the chapters to come, we know what works.

8

How America Has Changed Young Hearts and Minds in the Past

Teen Pregnancy

This is the story of another president and another important presidential speech touching on American family formation. This time, however, an American president's words led to actions rather than a backlash or a successful campaign to silence conversation on a critical social problem. And these were actions that produced quantifiable positive change, that changed hearts and minds—and that show what can be done when we work intelligently to address a social crisis.

The president was William Jefferson Clinton, and the day was January 24, 1995. The first-term president was delivering his State of the Union address to Congress and the nation. Republicans, under the leadership of Georgia congressman Newt Gingrich and the banner of the "Contract with America," had just trounced Clinton and the Democrats in the midterm election. The GOP had gained control of both the U.S. Senate and the House of Representatives for the first time in four decades. The party had won a majority of state legislatures for the first time in fifty years and a majority of governorships for the first time in more than twenty years. The "Republican Revolution" was on the march and a chastened Clinton was struggling to reestablish his relevance and win reelection.

Seeking an issue that would appeal to both conservatives and liberals and galvanize support among Republicans and Democrats alike, Clinton seized on the soaring rate of teen pregnancy. In his biography *Behind the Oval Office*, Dick Morris, the president's chief political adviser, famously said that in order to get reelected, Clinton had to "triangulate," which required that "the president needed to take a position that not only blended the best of each party's views but also transcended them to constitute a third force in the debate."[1] Teen pregnancy was an issue that Isabel Sawhill in the Office of Management and Budget and William Galston in the Domestic Policy Council had been urging the president to take on. Thus, on January 24, 1995, President Clinton used his largest platform, the annual State of the Union address, to make an unprecedented call to action on the crisis of children having children:

> We've got to ask our community leaders and all kinds of organizations to help us stop our most serious social problem: the epidemic of teen pregnancies and births where there is no marriage. . . . Government can only do so much. Tonight, I call on parents and leaders all across this country to join together in a national campaign against teen pregnancy to make a difference. We can do this and we must.[2]

Clinton was hardly the first to call attention to this American crisis. A little more than a decade earlier, *Time* magazine had put Angela, a white, fifteen-year-old girl, on its December 9, 1985, cover. Sporting a light pink blouse and a facial expression of adolescent angst, Angela was the quintessential girl next door, a blue-eyed, blond American teen looking toward a bright future.

Indeed, what earned Angela a spot on the *Time* cover was that she was so typical of what many American teens were facing in the mid-eighties—and therein lay the crisis. Angela was pregnant. She was in her third trimester, more than thirty weeks pregnant with soon-to-be-born son Corey, whom Angela would parent as a single mother. On the cover, next to the photo of Angela, were the words "Children Having Children: Teen Pregnancy in America" in big, bold letters. With an estimated 32 million U.S. readers each week, *Time* was trying to use its vast influence to sound the alarm that "teenage pregnancy was corroding America's social fabric." As chairman of *Time* Inc.'s Magazine Group, John A. Meyers, wrote in the "Letter from the Publisher" column, "Pregnant teenagers and unwed mothers were once virtually invisible and unmentionable. But now the hush has ended: yesterday's secret has become today's national problem."[3]

Perhaps for the first time, many Americans learned that more than a million American teenagers became pregnant each year. Four out of five were unmarried. They were teenagers from many different places and races, according to cover story writer Claudia Wallis, but they were also teenagers whose "tales and laments have a haunting sameness." Why was teen pregnancy a crisis and not the latest lifestyle choice? Wallis continued:

> Teen pregnancy imposes lasting hardships on two generations: parent and child. Teen mothers are, for instance, many times as likely as other women with young children to live below the poverty level. According to one study, only half of those who give birth before age 18 complete high school (as compared with 96% of those who postpone childbearing). On average, they earn half as much money and are far more likely to be dependent on

welfare: 71% of females under 30 who receive Aid to Families with Dependent Children had their first child as a teenager. . . . As infants, the offspring of teen mothers have high rates of illness and mortality. Later in life, they often experience educational and emotional problems. Many are victims of child abuse at the hands of parents too immature to understand why their baby is crying or how their doll-like plaything has suddenly developed a will of its own. Finally, these children of children are prone to dropping out and becoming teenage parents themselves. According to one study, 82% of girls who give birth at age 15 or younger were daughters of teenage mothers. . . . With disadvantage creating disadvantage, it is no wonder that teen pregnancy is widely viewed as the very hub of the U.S. poverty cycle.[4]

Despite *Time*'s earnest wake-up call, the problem of children having children only worsened. The U.S. teen-pregnancy rate hit a twenty-year high in 1990. In the George H. W. Bush years, vice president Dan Quayle's clumsy efforts to call attention to the issue merely confused and politicized the issue when he criticized TV character "Murphy Brown" for having a baby out of wedlock. (I will say more on that later in this chapter.)

Within weeks of President Clinton's State of the Union remarks, a chorus of bipartisan voices had echoed the president's call for action. Pennsylvania Senator Rick Santorum, an up-and-coming conservative Republican and frequent Clinton critic, wrote that "teenage pregnancy is the nation's most serious domestic crisis. . . . We must discourage young women from putting themselves in a situation where welfare is the only way out, which means reducing the rate of teenage pregnancy and out-of-wedlock births."[5] On March 2, 1995, prominent liberal Democrat Nita Lowey of New York introduced H.R. 1115, the Teen Pregnancy Prevention and

Parental Responsibility Act. Its goal was "Ending the Cycle of Inter-generational Dependency."[6]

Rather than creating a massive federal program, Clinton pushed to organize a national coalition of nongovernmental leaders to carry out his presidential mandate. The White House convened a series of meetings, including one chaired by the president himself in October 1995, to discuss the merits and possible activities of a nonpartisan, private sector–led and financed campaign to reduce teen pregnancy.

In the Presidential Briefing Book handed out in one of the meetings to approximately sixty leaders from across the country who were contemplating the launch of a national campaign, this wise appeal for participation was included: "No identifiable set of highly respected and credible national leaders has been willing to state clearly and repeatedly that teenagers ought not to become pregnant or be parents. Leaders may feel it's taboo—'too hot to handle'—but they should know that the President's statement in the 1995 State of the Union message that teenage pregnancy is 'the most serious problem facing our nation today' earned the loudest and longest applause of any portion of that speech."[7]

Many of the invited leaders were already engaged in state- and community-based efforts to curb teen pregnancy. But this diverse and growing coalition knew that the White House's backing—at least at the outset—would increase the visibility, influence, and power of their efforts on the ground.

Moreover, while agreement on the need to reduce teen pregnancy had been reached, how to do it was far from settled. Should condoms be distributed in schools? Should there be abstinence-only education? Should high schools for pregnant teens and young mothers be opened? How should the prickly issues of abortion and marriage be handled? How would the dramatic differences in teen-pregnancy rates by race impact the strategy? Should adoption be promoted as a choice for young women?

The Robert Wood Johnson Foundation became an early and generous supporter of the burgeoning campaign. The Foundation later produced a report stating that a neutral force was needed to become "an objective source of information on a topic that is often politically and ideologically controversial." Sawhill, who was at the Urban Institute by then, agreed to coordinate a national campaign and develop an organization to run it. From the outset, she and Urban Institute CEO Sarah Brown (then at the Institute of Medicine—now referred to as the National Academies of Science, Medicine and Engineering) emphasized the need to be bipartisan and inclusive. According to the Robert Wood Johnson Foundation's history of the project, "The Campaign's messages were to include support for teens delaying sexual activity as well as others providing teens with information about adequate contraceptive education and services, especially for those teens who are sexually active."[8]

One of the project's first tasks was to recruit diverse political leaders and cultural influencers in entertainment and media, philanthropy, academia, research, public health, and business. In February 1996, one year after Clinton's State of the Union, all this activity culminated in the creation of a new nonprofit, nonpartisan organization, the National Campaign to Prevent Teen Pregnancy, whose mission was "to improve the well-being of children, youth, and families by reducing teen pregnancy."[9] Led by former New Jersey Republican governor Thomas Kean (board chair), Sawhill (board president), and Brown (CEO), the twenty-five-member board was star-studded and widely diverse.

It prompted leaders of all persuasions to become strange bedfellows in reducing teenage pregnancy and intergenerational despair. And thus a star cause was born. At the federal level, bipartisan congressional advisory panels were set up, along with unprecedented coalitions of leaders from Hollywood, faith communities, business, and education, as well as cultural elites. As Sarah Brown shared with me in an interview for this book, "In addition, a strong advisory group of widely respected researchers was assembled—a step that provided depth and credibility to the group from the outset. As was said on day one, the new effort must rest on the best data and research available; that is, 'we need to begin by getting the facts straight.'"[10]

The campaign's initial goal was to reduce the teen-pregnancy rate by one third between 1996 and 2005. To achieve this goal, the National Campaign launched a multipronged effort with an emphasis on states and communities, research, faith-based organizations, public policy, and the media. It incorporated teen-pregnancy reduction messages into newspapers and magazines and on radio and television—especially those programs most viewed by teens as well as the parents of teens. Altogether, the campaign reached hundreds of millions of people.

The effort was so successful in its first ten years that the Robert Wood Johnson Foundation issued a 2009 report entitled "National Campaign Helps Reduce the Rate of Teen Pregnancy by One-Third in 10 Years" (Figure 8.1). The report included "Lessons Learned" for anyone considering a movement to shift norms and behavior.

The Clinton-inspired campaign to reduce teen pregnancy had succeeded. It was possible to change young hearts and minds— the metrics made this clear. Yet something happened along the way—something that made the campaign less than it was initially claimed to be and that requires our attention today if we are to lift a rising generation and give our young people a shot at successful lives.

FIGURE 8.1   Teenage birth rate, 1990–2019.

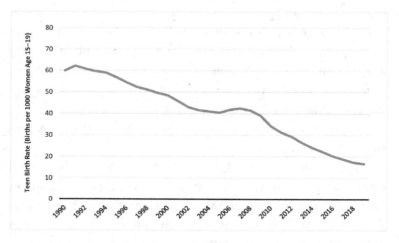

SOURCE: Centers for Disease Control and Prevention, National Vital Statistics Reports.
https://wonder.cdc.gov/natality-expanded-current.html.

THE DEFINING DECISION

Despite the campaign's extraordinary success in reducing teen pregnancies and births—and the valuable lessons learned for addressing other public health issues—the pivotal strategic choice at the beginning of the campaign cannot be overlooked. Perhaps the greatest lesson learned is what the campaign chose to focus on from the outset and what it chose *not* to focus on. Remember, President Clinton had identified the country's most serious social problem as the "epidemic of teen pregnancies and *births where there is no marriage*" (italics added) in his 1995 State of the Union address.[11] His March 20, 1995, letter to congressional leaders on welfare reform had been just as clear and inclusive. "We must discourage irresponsible behavior that lands people on welfare in the first place," he wrote, "with a national campaign against teen

	Lessons Learned
1	**When advocating for social change, set a measurable goal.** From the start, the Campaign aimed to reduce teenage pregnancy by one third within ten years. That target kept participants motivated and gave them a yardstick by which to measure progress.
2	**Work with people and organizations from across the political spectrum.** The Campaign cultivated congressional leaders from both major parties as well as a broad range of interest groups. If it had collaborated only with people who thought alike, it would not have accomplished as much.
3	**To enlist the support of a broad range of organizations, speak the language of each group.** For example, in working with faith leaders, Campaign staff spoke about values and morality. When addressing entertainment media, staff spoke about target audiences and ad revenue. With businesses, staff talked about the bottom line.
4	**Ask potential partners to contribute in ways that align with their values.** For example, Campaign staff found that faith leaders were eager to encourage parent-child communication, but most were unlikely to teach about contraception.
5	**When tackling a contentious social issue, begin with baseline public opinion data.** In hindsight, the Campaign CEO said that she should have done more public opinion polling from the outset to assess people's attitudes toward teen pregnancy and how those changed over time.
6	**When seeking to influence a large number of people, take a "wholesale" rather than a "retail" approach.** The latter means working one-on-one. The former means reaching large numbers of people through websites, teleconferences, publications, and partnerships with other organizations, such as the entertainment industry. As Campaign CEO Brown noted, "A single hour of television on the WB network or a one-page article in *Teen People* can reach millions of teens."
7	**When collaborating with the entertainment media, come prepared with concrete ideas on how to help people do their jobs.** When Campaign staff met with television producers and writers, they did not say the shows "should" cover teen pregnancy. Instead, they made it clear they understood the needs of writers and producers and offered ideas on how to incorporate messages into storylines for specific characters.

(continued)

	Lessons Learned
8	**Research plays a large role in public advocacy**. Particularly in an ideologically charged field, an effective organization needs to be seen as grounded in science. "It's easy to get buffeted by arguments and whims of the day unless you are grounded in good research, numbers and trends," said Campaign CEO Brown. "A strong grounding in science allows you to be more purposeful and avoid many political culture wars."
9	**When advocating for social change, keep in close touch with the targeted group—in this case, teens**. The Campaign developed a number of ways to do so, including its website, Youth Leadership Team, annual public service announcement contest with *Teen People* magazine, and Youth Network.[12]

pregnancy that *lets young people know it is wrong to have a child outside marriage*" (italics added).[13]

Teen pregnancy and births outside marriage were both serious problems. Yet, at its inception in 1995, Campaign organizers focused on addressing the former and avoided the latter. Why? The influence of *Murphy Brown* and the controversy surrounding her character likely played a role.

Murphy Brown was a fictional TV character played by well-known actress Candice Bergen on the show of the same name. The show became the nation's third most popular television series. In 1992, it boasted a weekly audience of nearly 20 million households. It also became the improbable center of a national cultural war waged around marriage and feminism.

Bergen's character was a single, childless forty-year-old, highly respected television news anchor. Murphy had overcome her share of challenges—including alcoholism and tobacco addiction—and succeeded in a male-dominated industry. She embodied the strong, financially independent woman and became an icon for young girls and women who dreamed of breaking the glass ceiling in their own lives. As a backstory in the show, Murphy Brown had been married to Jake Lowenstein, an "underground leftist radical" she had met after they were both maced and arrested in a 1968 protest. They had married but then divorced after only seven days. Fast forward twenty-five television years: Murphy Brown engages in a brief sexual relationship with Jake that results in her becoming pregnant. Lowenstein has no interest in being a parent, so Brown had a decision to make. On May 18, 1992, CBS aired the final episode of the fourth season. Rather than marriage, adoption, or abortion, Murphy Brown gave birth to a son, Avery, and chose to raise him as a single mother. What ensued may be the most influential three minutes and fifteen seconds in television history.

The episode begins with Murphy Brown reclining in her hospital bed soon after delivering her son. A nurse enters the room and brings Avery (played by a live baby) over for Brown to hold for the very first time. She talks to Avery about the frailties she'll show as his mother and the mistakes she will make along the way. The tear-jerking emotional scene culminates with Murphy, her voice halting and shaky, singing Avery Aretha Franklin's "You Make Me Feel Like a Natural Woman." As she finishes the song, she gently caresses Avery's tiny fingers, then turns and looks directly into the camera. The facial expression is that of a confident woman who, by choice, chance, or circumstance, made the decision to parent alone.[14]

The next day, the battle lines in the culture war were drawn. On May 19, 1992, vice president Dan Quayle gave a campaign speech at the Commonwealth Club of California to promote the reelection of George H. W. Bush. He was speaking in the aftermath of the Los Angeles riots, which followed the acquittal of four police officers who had been videotaped beating Rodney King, a black motorist who had been arrested for driving while intoxicated following a high-speed chase. Quayle's speech focused on the importance of preserving and promoting strong families in the fight against entrenched poverty, especially in low-income urban communities, which is where the riots took place. After laying out sobering statistics regarding intergenerational disadvantage and family breakdown, Quayle explained these as inevitable, symptomatic results of absent fathers.

> Nature abhors a vacuum. Where there are no mature, responsible men around to teach boys how to be good men, gangs serve in their place. In fact, gangs have become a surrogate family for much of a generation of inner-city boys. I recently visited with some former gang members in Albuquerque, New Mexico. In a private meeting, they told me why they had joined gangs. These teenage boys said that gangs gave them a sense of security. They made them feel wanted and useful. They got support from their friends. And they said, "It was like having family." "Like family?" Unfortunately, that says it all. The system perpetuates itself as these young men father children whom they have no intention of caring for, by women whose welfare checks support them. Teenage girls, mired in the same hopelessness, lack sufficient motive to say no to this trap.

Then Quayle pivoted. Instead of keeping the focus on a "poverty of values" in inner cities among particularly vulnerable young people, he turned his attention to cultural influencers who he believed were reshaping social norms and leading people to eschew marriage.

> Ultimately, however, marriage is a moral issue that requires cultural consensus and the use of social sanctions. . . . It doesn't help matters when primetime TV has Murphy Brown, a character who supposedly epitomizes today's intelligent, highly paid professional woman, mocking the importance of fathers by bearing a child

alone and calling it just another lifestyle choice. I know it's not fashionable to talk about moral values, but we need to do it. Even though our cultural leaders in Hollywood, network TV, and the national newspapers routinely jeer at them, I think most of us in this room know that some things are good and other things are wrong. And now, it's time to make the discussion public.[15]

The discussion became public indeed. While Quayle hoped to start a national conversation around family, hard work, integrity and personal responsibility, he instead unleashed a torrent of backlash. The *New York Daily News* May 20, 1992, front page carried a dramatic all-caps headline: "Quayle to Murphy Brown: YOU TRAMP!"[16] And the *New York Times* May 21, 1992, front page carried a picture of the final scene of Murphy Brown holding her baby, Avery, alongside Quayle's words criticizing her decision (see Figure 8.2).

The pushback was stunning. A few days later, Diane English, the creator and producer of Murphy Brown, responded to Quayle: "If the vice president . . . believes that a woman cannot adequately raise a child without a father, then he'd better make sure abortion remains safe and legal."[17]

None of this boiling controversy was lost on the pioneering leaders who were plotting the teen-pregnancy campaign in 1995. According to the Robert Wood Johnson Foundation report, "Organizers emphasized the need to avoid divisive debates over abortion and reproductive rights, and to focus on the common goal of preventing teen pregnancy. They made an intentional, strategic decision to ignore the vexing problems of marriage and abortion in order to forge a larger, more diverse coalition that could unify around a theme to stop 'children having children.'" When I asked Sawhill and Brown about the original design of teen-pregnancy

FIGURE 8.2   Murphy Brown and infant son, Avery.

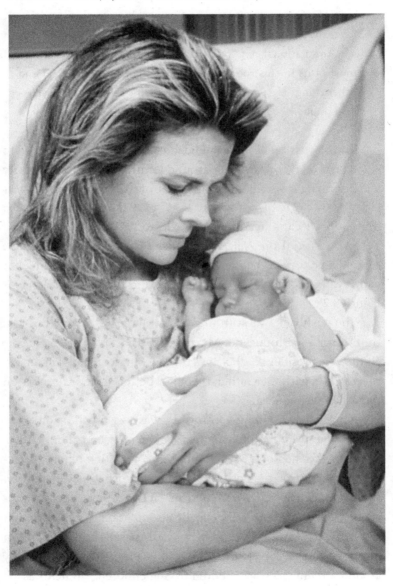

campaign in an interview for this book, Sawhill said, "My recollection is that our focus was primarily on age rather than marital status." Brown agreed: "We felt the national consensus was strong that teens need to grow up/be in school rather than be parents, whereas non-marital births included men and women in their 20s and more, and there were many different views about non-marital pregnancy/births." Thus, they initially named the organization the National Campaign to Prevent Teen Pregnancy, and not the National Campaign to Prevent Teen Pregnancy *and Nonmarital Births*.

A FOCUS ON TEEN PREGNANCY WAS NECESSARY, BUT NOT SUFFICIENT

Thus, at its inception in 1996, campaign organizers decided that drawing attention to nonmarital births would be strategically unwise. This may have been prudent, but others thought this was mistaken. Kay Hymowitz writes extensively on childhood, family issues, poverty, and cultural change in America. She sees the decision as a dodge to avoid talking about the real issue of family collapse due to the explosive growth in single parenthood. She wrote in her essay, "The Black Family: 40 Years of Lies,"

> There was just one small problem: *there was no epidemic of teen pregnancy*. There was an *out-of-wedlock* teen-pregnancy epidemic. Teenagers had gotten pregnant at even higher rates in the past. The numbers had reached their zenith in the 1950s. . . . Back in the day, however, when they found out they were pregnant, girls had either gotten married or given their babies up for adoption. Not this generation. They were used to seeing children growing up without fathers, and they felt no shame about arriving at the maternity ward with no rings on their fingers, even at 15 (italics in the original).[18]

FIGURE 8.3   Teen birthrate, 1950–2019.

SOURCE: Centers for Disease Control and Prevention, National Vital Statistics Reports. https://www.cdc.gov/nchs/data/nvsr/nvsr48/nvs48_16.pdf; https://wonder.cdc.gov/natality-expanded-current.html.

Indeed, while the reduction in teen-birth rates since the national campaign's launch in 1996 is impressive, it is clear that a downward trend had already been underway since the mid-1950s (see Figure 8.3).[19]

Hymowitz pointed out that the dramatic slide in teen births at the start of the twenty-first century was actually the tail end of a nearly seventy-year-long trend. Over most of this period, if a seventeen-year-old girl discovered she was pregnant, a hastily arranged "shotgun wedding" or adoption would typically ensue. The cultural norms governing relationships dictated that if a couple had sex, there was an implicit presumption that if the girl discovered she was "in a family way," the old playground chant would kick in: "First comes love, then comes marriage, then comes a baby in a baby carriage!"[20]

FIGURE 8.4 Nonmarital birth share to women aged 15–19, 1950–2019.

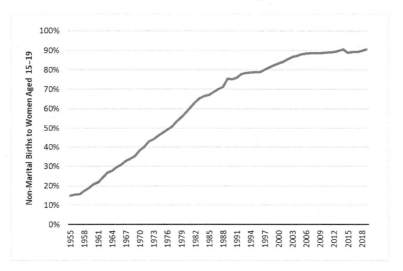

SOURCE: Centers for Disease Control and Prevention, National Vital Statistics Reports. https://www.cdc.gov/nchs/data/nvsr/nvsr48/nvs48_16.pdf; https://wonder.cdc.gov/natality-expanded-current.html.

What changed? Over the latter half of the twentieth century, teenage girls' passage into young adulthood was marked by greater access to education, employment, and opportunities that created a kind of future orientation. This became its own contraceptive form of self-regulating sexual behavior. Along with access to actual contraception, all these forces helped explain why teen pregnancies and births fell. Girls (and boys) did not want to risk not being able to take advantage of the doors opening up to them. During the same period, however, there had also been a meteoric rise in nonmarital birthrates for teens.

As Figure 8.4 indicates, in 1950 nearly 90 percent of teenage girls who became pregnant married before the birth of their child. By 2019, however, that number had completely reversed. Only

10 percent of pregnant teens got married and the vast majority chose single parenthood. The stigma had clearly decreased dramatically.

What explains the significant shift in attitudes regarding the necessity for marriage, especially when an unmarried couple faced the decision to bring their baby into the world? This wasn't just an issue for teens; nonmarital births and birthrates were rising for women of all ages and races. By 1990, two-thirds of black babies were born to single mothers, nearly three times the percentage from the mid-1960s. Among whites, 18 percent of infants were born to single mothers in 1990, a 500 percent increase over the 3 percent rate in 1965. Each year about a million more children of all races were born into single-parent homes.

In 1996, a number of social scientists tried to determine why nonmarital birth rates had soared beginning in 1970. Noted economist William Julius Wilson argued that communities in which men experienced high unemployment, loss of job opportunities due to economic dislocation, and poor education, led to a shortage of marriageable men, particularly among black men.[21] As noted political scientist Charles Murray, for his part, posited that well-intended War on Poverty policies such as welfare benefits for single mothers created perverse incentives that discouraged work, created dependency on public assistance, and deterred men from assuming their responsibility as fathers.[22] A team that included two renowned economists (who happened to be married to each other) produced a counterintuitive explanation for the growth in nonmarital births.

Former chair of the Federal Reserve and current U.S. Treasury secretary Janet Yellen, her Nobel Prize–winning husband George Akerlof, and University of California, Berkeley, economics professor Michael Katz wrote an extraordinary economic paper, "An Analysis of Out-of-Wedlock Births in the United States," which was published in the May 1996 issue of the *Quarterly Journal of Economics*. They argued that the huge increases in single-parent families headed by unmarried mothers was due to a "reproductive technology shock." The legalization of abortion and the dramatic increase in the availability of contraception (i.e., the birth control pill) were supposed to give women the tools to control the number and timing of the children they wanted to have. Paradoxically, however, their real impact was to raise rather than lower the number of unplanned pregnancies and out-of-wedlock birthrates. In another article, Akerlof and Yellen tied liberalized contraception and abortion to an erosion in the custom of shotgun marriages:

> Before 1970, the stigma of unwed motherhood was so great that few women were willing to bear children outside of marriage. The only circumstance that would cause women to engage in sexual activity was a promise of marriage in the event of pregnancy. Men were willing to make (and keep) that promise for they knew that in leaving one woman they would be unlikely to find another who would not make the same demand. Even women who would be willing to bear children out-of-wedlock could demand a promise of marriage in the event of pregnancy.[23]

The increased availability of contraception and abortion made shotgun weddings a thing of the past. Women who were willing to get an abortion or who reliably used contraception no longer found it necessary to condition sexual relations on a promise of marriage in the event of pregnancy. But women who wanted children, who did not want an abortion for moral or religious reasons, or who were unreliable in their use of contraception found themselves pressured to participate in premarital sexual relations without being able to exact a promise of marriage in case of pregnancy. These women feared, correctly, that if they refused sexual relations they would risk losing their partners. Sexual activity without commitment was increasingly expected in premarital relationships.

Advances in reproductive technology eroded the custom of shotgun marriage in another way. Before the sexual revolution, women had less freedom but men were expected to assume responsibility for their welfare. Today women are more free to choose but men have afforded themselves the comparable option. "If she is not willing to have an abortion or use contraception," the man can reason, "why should I sacrifice myself to get married?" By making the birth of the child the physical choice of the mother, the sexual revolution has made marriage and child support—and even the decision whether to wear a condom—a social choice of the father.

The Yellen-Akerlof-Katz study should have created shockwaves, but it has largely gone ignored. It established a logical link between well-intended interventions and unintended and potentially irreversible consequences. These consequences catalyzed a shift in cultural and social norms that weakened marriage, at least in certain communities. Given that stable families are the foundational building block to empowering agency within young people—and that a married, two-parent household is typically the best structure to facilitate stability—Figure 8.5 is telling. It lays out the percentage of births to unmarried women by age group in 1980 and 2019.

CAN WE RESURRECT MARRIAGE?

Figure 8.6 shows that the percentage of never-married adults is on a steady rise. Given such dramatic attitudinal and behavioral shifts, can the revitalization of that institution be made part of an effort to put young people on a path to control their own destiny? I think it can.

FIGURE 8.5   Percentage of births to unmarried women by age group, 1980 and 2019.

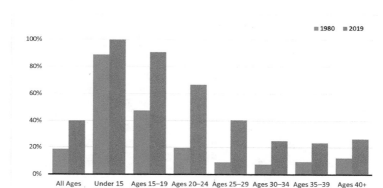

SOURCE: Centers for Disease Control and Prevention, National Vital Statistics Reports. https://www.cdc.gov/nchs/data/nvsr/nvsr48/nvs48_16.pdf; https://wonder.cdc.gov /natality-expanded-current.html.

The National Campaign to Prevent Teen and Unplanned Pregnancy showed that, when done well, major media campaigns sustained over time can play a significant role in shifting public opinion and cultural norms on contentious personal issues, particularly among young people. Indeed, in December 2017, the organization made a bold decision to make its work even more relevant to the rising generation by renaming itself Power to Decide.[24] The then-CEO Ginny Ehrlich wrote: "By ensuring that young people have the power to decide if and when to get pregnant, we help them keep their pathways to opportunity open. . . . We have doubled down on our commitment to ensuring that *all young people*—no matter who they are, where they live, or how much they or their families earn—have the power to decide if and when to get pregnant."

As a senior vice president at MTV overseeing campaigns such as *Choose or Lose* regarding voting in presidential elections, or *Fight*

FIGURE 8.6   Share of never-married adults reaches new high.

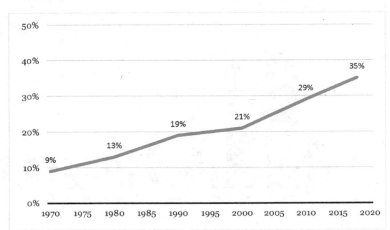

SOURCE: Institute for Family Studies. https://ifstudies.org/blog/the-share-of-never
-married-americans-has-reached-a-new-high.

For Your Rights to protect young people's sexual health, I saw that campaigns with empowering messages can nudge individual decision making for young people to act in their own best interest.

I believe a similar effort is needed to establish the importance of informed decision making about courtship culture and how to create stable marriages. It is important to note that by stable marriages I am referring to those permanent unions in which there is an absence of domestic violence, dual decision making about contraceptive choices, respect for taking roles in the workplace, and agreement about the importance of both parents shouldering child care expenses and responsibilities.

There's growing consensus on the need for public information campaigns that would promote a new cultural norm among young people in support of responsible parenthood and marriage in order to strengthen families and thereby strengthen individual agency for the next generation. Indeed, both the AEI/Brookings Working Group on Poverty and Opportunity and Harvard University's Closing the Opportunity Gap initiative have strongly recommended a large-scale marketing campaign that uses social and mass media and engages local institutions, including the church, schools, civic organizations, and neighborhood influencers, to change and normalize a new set of behavioral expectations concerning family formation.[25]

Almost thirty years since the launch of President Clinton's teen-pregnancy initiative, we are once again a deeply divided nation suffering through a time of increasingly polarized discourse. Yet it is instructive to look back at that time of similar discord when warring factions managed to find common ground and unite in a campaign that resulted in one of the greatest public health achievements in U.S. history: a dramatic reduction in teen pregnancies. As we saw previously in Figure 6.5, at the same time the campaign to reduce teen pregnancies and births was achieving historic success, a new crisis of nonmarital births was rising slightly up the age scale (women ages twenty to twenty-four). As Isabel Sawhill has noted in her work to improve opportunities for disadvantaged children in the United States, "The problem of unintended births has moved up the age scale." Sawhill believes "a similar consensus [that formed to combat teen pregnancy] could eventually emerge here too."[26]

Such a consensus could emerge, and it must if we are serious about achieving equality in opportunity and laying the foundation for all kids to obtain agency. Mass incarceration of young black men, the opioid crisis ravaging the white working-class community, the rise in deaths of despair due to social isolation and chronic loneliness—all these social ills are now reasonably being linked to nonmarital birthrates among young and less educated women. Yet, as Sawhill has stated, "For every child lifted out of poverty by a social program, another one is entering poverty as a result of the continued breakdown of the American family. If we could turn back the marriage clock to 1970, before the sharp rise in divorce and single parenthood began, the child poverty rate would be 20 percent lower than it is now."[27]

Our country needs another call to action, to finish the business President Clinton inspired almost three decades ago and address the social epidemic of rampant out-of-wedlock births to young women and men under 25. As Sarah Brown wrote to me, "Getting pregnant and raising a family is one of the most important and consequential decisions/pathways any of us ever make or choose. Accordingly, careful thought must be given over the years to pondering if, when, with whom and under what circumstances a pregnancy should be sought/invited."[28]

We know how to help teenagers and young adults better make these decisions. It will be difficult, but let's have the courage to try.

9

Dan Quayle Was Right, but His Strategy Was Wrong

What if—Vice President Dan Quayle hadn't shamed "Murphy Brown" for having a baby out of wedlock? What if he had instead expressed admiration for her decision to choose life and face the challenges of raising a child? What if he had instead criticized Murphy's ex-husband Jake Lowenstein for failing to live up to his responsibilities as Avery's father? What if the vice president had pointed out that the forty-something fictionalized TV anchor—who was well-educated, mature, affluent, and professionally successful—hardly represented the typical twenty-four-and-under single mothers of all races in our nation's most challenged neighborhoods. (It is not without irony that in her own personal life, actress Candice Bergen took a more traditional path of courtship by waiting until the age of thirty-five to get married before having a child at the age of thirty-nine, a classic case of *not* preaching what you practice.) Finally, what if Quayle had expressed empathy for the children of these all-too-real adults—if he had emphasized these kids' greatly reduced life chances because they lived in households headed by more typical single moms—rather than condemning the choices the adults in their lives had made. What if . . . ?

Maybe the Dan Quayle–Murphy Brown culture clash was inevitable, but maybe it was not. Had Quayle framed the issue in a different way, Murphy Brown might not have returned to the issue a few weeks later—in an episode that aired two weeks before the 1992 presidential election—and pummeled the vice president for blaming her for the nation's social ills and failing "to recognize that whether by choice or circumstance families come in all shapes and sizes and ultimately what really defines a family is commitment, caring and love."[1] The Bush White House might not have, as the *New York Times* reported, "first applauded, then dithered, then beat a befuddled retreat" on the issue.[2] Quayle might not have lost the first battle of this culture war in the face of Candice Bergen–Murphy Brown's powerful, compassionate, and inclusive defense of the new American family. He might have kept the focus on the issue of births outside marriage of *real* people, and that would have been a good thing. Why would it have been a good thing? It is because, as we'll see, on this issue Dan Quayle was right.

Barbara Dafoe Whitehead wrote just this—"Dan Quayle Was Right"—in the *Atlantic* one year after the controversy:

> If we fail to come to terms with the relationship between family structure and declining child well-being, then it will be increasingly difficult to improve children's life prospects, no matter how many new programs the federal government funds. Nor will we be able to make progress in bettering school performance or reducing crime or improving the quality of the nation's future work force—all domestic problems closely connected to family breakup. Worse, we may contribute to the problem by pursuing policies that actually increase family instability and breakup.[3]

Then, on the twentieth anniversary of Quayle's Commonwealth Club speech, the *Washington Post* asked Isabel Sawhill of the Brookings Institution and the National Campaign to Prevent Teen Pregnancy to write an essay on how the vice president's criticism of Murphy Brown had altered the cultural landscape. To the chagrin of many who had castigated Quayle as an insensitive and out-of-touch ideologue, Sawhill's piece was entitled "Twenty Years Later, It Turns Out Dan Quayle Was Right about Murphy Brown and Unmarried Moms."

"Twenty years later," she wrote, "Quayle's words seem less controversial than prophetic." The numbers spoke for themselves. The explosion in nonmarital births already underway in the early 1990s had only worsened over the following decades. In 1992, nearly 30 percent of all births were to unmarried women (already a sixfold increase since the early 1960s). By 2009, nonmarital births had risen to a staggering 41 percent of all births, which is today's new normal. (The figure is 40 percent for 2019.)

Sawhill laid out three reasons why Americans should be concerned about this seismic shift in family life and its adverse impact on children's ability to control their own destiny. First, she pointed out the inherent commitment associated with marriage as opposed to cohabitation: "Cohabitation is more fragile—cohabiting parents split up before their fifth anniversary at about twice the rate of married parents. Often, this is because the father moves on, leaving the mother not just with less support but with fewer marriage prospects. For her, marriage requires finding a partner willing to take responsibility for someone else's kids." Second, research shows that, on average, children in married, two-parent families fare far better than those in any other family configuration. They do better in school, are less likely to get pregnant or arrested. They have lower suicide rates and higher levels of education. They also earn more as adults.[4] "Meanwhile," Sawhill wrote in a 2012 op-ed for the *Washington Post*, "children who spend time in single-parent families are more likely to misbehave, get sick, drop out of high school and be unemployed."[5] Third, Sawhill highlighted marriage's economic benefits and single parenthood's economic difficulties.

The response to Sawhill's article was intense but the evidence was clear. As she later wrote in *Generation Unbound*, "While [Quayle] may have picked the wrong role model—since most unmarried moms are younger, are less educated, and make less money than the fictional news anchor—his concern about changes in the family were consistent with research showing that children, on average, benefit from being raised by their own married parents."[6]

Along the same lines, the American Enterprise Institute and the Brookings Institution had teamed up to create an ideologically diverse Working Group on Poverty and Opportunity. That group's final report in 2016 showed that an increase in households headed by single mothers resulted in more children born into poverty (see Figure 9.1).

Not surprisingly, the Working Group on Poverty and Opportunity's final report concluded that "improving the family environment in which children are raised is vital to any serious effort to reduce poverty and expand opportunity. Twenty-five years of extensive and rigorous research has shown that children raised in stable, secure families have a better chance to flourish."[7] And while "stable, secure families" can take different forms, they are most normally found in a loving, healthy marriage.

In the mid-1990s, Kaiser Permanente, the large hospital and health-maintenance organization, had partnered with the U.S. Centers for Disease Control and Prevention to conduct the first longitudinal study to examine the link between adverse childhood experiences and mental and physical health problems later on. It is still one of the nation's largest ongoing studies. Best known as the Adverse Childhood Experiences (ACE) Study, the researchers found that children who experience high numbers of adverse

FIGURE 9.1   Changes in family structure cause rise in poverty.

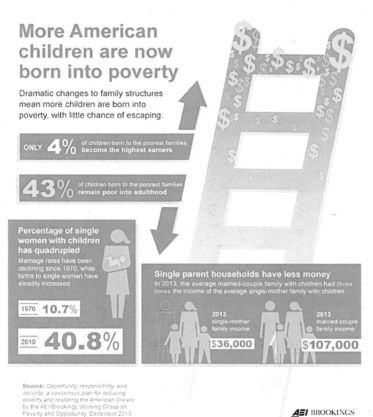

SOURCE: AEI/Brookings Working Group on Poverty and Opportunity, "Opportunity, Responsibility, and Security," December 2015. https://www.aei.org/research-products /report/opportunity-responsibility-and-security/.

childhood experiences—physical, verbal, or sexual abuse; physical or emotional neglect; household dysfunction or violence—are more likely to have chronic health conditions and engage in risky health behaviors in adulthood.

The original ACE study was conducted at Kaiser Permanente from 1995 to 1997. As a follow-up to taking their standardized physical exams, more than 17,000 HMO members were asked to complete a confidential questionnaire regarding events they may have personally experienced or observed in the first eighteen years of their life. The questionnaire (which follows) covered ten categories of adverse childhood experiences (ACES)—five ACEs experienced by the child (psychological, physical, or sexual abuse and physical or emotional neglect) and five the child might have observed in the household (parental breakup, domestic violence against the mother, substance abuse, mental illness, and incarceration).

The resulting ACE Score ranged from 0 (all "no" responses in the ten categories) to 10 (at least one "yes" in each of the ten categories). Researchers then compared the number of adverse childhood experiences to measures of adult risk-behavior, health status, and disease. The original study showed that individuals who had four or more ACEs were four to twelve times more prone to alcoholism, drug abuse, depression, and suicide than those who had none. They were two to four times more likely to smoke, have poor self-rated health, and have a sexually transmitted disease. They also experienced a 1.4- to 1.6-fold higher-than-normal incidence of physical inactivity and severe obesity.[8]

Unsurprisingly, each of the ten "ACEs" examined in this questionnaire most frequently stem from a child's experiences with members of their nuclear family, underscoring the importance of family environments for children's development. Even more concerning is that in studies that adjust for differences across age,

Ten Categories of Childhood Exposure	Yes / No Question
1. Psychological Abuse	Did a parent or other adult in the household often or very often swear at you, insult you, put you down, or humiliate you?
	Did a parent or other adult in the household often or very often act in a way that made you afraid that you might be physically hurt?
2. Physical Abuse	Did a parent or other adult in the household often or very often push, grab, slap, or throw something at you?
	Did a parent or other adult in the household often or very often ever hit you so hard that you had marks or were injured?
3. Sexual Abuse	Did an adult or person at least five years older than you ever touch or fondle you in a sexual way?
	Did an adult or person at least five years older than you, ever have you touch their body in a sexual way?
	Did an adult or person at least five years older than you ever attempt to have oral, anal, or vaginal intercourse with you?
	Did an adult or person at least five years older than you ever actually have oral, anal, or vaginal intercourse with you?
4. Emotional Neglect	Did you often or very often feel that no one in your family loved you nor thought you were important or special?
	Did you often or very often feel that your family didn't look out for each other, feel close to each other, nor support each other?
5. Physical Neglect	Did you often or very often feel that you didn't have enough to eat, had to wear dirty clothes, and had no one to protect you?

(continued)

Ten Categories of Childhood Exposure	Yes / No Question
	Did you often or very often feel that your parents were too drunk or high to take care of you nor take you to the doctor if you needed it?
6. Parental Breakup	Were your parents ever separated or divorced?
7. Domestic Violence of Mother	Was your mother or stepmother often pushed, grabbed, slapped, or had something thrown at her?
	Was your mother or stepmother sometimes or often kicked, bitten, hit with a fist, or hit with something hard?
	Was your mother or stepmother ever repeatedly hit over at least a few minutes or threatened with a gun or knife?
8. Substance Abuse	Did you live with anyone who was a problem drinker or alcoholic?
	Did you live with anyone who used street drugs?
9. Mental Illness	Was a household member depressed or mentally ill?
	Did a household member attempt suicide?
10. Incarceration	Did a household member go to prison?

sex, race, family income, poverty status, and parents' education level, "children from single-parent homes seem to be at higher risk for adverse childhood experiences than those who live with both parents."[9]

Dan Quayle may have been right on the substance but, according to David Frum, a former speechwriter for President George W. Bush, a paradigm shift took place beginning in the 1960s and 1970s, which required approaching the family issue in a new way. In a 2014 article in the *Atlantic*, Frum described how the order of decision making by ordinary Americans had shifted when it came to pregnancy. "When marriage was the near-universal norm in American society, a pregnancy out of wedlock pushed a couple toward one of four choices: shotgun wedding; adoption; abortion; or single motherhood, in that order of social acceptability. The result was a society in which both abortion and single motherhood were rare."

Frum recounts the changes in sexual mores, abortion, marriage, and the periodic reordering of unplanned-pregnancy decision making in the decades since, but here's where he believes we are today: "The order of choices in the face of an unexpected pregnancy has thus shifted again: single parenthood, abortion, shotgun wedding, and adoption."

Frum concluded that if the goal is to strengthen family stability for children and reestablish marriage as the best new (yet old) way to achieve that goal, it is a fool's errand to moralistically reprimand the choices a growing population of young adults are making today. His compelling alternative prescription is a new agenda of compassion and empathy—"one that emphasizes the life chances of children," and not adults, as its central tenet.[10]

In fairness, the vice president did try to connect the conditions that led to the Los Angeles riots to family dysfunction. He failed, however, to create an "empathy linkage" in the way that the teen pregnancy campaign would soon do. Imagine if Quayle had highlighted the real-world plight of the children of more representative, unmarried young mothers in such racially different communities as Los Angeles, Appalachia, and the Bronx? A more child-centered focus might have made a difference, especially if it stressed the importance of preventing the kinds of adverse experiences that infants and adolescents encounter and, quite predictably, lead to antisocial behavior and lower levels of self-efficacy later in life.

What if there were a path—a proven path—that likely prevents the kinds of adverse experiences that children and adolescents encounter that lead to antisocial behavior and lower levels of self-efficacy later in life? And what if that same set of choices kept almost 100 percent of parents and their children out of poverty? I would call that path the Success Sequence.

CHAPTER

10

The Success Sequence

The Empowering Alternative and the Other
Building Blocks of Agency

In 2013, more than twenty years after Dan Quayle's Commonwealth Club speech, New York City's Department of Health and Mental Hygiene revealed that in the five boroughs there were more than 20,000 teen pregnancies annually, 87 percent of which were unintended and mostly involved unmarried partners.[1] Robert Doar, commissioner of the city's Human Resources Administration, worked with Mayor Michael Bloomberg to launch a campaign to reduce teen pregnancies. In laying out his goals, Mayor Bloomberg announced: "This campaign makes very clear to young people that there's a lot at stake when it comes to deciding to raise a child. . . . By focusing on responsibility and the importance of education, employment, and family in providing children with the emotional and financial support they need, we'll let thousands of young New Yorkers know that waiting to becoming a parent could be the best decision they ever make."[2]

The campaign featured ads on buses and subway trains throughout the city; an interactive texting program featuring facts, games and quizzes; and a YouTube video to engage teens on the issue. It also featured public service advertisements such as

FIGURE 10.1   New York City success sequence ad campaign.

SOURCE: New York City Government. https://www.nydailynews.com/new-york/new-ad-campaign-teen-pregnancy-article-1.1278589.

Figure 10.1 and another with a baby addressing his mother with the words: "Honestly, mom . . . chances are he won't stay with you. What happens to me?"[3]

In a February 2014 policy brief produced by the Urban Institute, they observed that "this portion of the campaign has stirred up significant controversy, with some accusations that the ads stigmatize teen parenthood. Proponents of such efforts point out that other public health campaigns that stigmatized behavior, such as smoking, have worked."[4] Nevertheless, the campaign faced enormous pushback before it had an opportunity to meaningfully influence the beliefs of vulnerable New Yorkers, partially due to being a government-led rather than a private initiative. (This is an important lesson for any effort designed to sway public opinion and decision making on intimate matters such as sexual activity and child bearing.)

Much of the New York City campaign drew on research produced by Isabel Sawhill and Ron Haskins. In 2009, Sawhill, the Brookings Institution economist who had helped mastermind the historic reductions in teen pregnancy, had teamed up with a Brookings colleague, Ron Haskins, to write *Creating an Opportunity Society*, a book whose goal was to operationalize their belief that "everyone should have a shot at the American Dream."[5] At the center of their strategy was a simple series of behaviors: get at least a high school education, find a full-time job, and wait for marriage to have children—*in that order.* Haskins and Sawhill are today the most widely credited champions of what's known as the Success Sequence.[6]

The two scholars found that only 2 percent of U.S. adults who graduated from high school, maintained a full-time job (or had a partner who did), and delayed having children until after they were twenty-one and married lived below the poverty line. Roughly 71 percent ended up in the middle class or above.[7] Put differently, first graduating from high school, then securing full-time work, then getting married, and then having children offers individuals, as the New York City advertisement said, a 98 percent chance of avoiding poverty. (According to the most recent data, the figure for millennials—born between 1981 and 1996—is 97 percent by the time they reached ages twenty-eight through thirty-four.)[8]

The Success Sequence has attracted many admirers because of the simplicity of the three steps that young people, even if born into disadvantaged circumstances or raised by a young single parent, can themselves control and take in their lives. Yet the Success Sequence is not without its detractors. Some believe the steps are simply *too* simple. Others believe they mask a moralistic, conservative agenda to revitalize marriage—a worthy goal—especially in hard-hit communities in which family breakdown is an undeniable factor in perpetuating disadvantage.

Blogger and founder of the progressive think tank People's Policy Project Matt Bruenig, for example, thinks Success Sequencers are trying to impose a pro-marriage cultural narrative while ignoring the fact that full-time work does the "heavy lifting" in reducing poverty.[9] Richard Reeves, a Brookings Institute colleague of Sawhill, thinks the sequence overlooks a complex interplay of education, labor market, and racial discrimination in keeping even African American families who adhere to the sequence poorer than their white counterparts.[10] Michael Tanner, a scholar at the Cato Institute—the nation's premier libertarian think tank—cautions that "correlation is not causation."[11] Philip N. Cohen, a sociologist at the University of Maryland, argues against public funding of efforts to promote marriage. "The success sequence is a political meme repeated in highly similar form over more than a generation of public policy debates, without yet having any discernible impact for the better. The third 'step' or 'norm' in particular—marriage—has already been promoted with massive federal subsidies for almost two decades."[12] It is certainly true that President George W. Bush's Healthy Marriage Initiative had mixed results, and Cohen is right to question *government* efforts to positively shape intimate decision making such as the timing of marriage and childbearing. But privately organized efforts, such as the Campaign to Prevent Teen Pregnancy and faith-based efforts that I describe in Chapter 14, can have a profound impact in getting individuals to adopt behaviors such as those in the Success Sequence.

Where certain Success Sequence critics go badly wrong is in making insulting, if well-intentioned, pronouncements that rob individuals of the agency to make good decisions for themselves. Cohen, for example, writes, "The idea that delaying parenthood until marriage is a choice one makes is . . . prized by the white middle class, and the fact that black women often don't have that choice makes them the objects of scorn for their perceived lax morals."[13] This implies that black women do not value delayed parenthood or themselves have no choice but to become single parents. It recalls Brown economist Glenn Loury's classic line: "Racism is causing black folk to make the wrong choices?!? That's a disgusting, patronizing and infantilizing argument!"[14]

What is most curious about Success Sequence critics—beyond the fact that many of them have followed the Success Sequence in their own personal lives—is their alternative: a utopian fantasy in which the government takes care of all needs, regardless of one's personal choices. Bruenig, for example, argues that "our economic institutions, and especially our welfare state, should be designed to ensure that nobody is in poverty and that people can form the families they would like."[15] As Patrick T. Brown, a fellow with the Ethics and Public Policy Center, wrote in response,

> Forming the families they like often includes children, who are best served by a stable home life. No amount of cold hard cash is going to offer a kid the same stability and socioemotional benefits of avoiding a revolving door of live-in boyfriends. The ideological predisposition to downplay marriage ignores the fact that for a successful family life, including marriage in the Sequence has benefits for the partners and even bigger ones for their children.[16]

In general, the arguments against the Success Sequence have been handily rebutted. In response to one of the standard critiques, Bryan Caplan, professor of economics at George Mason University, retorts, "Even if the 'work does all the work' criticism were statistically true, it misses the point: Single parenthood makes it very hard to work full-time."[17] "Not everyone will be able to achieve this ordering of life events, but we believe it should be the guide star that society sets for each new generation," Sawhill and Haskin wrote in *Creating an Opportunity Society.* "The success sequence has fallen out of fashion in recent decades but is nonetheless still a tried and true means of ensuring that most children grow up in two-parent families. To those who argue that this goal is old-fashioned or inconsistent with modern culture, we argue that modern culture is inconsistent with the needs of children."[18]

In *Education for Upward Mobility*, Haskins offered compelling reasons why young people should know about the series of life decisions that yielded the most likely positive outcomes. First, studies make clear that increasing education, work, and marriage would reduce poverty rates and increase incomes. And second, those same studies also make clear that the choices many of our young people are making now often fail to promote their economic well-being. Haskin notes as well that they often make these decisions "without good advice or good examples in their families and neighborhood . . . and with little understanding of the long-term consequences of their choices." "There are no grounds to think that without some intervention, the life-course choices made by young people will improve anytime soon," he writes. "So the question before us is whether intervention programs that schools conduct can help young people improve these life-shaping choices."[19]

I believe these programs can help our young people make better life-shaping choices, and I believe our schools should institute these programs. More specifically, I believe that establishing the Success Sequence as the "guide star that society sets for each new generation" should be the task of all our mediating institutions. And it is an urgent one if we want young people to understand a fundamental building block of agency.

In a 2018 *Wall Street Journal* op-ed entitled "The 'Sequence' Is the Secret to Success," Wendy Wang, author of several research studies on youth empowerment, wrote about the high school–age daughter of a single mother who told Wang that she was well-aware that teen pregnancy was a bad idea. Yet the idea that school, then work, then marriage and then childbearing form a sequence that leads to success was totally foreign to her: "No one in my school talks about this," she said. "My mom never said anything either."[20]

Along the same lines, in 2017 I visited a ninth-grade class at a high school in a low-income community in New Orleans. I asked the students: "If I were to tell you that there is a series of decisions that, when followed by millions of young people, have resulted in 97% of those young people and their kids avoiding poverty and having economic success, would you want to know?"

There was, as you might imagine, a lot of interest. Even the teacher said, "Really?"

I then told them that I couldn't share this information with them because there are people who fear that they might be insulted if I did. They looked at me as if I were crazy. They demanded to know. They were, in effect, saying, "Tell us!"

So I did. I felt a moral obligation to share the information. What ensued was a rich, twenty-five-minute discussion about the Success Sequence. I touched on all the caveats—nothing in life is guaranteed, there is no one way to economic success, and so forth—but pointed out that there are different paths that have likely rewards and consequences. We talked about the Success

Sequence data and how differently ordered decisions in education, work, marriage, and children have different, statistically predictable outcomes.

In the end, none of the kids said, "I already knew that" or, for that matter, "Thank you, my life has changed forever." But these students had new, accurate information that was relevant to their futures, and I had no sense that the new information made them uncomfortable or ashamed because of their own home lives. On the contrary, I sensed that the kids felt *respected* that someone would treat them as responsible, future decision makers.

If we want young people to be critical thinkers, we need to give them accurate information to think critically about. What struck me about the New Orleans discussion was that these kids wanted to know this information once they knew it existed. Once I shared the data, a real discussion took place. And no one seemed to feel they were being told there is only one way to do life—a point I made at least a half-dozen times. According to Wendy Wang and Brad Wilcox: "It's not just about natural endowments, social structure, and culture; agency also matters. Most men and women have the capacity to make choices, to embrace virtues or avoid vices, and to otherwise take steps that increase or decrease their odds of doing well in school, finding and keeping a job, or deciding when to marry and have children."[21]

It's not just children who are receptive to the empowering data on the Success Sequence, but likely their parents too. My colleague Nat Malkus at the American Enterprise Institute explored this idea further with data from the American Perspectives Survey in a groundbreaking 2021 study. The survey asked adults whether they thought it was a good idea to teach "students that young people who get at least a high school degree, have a job and get married— before having children—are more likely to be financially secure and to avoid poverty in later life."

The response was overwhelmingly in support. More than three in four parents supported teaching the Success Sequence in schools. Even more importantly, this trend held true across every group the study examined. Rich and poor, highly educated and less educated, black and white, young and old, Democrat and Republican—a strong majority of Americans from every background believed the tenets of the Success Sequence should be taught in our schools.[22] And despite concerns that teaching these types of lessons to children might be viewed as insulting or patronizing, seven in ten parent respondents who were most distant from adhering to the "success sequence"—because they had not graduated high school, were unmarried parents, or were currently not working—supported teaching it to students.

Someday this topic will not be taboo. Someday we will be able to talk with middle and high schoolers about the decisions many of us have made in our own lives as adults because we want our kids to have better chances in life. Someday can't come soon enough for kids who need real information and guidance as they embark on high school, college, and young adulthood.

We do our children no favors in withholding from them the very knowledge that can unleash their ability to lead a complete life of their choosing. The reason the Success Sequence can be so important to the rising generation is that it confirms this abiding life-shaping truth: While a young person has no control over the family *they are from*, they do have the power to determine the family *they will form*—and that can make all the difference.

CHAPTER
11

The Bill & Melinda Gates Foundation and the Foundation of Family

When my wife and I became parents for the first time in 2009, we experienced firsthand the awesome responsibility of raising a newborn child. The daily minutiae of parenting were exhilarating but simultaneously overwhelming and exhausting for both of us. And we were a married, educated, and stable couple. We had good jobs, a home, and incomes that afforded us a decent quality of life. We could not fathom how we would have coped if one of us had been on our own, half our age, less educated, unemployed, and thrust into the role of a young, single parent.

I was working at the Bill & Melinda Gates Foundation on the postsecondary success team, which handed out more than $470 million in philanthropic donations that year. Our goal was to increase the number of primarily low-income young adults who earned a college degree or an industry credential after high school. I loved the work. But my wife and I wanted our daughter to be closer to family in New York and the bicoastal commute from the Foundation's Seattle headquarters to our New York home was just not sustainable. Seeing everything we were pouring into our young daughter made me appreciate viscerally how important it was to "start early with the end in mind," as John Bridgeland, my old White House boss, would say, when it came to building our own child's future. So I left the foundation in 2010.

One of the lessons I learned at the Gates Foundation was that as a country we are failing in our efforts to improve educational outcomes partly because we spend billions of dollars way too late to help high school and college students who never learned the basics in preschool and elementary and middle school. Another was that not enough children in utero and aged birth to five receive the kinds of nurturing support necessary for healthy development. In the years since leaving the Foundation—the years since my "Who's Your Daddy" epiphany—I have come to believe that our schools and our philanthropy were not investing early enough. Whether due to willful blindness, timidity, or plain ignorance, our leaders were failing to address the consequences of increasing numbers of American children being raised in unstable and fragmented families.

Research psychologist Nicholas Zill summed up my thinking in a 2016 article ("How Family Transitions Affect Students' Achievement") in *Family Studies* journal: "It is not generally appreciated how much burden has been placed on our public schools by the revolutionary increases in divorce, cohabitation, and unmarried childbearing that took place over the last half century. We expect schools not only to cope with these changes, but also to solve any student achievement or behavior problems that might arise from dysfunctional family dynamics."[1]

My own views on the importance of family structure crystallized when I read the 2017 speech ("Our Education Efforts Are Evolving") Bill Gates gave to the Council of Great City Schools in Cleveland, Ohio.[2] Gates summarized the lessons that he and wife,

Melinda, learned after investing $1 billion in "school improvement and redesign efforts" over 17 years. "By and large, schools are still falling short on the key metrics of a quality education—math scores, English scores, international comparisons, and college completion." Moreover, he said, the same disparities in achievement and postsecondary success still exist for children of color and low-income students.

Why had progress been so meager despite the Foundation's and others' massive investment of time and money? In Cleveland, Gates cited the challenges of moving ideas from the pilot stage to wide-scale usage and argued that "the financial and political costs of closing existing schools and replacing them with new schools was too high."[3]

In a speech of more than 3,000 words, however, Gates never mentioned "family" or "parent," the rapid rise of children raised in fragile families, or the millions of babies born outside marriage to women aged twenty-four and under from 2000 to 2017. I was stunned. To their credit, Bill and Melinda Gates were undaunted. Ever the self-described impatient optimists, they committed to spending another $2 billion over the next five years to improve educational outcomes.

Three years later, in their 2020 annual letter, on the Gates Foundation's twentieth anniversary, Bill and Melinda Gates once again expressed their frustration: "When it comes to U.S. education, though, we're not yet seeing the kind of bottom-line impact we expected. The status quo is still failing American students." Unlike the Foundation's global health work, where a vaccine can make an instantaneous difference, of the education arena, Melinda wrote, it is "hard to isolate any single intervention and say it made all the difference. . . . Getting a child through high school requires at least 13 years of instruction enabled by hundreds of teachers, administrators, and local, state, and national policymakers," she

continued. "The process is so cumulative that changing the ultimate outcome requires intervention at many different stages."[4]

In fact, there *is* a single intervention that exists over the
thirteen-year span of a child's K–12 education, and it can make
all the difference to that child: a loving and stable family, which is
most reliably found in a married, two-parent household. In "The
Impact of Family Formation Change on the Cognitive, Social, and
Emotional Well-Being of the Next Generation," for example, sociologist Paul R. Amato quantified what he calls "perhaps the most
profound change in the American family over the past four
decades." Using data from the National Study of Adolescent Health,
Amato estimated that more than 1.2 million *fewer* children would
have been suspended from school if two-parent households had
remained at levels that existed before the 1960s explosion in out-
of-wedlock births. In addition, nearly 750,000 *fewer* youngsters
would have had to repeat a grade in 2002. That would have been
about a million fewer children in the so-called school-to-prison
pipeline at that time, and many fewer adults locked up today.[5]

And yet, in their 2020 annual letter, neither Melinda nor Bill
Gates makes a single mention of the word "family," much less any
strategy to educate students about the timing and readiness needed
to form stable families and give themselves and their children a
better shot at successful lives.

Sadly, as I was writing this book, Bill and Melinda Gates
announced their divorce after twenty-seven years of marriage.
According to an exclusive report in *People* magazine, the couple
timed their divorce to coincide with a milestone in the education
of their youngest of three children, who was turning eighteen. "It's
absolutely because their youngest child is graduating from high
school, and the idea was that they stayed together through that,"
a source told *People*. "They limped through until their kids were
out of school like a lot of people."[6]

Bill and Melinda Gates seemed to recognize the importance of the stability of the married, two-parent family when it came to their own children. It will be interesting to read their future Annual Letters. Will the two Foundation heads, after spending another nearly $2 billion on education, finally acknowledge the critical role family structure plays in the lives of other people's children? And most importantly, will they prioritize the role that schools can play in helping young people make better decisions about the timing of family formation as they enter young adulthood? I hope the answer is yes, especially given what my colleagues and I often talked about as the "Gates effect"—the extraordinary influence that the Foundation's goals and grants wield with policymakers, philanthropists, researchers, K–12 practitioners, and virtually every institution that is trying to improve outcomes for kids.

I hope.

How FREE Can Usher in a New "Age of Agency" for Young Americans

12

The FREE Framework
to Build Agency

When I first told my Mum that I was writing a book to inspire a new generation of young people to lead lives of their own choosing, her eyes filled with pride. Even with her faltering health and fading memory, she looked at me with the blessings only a mother can confer on her child. Then, those same wise eyes narrowed and she asked, "Just exactly what are you going to tell them?" I said I was going to, in some way, tell her and Dad's story—the adventure these two Jamaicans had embarked on together to make a life of their own choosing—because, like for most of us, my path to a life of agency and the lessons I learned on the way were made possible by my own parents.

Vincent Rowe and Eula Seivright met in 1954. Vincent was twenty-two and Eula was nineteen. She worked as a nurse at a sugar cane producer on Jamaica's north coast. He worked at the same refinery and had risen to a senior role in the accounting department, thanks to his mathematical skills. Mum would describe how he would pick her up on horseback to go riding in the country on weekend dates. Years later, if my Dad made some bonehead mistake—say, forgetting their wedding anniversary—she would jokingly ask, "Why can't you still be as romantic as you were back then?"

As Eula and Vincent got to know one another, they shared their hopes and dreams for the future. He was good with numbers and wanted to pursue a degree in engineering, something that would have been more challenging if he had stayed in Jamaica. He decided the best path for him was to attend university in Great Britain, something he could do since Jamaica was then still part of the British Commonwealth. Dad spent years scraping together the necessary funds. He ultimately saved enough to leave Jamaica and set out on his own to London in search of a better future. After securing a job and settling in for a few months, Vincent was ready for the next big step. Marriage laws in Britain and Jamaica required that a prospective groom secure parental consent to marry a woman who was under the age of twenty-one. So Vincent put pen to paper and wrote the letter of a lifetime to ask Eula's mother and father for their permission to take her hand in marriage. My Mum said when the letter arrived from overseas, there was much consternation and discussion with the family and local pastor.

I always wondered if my parents' saying yes to me when I begged to stay in my junior high school had something to do with the moment in their own young lives when my Mum had asked her parents to let her set her own course and leave her tiny town in the foothills of Jamaica (see Figure 12.1). In any case, in 1955, Mum bravely boarded a huge passenger boat for the 5,000-mile journey to England. Once married, Eula and Vincent started working and going to school in London. Dad was a city bus driver and Mum was a nurse. It was a hardscrabble and wonderful life in their small flat, especially after my brother and I, seven years later, arrived on the scene. Then, Eula and Vincent embarked on another adventure. They moved to the United States. Dad had landed a job as one of the early black engineers at IBM and my Mum became an analyst at Manufacturers Hanover Trust bank.

FIGURE 12.1   Vincent and Eula Rowe.

The family they established and the stability they ensured became the foundation for everything I have been able to create in my own life.

I learned from my parents never to be scared to go on an adventure, especially if you are going on it with a partner who loves you and has your back. Life will be hard; life will be a struggle; and life will present hurdles. But life is also a series of opportunities. There are pathways and partners you can choose that can make all the difference in increasing your odds of personal fulfillment. And there's the point: you have the power to choose. That is why I have written this book: to help a rising generation realize that they have the power to shape their own destiny, even in the face of life's inevitable obstacles. They have the ability to put their own lives in motion, in the direction they seek, if they so choose. This is agency—the force of one's free will guided by moral discernment.

Of course, young people do not cultivate personal agency on their own. To develop the capacity for moral discernment and their ability to create good or bad outcomes in their lives, they must engage what I call the four building blocks of agency. It is a forward-looking framework I call FREE, which encompasses the four pillars of

Family
Religion
Education
Entrepreneurship

I'll flesh out each of these elements over the next four chapters, but here they are in a nutshell.

FAMILY

Family does not mean the family that you were born into. Rather, it is the family you will form in the future. It is society's first and most vital mediating institution. Family may take many forms but, as we've seen, the form linked overwhelmingly to positive outcomes for children and adults is the married, two-parent household.

Almost all Americans will get married at some point in their life or be in a serious relationship to form a family or serious partnership of two. Further, according to the PEW Research Center, 85 percent of Americans will become a parent in their lifetime and create an intergenerational family.[1] The question is what can our educators, mediating institutions, private and public organizations—and the culture, writ large—do to ensure that our students understand the timing and structure of family formation that offers the greatest likelihood of success for them and their children?

RELIGION

While there is a general decline in religiosity, particularly among young Americans, it is still the case that a personal faith commitment can be a force for good in one's own life and strengthens the family. It's also the case that faith-based organizations need to be recognized, revitalized, and engaged for two simple reasons. One, they have a capacity to speak with moral authority in ways that the government cannot. And two, they can shape social norms to encourage behavior that advances the human condition.

EDUCATION

As our country is having important conversations about how to create an opportunity society and upward mobility for people of all races, it is easy to forget that the disparities we seek to eliminate, originate early in life—long before they show up as statistical gaps in adult financial wealth, home ownership, incarceration rates, or educational achievement. In the school district in which I have led public charter schools for the last decade, only 2 percent of the high school graduates can do basic reading and math without requiring remediation. If we truly care about creating an age of agency, we should be wary of fashionable "racial equity" goals that create ceilings of mediocrity rather than excellence for all. The first "E" in the FREE framework requires young people to take ownership of their own learning and habits—study, attendance, homework completion, self-discipline—that are the foundations of learning. It also involves advocating for policies like school choice that level the playing field of opportunity for everyone.

ENTREPRENEURSHIP

While entrepreneurship is usually defined as the act of someone launching their own business, the final "E" in FREE calls on students to cultivate an entrepreneurial mind-set about their own lives. It means encouraging students to approach their jobs and careers not only as employees but also as prospective employers, as founders—as someone who owns his or her own future. This concept of entrepreneurship is what former American Enterprise Institute president Arthur Brooks calls "earned success." Brooks writes:

> Earned success involves the ability to create value honestly—not by inheriting a fortune, not by picking up a welfare check. It does not mean making money in and of itself. Earned success is the creation of value in our lives or in the lives of others. Earned success is the stuff of entrepreneurs who seek value through innovation, hard work and passion. Earned success is what parents feel when their children do wonderful things, what social innovators feel when they change lives, what artists feel when they create something of beauty.[2]

As my parents, Eula and Vincent, said, life will present a host of hurdles. But whether and how you overcome life's hurdles makes all the difference. "Between stimulus and response there is space," Viktor Frankl famously wrote in *Man's Search for Meaning.* "In that space is our power to choose our response. In our response lies our growth and our freedom."[3]

In that space is our agency. And the opportunity to live FREE.

CHAPTER

13

Family

The future of the family is a matter of enormous and incalculable importance, and the strength, health, and integrity of marriage and family life constitute an absolutely essential precondition for all other social, economic, and political goods.

—Wilfred McClay, Free Societies
as Schools of the Soul

In 1860, Milton Bradley created the Checkered Game of Life board game. His patent application made it clear that "in addition to the amusement and excitement of the game, it is intended to forcibly impress upon the minds of youth the great moral principles of virtue and vice."[1] The game's red-and-ivory checkerboard presented a sixty-four-square obstacle course featuring character traits—bravery, idleness, industry, honesty—that could lead to wealth, suicide, prison, disgrace, fame, ruin, or happiness.[2]

The deeply religious Bradley explained that the game represents "the checkered journey of life." The most successful player would "gain on his journey that which shall make him the most prosperous, and to shun that which will retard him in his progress." Part of your life outcomes were in God's hands; other parts were in yours. As each player twirled a wooden teetotum, they were offered key life decisions and character traits to choose from (e.g., "Bravery or Idleness" and "College or Fame") that led to next steps. While landing on "Cupid" meant going directly to "Matrimony," landing on "Gambling" led directly to "Ruin."

For Bradley, challenging circumstances at any point in life did not have to dictate outcomes. If a player landed at the Poverty square immediately after Infancy, they needn't fear. It is "not necessarily a fact that poverty will be a disadvantage."[3] "School" and "Ambition" were both accessible from "Poverty." "Perseverance" could lead to "Success." The game's original message was clear: choices matter. Redemption was an ever-present possibility. Honor was in your grasp, even if you had committed a crime. The traits a player chose to adopt determined whether they achieved the overarching goal of the game—to live to a "Happy Old Age."

The Checkered Game of Life sold millions of copies. On its centennial in 1960, however, Hasbro Company, which had purchased the Milton Bradley Company, released a new version with a truncated name: Game of Life. The revamped edition bore no resemblance to the original. There was no teetotum, no vices like "Disgrace" or "Idleness" to be avoided, no virtues like "Honesty" or "Perseverance" to be embraced. The new version defined success as a function of how much money a player amassed and involved practical matters like choosing a college or profession, buying insurance, securing a mortgage, or playing the stock market. In a 2012 lecture to Harvard University students, historian Jill Lepore described the 1960 Game of Life as "incredibly grubby . . . just a shamelessly amoral and cash-conscious monster of a board game."[4]

Perhaps in a nod to Milton Bradley's inclusion of Matrimony, the 1960 Game of Life did put its thumb on the scale in one area. Each player had to go to church and get married if they wanted to succeed. And you could only add a baby girl or boy if you were already married. The new requirement—Bradley's original version simply presented marriage as a virtuous choice—prompted no moral outrage. It merely reflected cultural norms concerning marriage and childbearing in 1960, since at the time 95 percent of all babies were born within marriage. Imagine what the reaction would be today.

Indeed, nearly fifty years later, in 2007, Hasbro again revamped the Game of Life. According to Hasbro's promotional materials, "The Game of Life: Twists and Turns" puts a new and modern spin on Hasbro's classic family board game. It is a game of choices, where players can 'test drive' different lifestyles, take their chances and experience the twists and turns of real life."[5]

There are no absolutes in the new version—virtually anything goes. The only commonality is that each player is given a branded Visa credit card (ironically, with the name of Milton Bradley). Marriage is no longer required. If a player lands on a space that offers the marriage option, choosing that option does not guarantee a particular outcome. Moreover, if a player chooses that option, all other players have $1,000 automatically drained from their bank account for a wedding gift. Thus, in today's Game of Life: Twists and Turns, marriage is not mandatory, and moreover, your friends have a perverse incentive to encourage you not to get married.

As Lepore noted in her Harvard lecture, the new version's "only object is to experience all that life has to offer. With Milton Bradley's Visa card in hand, you can do whatever you want. It doesn't matter. No one cares. There are no consequences."[6] However, *real life*, unlike the Game of Life, is not a game. There are choices in real life and those choices have consequences for adults and their children—all of which brings us to the role of the Family in FREE.

As we have seen, the family our students will form matters monumentally to their ultimate success and personal agency—and the type of family that has been found to be most beneficial for the prospects of young adults and their future children is an intact, married, two-parent household. It bears repeating that millennials are taking divergent paths toward adulthood and family formation, paths associated with markedly different economic outcomes. Millennials are much more likely to flourish financially if they first earn at least a high school degree, then find full-time work, and then marry before having any children. According to an Institute for Family Studies report, 97 percent of millennials who make this ordered series of decisions—the Success Sequence—are not poor by the time they reach their prime young-adult years (ages twenty-eight through thirty-four).[7]

Despite all this—and despite the fact that there has been a resurgence in the number of children living with two parents in recent years—there is reason for both worry and action. In 2016, the National Center for Health Statistics division of the Centers for Disease Control and Prevention released a report on attitudes toward marriage, childbearing, and sexual behavior. It found that the percentage of respondents aged fifteen through forty-four who thought it was "okay for an unmarried female to have and raise a child" had increased over time. Among women, 70 percent agreed in 2002 and 78 percent agreed in 2011–2013. Among men, 59 percent agreed in 2002 and 69 percent agreed in 2011–2013. An even higher percentage of women aged fifteen through twenty-four (77 percent) agreed with the statement in 2011–2013, while only 60 percent of men in the same age group agreed.[8]

If we want to inspire the rising generation to have more children born into stable, married, two-parent households—one of the best predictors of a life of agency—I recommend four steps:

1. Re-create or revitalize a social norm concerning work, marriage, responsible family formation, and parenthood.
2. Make family structure a standard measurement category of child outcomes.
3. Implement family-friendly policies that do not penalize marriage.
4. Declare the reduction in nonmarital births to women aged twenty-four and under to be a "winnable battle."

CREATE OR RENEW A SOCIAL NORM CONCERNING EDUCATION, WORK, MARRIAGE, AND THE TIMING OF FAMILY FORMATION

In 2015 the Closing the Opportunity Gap initiative recommended a

> large-scale social marketing campaign that uses the media, and especially social media, to change social norms. . . . The group identified four messages for this campaign: 1) Children require a stable, committed partnership between their parents; 2) Parents should follow the "success sequence," which involves first graduating from high school, then getting a job, then getting married, and then having children (a sequence that creates a 97-percent chance of avoiding poverty);[9] 3) Partners should not have a baby until they really want one;[10] and 4) Low-income single parents raising unplanned children reduce the child's later chances for

success (for example, likelihood of graduating from high school or college, escaping poverty, and being married).[11]

A similar recommendation came from a joint effort of the American Enterprise Institute and the Brookings Institution. In its Working Group on Poverty and Opportunity's 2015 report,[12] the group said that "political leaders, educators, and civic leaders—from both the political left and right—need to be clear about how hard it is to raise children without a committed co-parent." It pointed out that we have effectively reduced major public health problems such as smoking and teen pregnancy by changing cultural attitudes facilitated through public information campaigns.[13] The group proposed a campaign of similar scope to emphasize the value of committed coparenting and marriage.[14]

The Culture of Freedom Initiative organized by the Philanthropy Roundtable can be a model for such a campaign. This privately funded 2016–2018 campaign identified "replicable strategies to revive the cultural factors that expand access to the American Dream." Its theory of action was to strengthen two elements of social capital that are closely associated with upward mobility and human flourishing: family and faith. Project organizers launched a hyperlocal, microtargeted set of tactics to promote human flourishing: decrease divorce rates and out-of-wedlock births and increase marriage rates and regular church attendance. They first implemented the model in three cities—Dayton, Ohio; Jacksonville, Florida; and Phoenix, Arizona—before going nationwide. Initial results of the campaign indicate that the initiative may have played a significant role in reducing the divorce rate in Jacksonville. In addition, they engaged a broad network of religious congregations committed to strengthening marriage.[15] The Culture of Freedom Initiative (now called Communio) and the campaign to reduce teen pregnancy are compelling models for local and national campaigns to promote the Success Sequence and to strengthen families.

MAKE FAMILY STRUCTURE A STANDARD MEASURE OF CHILD OUTCOMES

Family structure is often missing from data measuring student progress. The New York State Education Department, for example, provides an easy-to-use data site that allows users to access data in reading and math test scores as well as graduation rates. Student information can be filtered by many factors, including school, gender, race or ethnicity, migrant status, geographic district, English language learner status, economic status, and disability status. Yet the site provides no way to disaggregate student outcomes by family structure. No other state seems to do so either. At the federal level, the National Assessment of Educational Progress (NAEP) offers a Data Explorer tool that allows users to "create statistical tables, charts, maps . . . by grade, subject, and jurisdiction."[16] By law, NAEP reporting must include information on race, ethnicity, socioeconomic status, gender, disability, and limited English proficiency.[17] Yet here, as in New York and other states, there is no way to review results by family structure. It should not be this way.

In the world of neuroscience, the phenomenon of being oblivious to the obvious is called "inattentional blindness." The current filters and categories we use to evaluate progress in student achievement focus primarily—and stubbornly—on race, class, gender, and geography. In disregarding family structure, the data obscure a massive demographic shift that might explain other well-documented achievement gaps. The omission of family structure and stability as a measure that is crucial to child development and agency is no benign oversight—it has consequences. The dearth of child educational data parsed by family structure makes it easier to come to erroneous, single-cause conclusions. It masks opportunities to implement *different* types of interventions that could, in fact, improve life outcomes for the next generation. If we truly want to improve outcomes for children, we must have the moral courage to measure student achievement outcomes by family structure groupings as routinely as we already do by race, class, and gender. We must overcome our "inattentional"—or perhaps *intentional*—blindness.

Health-care leaders and analysts have made the commonsense decision to study causal and correlational links between family structure and child-health outcomes. These analyses are yielding new explanations for entrenched problems and ushering in a new wave of family-focused prescriptions in the health arena. It is time education leaders and analysts do the same. The first step is including family structure in all the data we collect on student outcomes. If the National Center for Health Statistics can figure how to incorporate family structure as a metric for measurement, surely the technical experts at the National Center for Education can do the same. And so can state experts in education, imprisonment, crime, and other areas that affect children's lives and their ability to lead self-determined lives.

IMPLEMENT FAMILY-FRIENDLY POLICIES THAT INCENTIVIZE WORK AND DO NOT PENALIZE MARRIAGE

While the government has a mixed record of influencing intimate decisions such as the appropriate timing of family formation, there are policies that can support stronger family formation. Eliminating marriage penalties from means-tested tax and transfer programs is one way. Incentivizing work, as is done with the Earned Income Tax Credit, is another.

Because of the many federal benefits—Medicaid (government-provided health insurance), SNAP (food stamps), and many tax credits—lower-income couples with children often face a financial penalty if they choose to marry rather than cohabitate.[18] For working-class couples, these taxes on marriage can slash their income by as much as 30 percent.[19]

DECLARE THE REDUCTION IN NONMARITAL BIRTHS TO WOMEN TWENTY-FOUR AND UNDER TO BE A "WINNABLE BATTLE"

The U.S. Centers for Disease Control and Prevention (CDC) have had success with the Winnable Battles campaign. The organization targets "public health priorities with large-scale impact on health and known effective strategies to address them."[20] The CDC then sets clear goals, and agencies across the federal government align their policies with these goals. The result has been significant progress in reducing the health burden from diseases and conditions targeted under Winnable Battles. Past Winnable Battles have led to reductions in smoking and teen pregnancy. The CDC should make reducing nonmarital births, particularly to women aged twenty-four and under, a whole-of-government Winnable Battle.

CHAPTER 14

Religion

*Of all the dispositions and habits which lead
to political prosperity, religion and morality are
indispensable supports.*

—George Washington, 1796 farewell address

On the eve of a snowy nor'easter in March 2017, I sat in awe in the magnificent Central Synagogue in midtown Manhattan. I couldn't decide if I was more inspired by the soaring home of one of New York City's largest and oldest Jewish Reform congregations or the diverse assemblage of clergy in ritual garb—Jews, Christians, Muslims, Hindus, Buddhists, and Sikhs—seated at the front of the synagogue.

An hour before the event, Governor Andrew Cuomo had declared a state of emergency across the entire state. A severe winter storm was expected to bring heavy snow and high winds across the region, yet despite the impending blizzard, these religious leaders had come together for an extraordinary interfaith gathering to mobilize New Yorkers in an important cause. I was one of 1,200 people in the sanctuary that night for an event organized by the

Raise the Age Coalition. This was a kaleidoscope of faith, nonprofit, social-justice, law-enforcement, and legal-aid community leaders working to raise the age of criminal responsibility to eighteen so that sixteen- and seventeen-year-olds who committed nonviolent crimes would receive more fitting, youth-oriented interventions and evidence-based treatment.

It was a righteous, research-backed cause and the legislation ultimately passed in 2018.[1] But what I remember most from that winter evening were the stories the young offenders told. For many, their journey of bad choices didn't begin late in their teenage years. Instead, it began in their troubled families. They told of growing up in dysfunctional homes, suffering the pain of an absent father or watching an overwhelmed single mother who did her best but could not shield them from the ravages of the street. For me, their stories underscored the importance of developing healthy and stable families (the "F" in FREE). But the faith-based event itself underscored the importance of religion and religious institutions in promoting conditions and choices that lead to flourishing lives of agency (the "R").

When it comes to family life, religious couples report the highest levels of marital satisfaction.[2] Studies have also shown that religious attendance is associated with a lower likelihood of divorce and family disruption among married couples.[3] Indeed, Pope John Paul II called family the "first and vital cell of society." He believed that "healthy relationships in marriage and the family are of the greatest importance in the development and well-being of the human person."[4]

The Raise the Age event was a powerful reminder of the faith community's unique ability to spur "sacred action" to help young people avoid the cycle of dysfunction and criminality. While that night was about the religious community preventing still-impressionable teenagers from being treated like hardened adult criminals, I couldn't help but think about the countless other times people of faith had come together to improve the lives of rising generations. Beyond the fulfillment usually experienced when individuals make a powerful faith commitment in their own life, there are the benefits of joining a community of kindred spirits. That is why embracing religion can be an important step in leading a self-determined life of human flourishing, forging stronger family bonds, and enjoying better social connectedness.

RELIGION AS A SOURCE OF MEANING, FULFILLMENT, AND SATISFACTION

In late 2017, the Pew Research Center conducted two major surveys asking Americans what makes life meaningful. The answer across a wide variety of social and demographic subgroups was clear and consistent: *family.* In other studies, Pew found that, globally, people are much more likely to say they are "very happy" if they attend a house of worship at least once per month.[5]

Indeed, a wide range of research shows that people who attend a house of worship more frequently,[6] pray more,[7] and more strongly identify themselves as religious[8] are all more likely to report greater levels of happiness[9] and well-being. Moreover, valuing religion is associated with a lower risk of depression.[10]

One aspect of agency is strong social-emotional development. Analysis of the General Social Survey—one of the premier national assessments of a variety of social outcomes—suggests that belief in a supportive higher power is associated with greater levels of self-esteem. One comprehensive literature review found that several components of religious involvement[11] reduce the likelihood of criminal behavior and significantly decrease binge drinking, marijuana use, and dependence on hard drugs over time, even among individuals who are already drug offenders.[12]

These social-emotional benefits associated with religion need to be acknowledged and promoted, especially at a time when social isolation—even prior to the COVID-19 pandemic—is on the rise among young and old Americans. In January 2020, for example, Cigna, a global health service company, released a study finding that nearly 79 percent of Gen Z respondents and 71 percent of millennials reported feeling lonely, compared to just half of baby boomers.[13] Religion can provide an antidote to loneliness in the real world. In an era when members of the millennial generation are now being referred to as "Mil(lonely)als," the Walton Family Foundation found that Millennials and Gen Z–ers were much more likely to say they felt "somewhat" or "very" connected to the people in their local community if they were frequent attendees of religious services.[14]

RELIGIOUS SUBSTITUTES DON'T WORK

Despite these benefits, religious practice in the United States is declining. About one quarter of Americans now identify as "nones," having no religious preference in particular.[15] Millennials and other young Americans consistently show the lowest rates of religious affiliation and the lowest frequency of attendance at religious services.[16] The challenge, of course, is that human beings of all ages have to believe in *something*. There is an innate desire to be a part of something larger than ourselves. Abraham Kuyper argued that "all ideological movements—secular or religious—were fundamentally faith-based" and that human beings are innately created to be "rooted" in a belief system. The late theologian warned that "rootless individuals and communities are particularly vulnerable to being absorbed into rising ideologies who clearly point to some foundation or direction."[17] As G. K. Chesterton once said, "When men choose not to believe in God, they do not thereafter believe in nothing, they then become capable of believing in anything."[18]

In the absence of traditional religion, a new form of identity politics has risen to fill this spiritual vacuum. In *Woke Racism: How a New Religion Has Betrayed Black America*, Columbia University professor John McWhorter describes how a well-meaning but pernicious form of "antiracism" has become, not simply a progressive ideology, but a religion—one that's illogical, unreachable, and unintentionally neoracist. McWhorter argues that this illiberal neoracism is actually hurting black communities and weakening the American social fabric. And he's right.[19]

And here's the great tragedy of our new religion of woke racism. As my American Enterprise Institute colleague Brad Wilcox, a sociologist at the University of Virginia, reveals in *Black Men Making It in America*, black men who attended traditional religious services regularly at a young age were 10 percentage points more likely to make it into the middle class when they reached adulthood than peers who did not.[20] Real religion—not faux religions like the new church of "Wokeness"—matters in black lives and, indeed, all lives.

A PATH FORWARD TO RESTORE RELIGION'S PROPER PLACE IN AMERICAN CULTURE

In developing the power of personal agency, young people do not need shabby substitutes for traditional religion. Rather, they need more compelling reasons to make a real personal faith commitment. They also need revitalized religious institutions that can create better conditions for our young people. They also need public and private entities willing to engage with religious institutions in the "sacred action" of building agency.

Like the Raise the Age Coalition, more faith-based institutions are demonstrating their power to help young people reach their potential. Take, for example, the Culture of Freedom Initiative and Seton Education Partners.

Culture of Freedom Initiative

The overall goal of the Philanthropy Roundtable's Culture of Freedom Initiative was to strengthen marriage and improve family life, one relationship at a time, through a hyperlocal, microtargeted strategy. What, specifically, did this look like? In Jacksonville, Florida, for example, Community Organizing and Family Issues (COFI) combined a digital air campaign with an extensive, in-person ground game to convey to residents that marriage matters. From 2016 to 2018, the initiative generated more than 28 million digital impressions with the message that it is never too early nor too late to invest in your marriage. It also sponsored marriage and relationship education programs. In the end, the local effort connected approximately 50,000 adults to fifty local churches and forty nonprofits committed to helping individuals strengthen their marriage.

Culture of Freedom provided individual pastors with "big data" insights on the specific needs of their community and the opportunities for action. It also provided data to participating institutions for new pilot programs to strengthen family life and church connections. To help churches and nonprofits expand their membership and reach, COFI offered additional financial assistance. As part of COFI, local congregations launched programs to connect their members to everything from healthy marriage and relationship classes to comedy date nights for couples. COFI Jacksonville coincided with a 24 percent decline in the divorce rate per 1,000 persons in Duval County from 2015 to 2018—a rate of decline that was 21 percent *faster* than in demographically similar coun-ties across the United States.[21]

Culture of Freedom has formally spun off from the Philan-thropy Roundtable and is now called Communio. Its goal remains the same, and its scope is now national. Communio is a serious force for the revitalization of faith and family in many cities around our nation—and a model for similar efforts.

Seton Education Partners

In 2009, at the height of the Great Recession, Scott W. Hamilton and Stephanie Saroki de García launched Seton Education Partners in response to the collapse of urban Catholic education across the country. Over the previous four decades, Catholic schools had seen enrollments plummet by more than 50 percent. More than 1,500 Catholic elementary schools in low-income communities had closed or been consolidated. García and Hamilton recognized that this meant fewer schools that nurture the whole child, including the spirit—and fewer education options—for hundreds of thou-sands of families.[22]

In response, Seton pioneered several school models to provide holistic education in our nation's underserved communities. Seton launched the nation's first blended-learning Catholic school, Mis-sion Dolores Academy, in San Francisco. This model combines adaptive learning software on computers with teacher-led small group instruction. The goal is to create more individualized learn-ing time for children. Seton has now replicated this program a dozen times in eight other cities, thus saving and strengthening once-struggling Catholic schools.

In 2013, Seton launched a classically inspired public charter school in the South Bronx and coupled the school with El Camino, an optional, privately funded after-school faith-formation program.

Seton has successfully replicated this model and plans to soon serve more than 3,200 children and their families in the Bronx. In 2020, it also launched the Romero Academy, an independent Catholic school, in Cincinnati.

Seton's charter and Catholic schools emphasize helping students, their families, and staff grow in virtue. Starting with the cardinal virtues of prudence, justice, fortitude, and temperance, character formation is central to each school's ethos—from its culture and daily routines to curricula and professional development. During "The Quietest Moment of the Day," children spend a few minutes in silence reflecting on how they demonstrated—or could have better demonstrated—perseverance, patience, mercy, or kindness. Moreover, schools celebrate children and adults who model virtue.

Several principles undergird Seton's philosophy of education, regardless of the particular type of school:

> "Start with Dignity"—Seton believes each person has worth independent of what he or she does, and that each person is meant to live a life of deep meaning and purpose. Seton encourages everyone—children, their families, and all staff—to put human dignity first.
>
> "Acknowledge Families as the First Educators"—Seton schools exist to lift up parents so they can serve as the first (and primary) educators of their children. In practical terms, this means supporting parents through home visits, "Coffee and Conversations," "Parent University," and "Family Faith Nights" programs to facilitate this two-way "partnership" with parents working to raise young men and women of character.

"Value Free Choice"—Seton rejects the view that human beings are determined entirely by their environment. While circumstances do impact and shape a person, they are not the sole determining factor of one's life. Each person is responsible for their own choices and can choose to grow from mistakes and hardships. A good education helps children understand the gift of liberty and how to exercise their free choice as well.[23]

More than 95 percent of Seton students are a member of a minority group and more than 90 percent live below the poverty line. These students are poised to receive a world-class education through Seton's network of schools. For example, students in Seton's Brilla elementary school network "grew 1.5 times faster than the national average in both reading and math," making Brilla the third highest performing elementary school in New York State among those serving children from similar backgrounds.[24] Seton is now poised to grow. In 2020 it was granted the right to open a public charter school in Texas and was exploring growth opportunities in other states. "If the country faces cultural problems, we stand a much better chance of fixing them not through government, but through spiritual revival and the building of new, energetic, and vital religious communities distinct from the state," Brown University economist Glenn Loury wrote in 2005. "The mention of God may seem quaint, or vaguely inappropriate, but it is clear that behavioral problems involve spiritual issues."[25] Loury's words may be even more true today.

As we move to create a culture of agency, it is essential to the formation of FREE children that there be more private organizations like Communio and Seton Education Partners and coalitions like Raise the Age. We need to increase the reach of all our faith communities and leverage their inherent strengths to address the nation's most painful social ailments in order to shape the hearts and minds of the next generation. This is "sacred action" indeed.

CHAPTER

15

Education

Education means emancipation. It means light and liberty.
It means the uplifting of the soul of man into the glorious
light of truth, the light only by which men can be free.

—Frederick Douglass

"Son, as a boy growing up in Jamaica, I learnt to be a 'mon.' I was a mon, full-stop," my father would say, "It wasn't until I came to this country that I realized I was a *black* mon." Speaking in the patois of his beloved Caribbean nation, my now deceased father often told me about the struggles he experienced after emigrating to America. He described what it was like to grow up in an island country where your success or failure was more likely determined by individual effort rather than your racial group identity, since virtually everyone in Jamaica was black. He contrasted that to life in the United States, where he was constantly reminded of what he could not or should not do simply because of his race.

He marveled at how Americans, black and white alike, obsessed over skin color. There was a certain way to "talk black and act black," or "talk white and act white." (Other races didn't seem to matter.) My father found it especially maddening that certain negative behaviors or conditions—committing crime or living in poverty, for example—were so often equated with being black even though the number of non-Hispanic whites in prison or on welfare exceeded any other racial category. He was stunned by how black people were almost always portrayed as either victims or perpetrators of the most self-destructive actions. He was also appalled that positive behaviors—studying hard, getting good grades, being a good father—were so often associated with being white and *not* being *black*, and that black kids who studied hard and got good grades were seen as somehow betraying their race. I miss my father dearly, but I'm glad he was not around to see the National Museum of African American History and Culture's "Aspects of Whiteness" web posting (see Chapter 5).

My parents thought the negative stereotypes weren't just wrong but also debilitating, especially for black children. My parents didn't want their children to succumb to them. They rejected the very idea that we had to accept or tolerate these false caricatures. "You are not oppressed," Dad used to say to me. While they had come to the United States during a tumultuous time in race relations in the late 1960s, my parents knew that opportunities for black Americans, and indeed for all Americans, were expanding. The country was changing. Despite the contradictions between its founding ideals and the history of slavery and Jim Crow discrimination, America had made steady progress in dismantling laws that imposed a racial hierarchy and stifled black advancement. Indeed, the Civil Rights Act of 1964 and the Voting Rights Act of 1965 had just been signed.

Dad always told me and my brother that we had to be prepared for opportunities when they came our way. If he were alive today, he would be stunned to see current data from Harvard University on black admissions to its freshman class. In 2017–2018, if you were a black applicant and Harvard ranked you in the top two (of ten) academic categories, you had a better than 55 percent chance of being admitted.[1] And Harvard is no outlier. You will likely find that kind of disproportionate opportunity for black kids, and minority students in general, at virtually every institution of higher education in the country.

This is why I have dedicated much of my professional life to ensuring that kids of all backgrounds have access to great, tuition-free public education, regardless of race, family structure, class, or zip code. I want all our children to be prepared for the enormous opportunities now out there. In 2010, I made a ten-year commitment to serve as CEO of Public Prep, a network of single-sex elementary and middle schools in the South Bronx and Manhattan's Lower East Side. We had more than 2,000 kids—most low-income and most black and Hispanic. Many of our parents, like my mother and father, wanted their kids to be prepared for their shot at the American Dream. I'm proud to say that Public Prep alumni now attend some of the nation's finest high schools and colleges. In 2022 I plan to launch Vertex Partnership Academies, a new network seeking to be International Baccalaureate (IB) high schools that will offer both the IB Diploma and the IB Careers pathway. Vertex will be grounded in the concepts of equality of opportunity, individual dignity, and our common humanity as well the cardinal virtues of courage, justice, temperance, and wisdom. Our first campus will open in the Bronx.

The first "E" in FREE calls on each young person to commit to study hard and meet the highest educational expectations. It is therefore essential that these students and their families have a wide range of high-quality education options to choose from—

kindergarten through Grade 12 institutions that, like Vertex Partnership Academies, promote the academic and character development required to empower young people to make reasoned and morally uplifting decisions in their own lives. This is what Martin Luther King, Jr., had in mind when he defined the purpose of education. Teaching kids "to think intensively and to think critically" is important, he wrote,

> But education which stops with efficiency may prove the greatest menace to society. The most dangerous criminal may be the man gifted with reason, but with no morals. . . . We must remember that intelligence is not enough. Intelligence plus character—that is the goal of true education. The complete education gives one not only power of concentration, but worthy objectives upon which to concentrate. The broad education will, therefore, transmit to one not only the accumulated knowledge of the [human] race but also the accumulated experience of social living.[2]

If we want the rising generation to usher in a new age of agency, we must make the following five changes in K–12 and higher education:

1. Eliminate barriers to school choice nationwide;
2. Teach the Success Sequence as a probabilities class in middle, high, and post-secondary schools;
3. Focus on the "Distance-to-100" gap rather than the racial achievement gap;
4. Expand content-rich curricula, with a particular focus on civics and historical content;
5. Replace race-based affirmative action with class-based preferences in higher education.

ELIMINATE BARRIERS TO SCHOOL CHOICE NATIONWIDE

State constitutions typically require children to be in elementary, middle, or high school from age five to age sixteen or eighteen, yet compulsory schooling does not mean compulsory designation or assignment of the school to meet that requirement.

While the concept of compulsory education is universal, the ability for all Americans to choose what works for their own child is not. School choice already exists for middle- and upper-income families. In general, they have the financial means to enroll their children in private or parochial schools or move to neighborhoods that have good public schools. That is not the case for children in most need of a high-quality education—low-income children. True school choice does not exist for their families. These students are most often consigned to their neighborhood school, no matter the quality of that school and no matter that school's success or failure in educating its students.

In my time running public charter schools, the most surreal experience is the annual lottery in which parents compete for a few hundred open seats in our network. Each year, following the electronic drawing, we had the privilege of calling parents and telling them that their child had just been admitted. They were always overjoyed. Conversely, we had to tell the nearly 5,000 families that their child did not gain enrollment via the lottery. The best we could do was put them on a long wait list. Their chances of admittance were slim. It was heart-breaking and depressing for all of us.

One year the *New York Post* ran a front-page story about one of our wait-listed parents and her son. Next to her full-page picture was the headline "Let my son in!"[3] This parent was frustrated with the artificial cap the state placed on charter schools—a cap that prevented the opening of new public charter schools in low-income communities with manifestly failing traditional public schools. She was not alone. That same year a McLaughlin & Associates poll found that more than 72 percent of New Yorkers with household incomes under $60,000 wanted the cap lifted.[4] Nationwide, according to the National Alliance for Public Charter Schools, charter schools serve 3.3 million students but 5 million more would attend if space were available.[5] It does not have to be this way. State legislators should make space available by allowing new and existing charter schools to meet parental demand. Low-income families are asking for nothing more than the opportunity to send their children to a great public school.

There are several other ways to give families the opportunity to choose excellent schools for their children. Educational Savings Accounts (ESAs) are one great option. Arizona was the first state to implement an ESA program. When an Arizona parent removes their child from public school, they are given a restricted-use debit card with about 90 percent of the money the state would otherwise spend on their child's education. Parents can then apply these funds toward educational ends—such as paying tuition at a local private school, paying for music lessons, or purchasing textbooks to homeschool their child. Even though ESAs don't equal the entire sum that state, local, and federal programs spend on the average child's education, the cash value of these accounts can help many families send their kids to an otherwise unaffordable school. The program has been a big hit in Arizona, and it could be a model for other states that are looking to open excellent educational pathways for more students.[6]

States can also offer tuition vouchers to low-income students who wish to attend a private school. Wisconsin and the District of Columbia, for example, have some of the nation's most expansive voucher programs. Low-income families in these states are eligible for up $10,000 each year in private-school tuition support.[7]

States preferring a more indirect form of support can implement "tuition tax credit" programs. Families that send their child to a private school or homeschool them receive a tax break of, say, $5,000. These tax credits can be made fully refundable (families still receive the credit even when they do not owe any taxes) in order to maximize their impact for low-income families. While no states currently offer a tuition tax credit program for families who choose an alternate educational path for their children, some do offer tax relief for these families. Minnesota, for example, considers private-school tuition tax deductible.[8]

As David S. D'Amato wrote in *Forbes*, "If we want better schools—schools that fulfill their duties by providing a quality education at reasonable cost—we need choice, competition and the accountability they engender."[9]

TEACH THE SUCCESS SEQUENCE AS A PROBABILITIES CLASS IN MIDDLE, HIGH, AND POSTSECONDARY SCHOOLS

Parents want their kids to learn empowering strategies that give them a better chance to overcome life's inevitable hurdles. I think we all know this in our hearts and minds. I've certainly seen it in my charter school work. But we also have compelling evidence on the subject. A July 2020 national survey commissioned by the Heritage Foundation found that 72 percent of all parents and 60 percent of all school board members agreed that schools should explicitly teach that graduating high school, getting a job, and getting married before having children will make students more likely to avoid poverty.[10]

The Success Sequence could be taught as one of many possible decision pathways in a probability or statistics class. This would allow kids to explore data indicating how various life decisions differentially affect their likelihood of achieving economic prosperity in adulthood. The data would have to be presented as descriptive, not prescriptive. For example, there is a sharp contrast between millennials who married first and those who had a baby first. According to the Institute for Family Studies' Millennial Success Sequence report, fully 86 percent of young adults who married first have family incomes in the middle or top third. By contrast, only 53 percent of millennials who put childbearing first have incomes in the middle or top third.[11]

The goal would be to help middle and high school students develop personal agency over the forces they *do control* in their education, work, and relationships in order to give them the best shot to overcome the forces they *do not control*—life's hard knocks, the effects of discrimination, and other forces that might lead to poverty. Since these lessons would be designed for young people whose parents may not have followed the most advantageous path in their own lives, it would be important that teachers meet with parents beforehand to talk about the reason for this class. The goal is certainly not to shame parents for decisions they may have made. Rather, it is to communicate the fact that the structure and stability of the families their children form will matter monumentally to their ultimate success. This may be the best information we can give them to build the personal agency necessary to overcome racism, poverty, or any other type of adversity.

Parents need educators to be the adults in the room and not be cowed into silence by political correctness or fear of being accused of moralizing. They need educators who will talk openly to students about the best path to achieve their dreams for their children.

An example of a curriculum that includes the Success Sequence can be found in the Appendix. "Is It a Healthy Relationship?," comes from Marline Pearson's "Love Notes 3.0." It is designed to help teens and young adults learn how to make wise choices about partners, sex, relationships, and pregnancy and how to assess the health of their relationships.[12] In a federally funded randomized control trial over five years, "Love Notes" was shown to be extremely effective as an innovative pregnancy prevention strategy for at-risk youth.[13] The program cut teen pregnancy by almost half among students who participated in the course.

Educators have a responsibility to point out the paths into adulthood that will most likely lead to agency and economic success and away from dysfunction and poverty. The Success Sequence's data-driven approach can help their students make the best decisions in their own lives.

FOCUS ON DISTANCE TO 100 VERSUS CLOSING RACIAL ACHIEVEMENT GAPS

The multidecade obsession with closing racial or class achievement gaps has not only failed to close those gaps, it has done nothing to substantially increase overall achievement levels. Four researchers, Eric A. Hanushek, Paul E. Peterson, Laura M. Talpey, and Ludger Woessmann, recently examined this question. Their widely read 2019 study in *Education Next*, "The Achievement Gap Fails to Close," found that the relationship between socioeconomic status and achievement—what they call the "opportunity gap"—has not grown over the past 50 years, but neither has it closed. "Instead," they concluded, "the gap between the haves and have-nots has persisted."[14]

These macro-results are hardly surprising. In May 2021, the Rhode Island State Board of Education asked me to testify on how

FIGURE 15.1   Percentage of eighth graders in Rhode Island scoring proficient on NAEP Reading Assessment, by race.

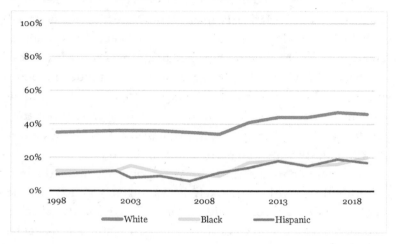

SOURCE: NAEP Data Explorer and Rhode Island Department of Education. https://nces.ed.gov/nationsreportcard/data/.

to improve educational outcomes. In preparing for the hearing, I compiled eighth grade National Assessment of Educational Progress reading proficiency scores for Rhode Island students since 1998, the first year the Nation's Report Card was administered there. As Figure 15.1 indicates, the racial achievement gap has essentially remained the same for two decades. And here's the sad point: if Rhode Island had, in fact, closed the black- or Hispanic-to-white achievement gap without improving outcomes for *all* students, black and Hispanic students would still be mired in mediocrity. They would have merely moved from slightly less than mediocrity to full mediocrity because every year since 1998, less than half of the state's white eighth graders achieved NAEP proficiency in reading.[15]

These numbers highlight our massive national failure to effectively teach literacy and build verbal proficiency across *all* races.

FIGURE 15.2   Number of eighth graders in Rhode Island scoring below proficient on NAEP reading assessment (2018).

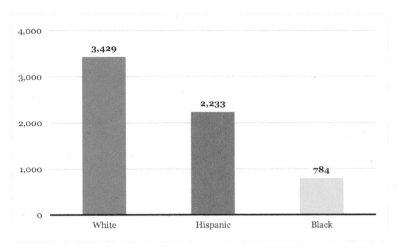

SOURCE: NAEP Data Explorer and Rhode Island Department of Education. https://nces.ed.gov/nationsreportcard/data/; https://www.ride.ri.gov/informationaccount ability/rieducationdata/enrollmentgraduationdata.aspx.

They also shatter the false assumption that racism is the sole, or even the primary, cause of low proficiency rates among black and Hispanic Americans. "Systemic racism" can hardly be the cause of such poor performance among thousands of white students (Figure 15.2). In my view, however, our multidecade obsession with closing achievement gaps has done something even worse. It encourages monocausal thinking, which keeps us from identifying solutions *across* categories. If systemic racism is truly the primary cause of racial disparities, then the solutions need to be systematically or institutionally focused on race. But this strategy has clearly failed.

There is an alternative approach that I refer to as "Distance to 100." Distance to 100 would emphasize eliminating the gap to 100 percent proficiency for all students. Indeed, we would start by asking why only roughly a third of all American students are reading at proficiency. That Distance to 100—nearly 70 percent— is more than double the class- or race-based achievement gaps.

If we adopted this approach, we would soon discover that the reason a majority of white students have consistently not been reading at grade level overlaps with the reason a majority of black students have not been reading at grade level. For decades, education researchers from E. D. Hirsch to Dan Willingham to Natalie Wexler have made the case that a lack of focus on building knowledge in early reading instruction has had a devastating impact on all American children. Natalie Wexler[16] outlines the dilemma in her book *The Knowledge Gap: The Hidden Cause of America's Broken Education System—And How to Fix It*:[17]

> American elementary education has been shaped by a theory that goes like this: Reading—a term used to mean not just matching letters to sounds but also comprehension—can be taught in a manner completely disconnected from content. Use simple texts to teach children how to find the main idea, make inferences, draw conclusions, and so on, and eventually they'll be able to apply those skills to grasp the meaning of anything put in front of them.
>
> In the meantime, what children are reading doesn't really matter—it's better for them to acquire skills that will enable them to discover knowledge for themselves later on than for them to be given information directly, or so the thinking goes. That is, they need to spend their time "learning to read" before "reading to learn." Science can wait; history, which is considered too abstract for young minds to grasp, must wait. Reading time is filled, instead, with a variety of short books and passages unconnected to one another except by the "comprehension skills" they're meant to teach.
>
> As far back as 1977, early-elementary teachers spent more than twice as much time on reading as on science and social stud-

ies combined. But since 2001, when the federal No Child Left Behind legislation made standardized reading and math scores the yardstick for measuring progress, the time devoted to both subjects has only grown. In turn, the amount of time spent on social studies and science has plummeted—especially in schools where test scores are low.

And yet, despite the enormous expenditure of time and resources on reading, American children haven't become better readers.[18] For the past 20 years, only about a third of students have scored at or above the "proficient" level on national tests. For low-income and minority kids, the picture is especially bleak: Their average test scores are far below those of their more affluent, largely white peers—a phenomenon usually referred to as the achievement gap. As this gap has grown wider, America's standing in international literacy rankings, already mediocre, has fallen.

All of which raises a disturbing question: What if the medicine we have been prescribing is only making matters worse, particularly for poor children? What if the best way to boost reading comprehension is not to drill kids on discrete skills but to teach them, as early as possible, the very things we've marginalized—including history, science, and other content that could build the knowledge and vocabulary they need to understand both written texts and the world around them?

In short, we should focus on what's required to improve everyone's achievement, on those factors that truly are holding all kids back—unstable families, lack of access to content-rich curriculum, lack of school choice, and similar obstacles. As Hanushek and his coauthors state, "The stubborn endurance of achievement inequalities suggests the need to reconsider policies and practices aimed at shrinking the gap. Although policymakers have repeatedly tried to break the link between students' learning and their socioeconomic background, these interventions thus far have been unable to dent the relationship between socioeconomic status and achievement. Perhaps it is time to consider alternatives."[19] Distance to 100 may be that empowering alternative.

EXPAND CONTENT-RICH CURRICULA, WITH A FOCUS ON CIVICS AND HISTORY

As already described in this chapter, our country has been mired in a decades-long literacy crisis. In crisis, however, there is always opportunity, and the opportunity here is twofold: the overwhelming need to teach our students American history aligns neatly with the need to address the nation's literacy crisis. Properly done, the promotion of civic literacy can simultaneously increase basic literacy in our students. Both, it seems to me, are essential elements of agency.

So how do we achieve both? We reintroduce content-rich readings into the curriculum. We have our youngest students *"read to learn"* simultaneously to the process to *"learn to read."* And as Natalie Wexler noted, we revamp our curriculum and school days *"to teach* them, as early as possible, the very things we've marginalized—including history, science, and other content that could build the knowledge and vocabulary they need to understand both written texts and the world around them" (italics added).[20]

A good place to start would be history. Most people can agree that all kids should learn a more complete history of the United States through more content-rich curricula. The good news is that there are uplifting alternatives to the *New York Times'* fatally flawed 1619 Project (discussed in Chapter 4).

Former District of Columbia Chancellor Kaya Henderson created Reconstruction "to show our kids that they are descendants of powerful, creative, and resilient ancestors whose contributions permeate every aspect of life across the globe; and that they too are called to contribute to this rich legacy."[21] There is also the freely available curriculum from the Woodson Center's 1776 Unites project.[22] Founded by Robert Woodson, this initiative puts a special focus on voices in the black community that celebrate black excellence and reject the victimhood culture. It showcases the millions of black Americans who have prospered by embracing our nation's founding ideals. The curriculum features lessons on the Rosenwald Schools and other lesser-known stories of black resiliency in the face of adversity. As of this writing, it has been downloaded more than 25,000 times by teachers in all fifty states. It is now taught in public, private, and parochial schools; after-school programs; prison ministries; and home schools.

We should be encouraging the creation and adoption of more such curricula. I think we'll find that making better citizens will lead, at long last, to making better readers.

REPLACE RACE-BASED AFFIRMATIVE ACTION WITH CLASS-BASED PREFERENCES IN HIGHER EDUCATION

In 2017–2018, if you were a black applicant and Harvard ranked you in the top two academic categories, you had a 55 percent chance to be admitted. But a closer look at the admissions protocols reveals that racial preferences in higher education are impeding opportunities for low-income students of all races. As Figure 15.3 indicates, Harvard places each applicant into one of ten categories in an "academic index" (a metric created by Harvard based on test scores and grade point average).[23]

Based on this data, Harvard was four times more likely to admit a black applicant ranked in the top academic category than white students (56.1 percent versus 15.3 percent) and Asian

FIGURE 15.3   Harvard's preferences for underrepresented minorities.

Academic Decile	White	Asian American	African American	Hispanic	All Applicants
10	15.3%	12.7%	56.1%	31.3%	14.6%
9	10.8%	7.6%	54.6%	26.2%	10.4%
8	7.5%	5.1%	44.5%	22.9%	8.2%
7	4.8%	4.0%	41.1%	17.3%	6.6%
6	4.2%	2.5%	29.7%	13.7%	5.6%
5	2.6%	1.9%	22.4%	9.1% ·	4.4%
4	1.8%	0.9%	12.8%	5.5%	3.3%
3	0.6%	0.6%	5.2%	2.0%	1.7%
2	0.4%	0.2%	1.0%	0.3%	0.5%
1	0.0%	0.0%	0.0%	0.0%	0.0%

SOURCE: *Students for Fair Admissions Inc. v. President & Fellows of Harvard College* Supreme Court case. https://www.supremecourt.gov/DocketPDF/20/20-1199/169941/20210225095525027_Harvard%20Cert%20Petn%20Feb%2025.pdf.

students (56.1 percent versus 12.7 percent) with the same academic ranking. Moreover, an Asian American in the fourth-lowest decile had virtually no chance of being admitted to Harvard (0.9 percent), but an African American in that decile had a higher chance of admission (12.8 percent) than an Asian American in the *top* decile (12.7 percent).

This data was compiled by Students for Fair Admissions, a nonprofit membership group of more than 20,000 students, parents, and others who believe that racial classifications and preferences in college admissions are unfair, unnecessary, and unconstitutional. Students for Fair Admissions is currently pursuing a legal case against Harvard University, alleging racial discrimination against Asian applicants in undergraduate admissions. According to the Northwestern Law Review, the case "is one of the most notable recent equal protection challenges to be advanced almost exclusively on the basis of statistical evidence . . . and could well end affirmative action in higher education and beyond if it winds up at the Supreme Court."[24]

Forty-four years after the U.S. Supreme Court upheld a university's right to allow race to be one of several factors in university admissions (*Regents of the University of California v. Bakke*, 1978), and nineteen years after it ruled that the Constitution's Equal Protection Clause did not prohibit a law school's "narrowly tailored use of race in admissions decisions to further a compelling interest in obtaining the educational benefits that flow from a diverse student body" (*Grutter vs. Bollinger*, 2003), the high court may someday soon scuttle race-based preferences altogether. That would be a good thing.[25]

Why? For one, Harvard's race-based admissions are twice as likely to go to *nondisadvantaged* black applicants as to *disadvantaged* ones.[26] In other words, qualified low-income black applicants are taking a back seat to economically advantaged black and other applicants. Of course, economically advantaged African Americans should have a fair shot to get into any of the best schools in the country, but admission to the best schools in the country should be based on their own merit, and they should not be given an artificial preference over students of other races who come from an economically disadvantaged background.

If Students for Fair Admissions wins its case and the Supreme Court ends racial preference in higher education, would a large segment of these economically advantaged black and other students still be able to earn admission even without racial preferences? The answer is likely yes. According to MarketWatch, "The black students that elite colleges do admit increasingly come from either mixed-race backgrounds or immigrant families from Africa or the Caribbean." MarketWatch went on to note that one long-term study shows that at "highly selective private colleges, . . . students from black immigrant families plus students with one black and nonblack parent [rose] from about 40 percent of black students in the 1980s . . . to about 60 percent in the late 1990s."[27]

This phenomenon was explored in a 2012 study, "Exploring the Divergent Academic Outcomes of U.S.-Origin and Immigrant-Origin Black Undergraduates":[28]

> Immigrant-generational differences among black students stem from their differing cultural perspectives on education. John Ogbu and colleagues (Ogbu, 1991, 2003; Ogbu & Simons, 1998) have offered the Cultural-Ecological Theory of School Performance to explain performance differences between immigrant-origin and U.S.-origin Blacks.[29] According to John Ogbu, the achievement differences between these two groups stem from the different cultural adaptations of voluntary immigrants versus involuntary immigrants (or involuntary minorities). Voluntary minority immigrants attribute the discriminatory treatment they receive in their host societies to their status as "guests in a foreign land" and believe that the barriers they face are temporary challenges they can overcome through hard work, greater acculturation, and academic attainment (Ogbu, 1991; Ogbu & Simons, 1998). Ogbu argues that these perspectives lead voluntary immigrants to place greater value on educational success, as a collective, relative to involuntary minorities who entered their host societies through conquest, colonization, and enslavement (Ogbu, 1991; Ogbu & Simons, 1998). Involuntary minorities tend to view discriminatory treatment as permanent and institutionalized. According to Ogbu, these groups often do not believe that education will enable them to overcome systemic oppression and attain economic success or societal status and, accordingly, invest less time and resources in an effort to achieve academic success.

In brief, a community of black students is demonstrating that the racism some might deem systemic, institutional, and structural is actually *surmountable*.

There is overwhelming evidence that black students, particularly from African and Caribbean nations that place high value on academic success, as well as those native-born black people who are raised in stable, two-parent households, disproportionately enter elite universities. Racial preferences in education and elsewhere may soon not exist, and as a testament to this nation's progress in empowering young black people to reach their potential, may no longer even be necessary. Class-based preferences would give low-income kids of all races greater opportunity in higher education, and thus greater opportunities to build personal agency.

Nearly forty years ago, in April 1983, the Nation at Risk report raised the alarm that our country was falling behind in preparing young people for the challenges ahead:

> "Our concern . . . goes well beyond matters such as industry and commerce. It also includes the intellectual, moral, and spiritual strengths of our people which knit together the very fabric of our society. The people of the United States need to know that individuals in our society who do not possess the levels of skill, literacy, and training essential to this new era will be effectively disenfranchised, not simply from the material rewards that accompany competent performance, but also from the chance to participate fully in our national life. A high level of shared education is essential to a free, democratic society and to the fostering of a common culture, especially in a country that prides itself on pluralism and individual freedom.[30]

My hope is that the five steps outlined here will make it more possible for young people to receive a solid foundation in education that enhances their ability to exercise individual freedom and agency.

16

Entrepreneurship

*I discovered that I am the maker of my own life, that the
individual matters, and any individual person has the
moral capacity of changing his or her own life.*

—Ismael Hernandez

Writer James Truslow Adams coined the term "The American Dream" in 1931—ironically enough, while in the teeth of the Great Depression. The American Dream promised that "life should be better and richer and fuller for everyone, with opportunity for each according to ability or achievement," said Adams. "It is a dream of social order in which each man and each woman shall be able to attain to the fullest stature of which they are innately capable, and be recognized by others for what they are, regardless of the fortuitous circumstances of birth or position."[1]

Adams's definition captures the cross-generational promise of upward mobility that has been fundamental to the American story since its inception. Yet ninety years after Adams coined the term— ninety years that have seen the United States lead the world in wealth creation and upward economic mobility—a growing number of young people question the durability of the American Dream. Indeed, a global UNICEF study of twenty-one countries released in November 2021 showed that 56 percent of Americans aged fifteen to twenty-four said that children today would be worse off economically than their parents.[2]

My primary concern, as someone who runs schools, is that both the "blame-the-system" and "blame-the-victim" narratives in tandem suppress the countervailing steps young people can take to help them achieve agency and shape their own futures. Without an intervention, more young people may take on a persona of a victimized soul and adopt a mindset of "yes, I can't" versus "yes, I can."

This is where the second "E" in FREE comes in: Entrepreneurship. An entrepreneur is usually viewed as someone who creates a for-profit business. My definition of an entrepreneur includes that idea, but it is broader to encompass one who takes ownership of all facets of their life to create financial, social, and other forms of wealth.

To understand this broader concept of entrepreneurship, compare it to "learned helplessness," the term psychologist Martin Seligman coined in the late 1960s. In both human and animal studies he found that subjects exposed repeatedly to adverse situations over which they had no control developed over time an acceptance of *inescapable* (emphasis mine) powerlessness. For years, learned helplessness was understood as "a behavior pattern involving a maladaptive response characterized by avoidance of challenges, negative affect, and the collapse of problem-solving strategies when obstacles arise."[3]

Five decades later, however, Seligman made a fascinating disclosure about the concept of learned helplessness: "The original theory got it backward." In "Learned Helplessness at Fifty: Insights from Neuroscience," Seligman and coauthor Steven F. Maier wrote that "helplessness was not learned in the original experiments. Rather, passivity and heightened anxiety are the default mammalian reaction to prolonged bad events. What can be learned is cortical—that bad events will be controllable in the future."[4]

In other words, while a baby or young person's naturally occurring sense of helplessness or dependency can be negatively reinforced, it can also be counteracted by strategies that instill hope and a sense of control and ownership. Helplessness can be unlearned. Learned optimism can be the empowering alternative, the default habit to overcome a victimhood narrative that depresses human motivation.

Entrepreneurship is the exact opposite of learned helplessness. It is the force that enables young people to become problem solvers when obstacles arise. By embracing the concept of entrepreneurship, you can better envision yourself as an owner, a steward, a curator of your own life: someone who has the ability to handle temporary setbacks and who can leverage the factors within your control to reshape outcomes, even when conditions may suggest otherwise.

Consider the $164,100 wealth gap between black and white Americans.[5] As we saw in Chapter 2, it becomes a $158,870 wealth gap *in favor of blacks* when family structure and education are taken into account. Again, individual choices do make a difference. Industriousness, self-discipline and a strong work ethic matter—and they carry with them an undeniable dignity. Imagine if, instead of the "no matter what, you are disadvantaged" message, young people of all races understood that nothing is predetermined in their lives and that they themselves have the greatest influence over their own futures.

There are many ways that a rising generation can develop this sense of ownership. Society's institutions—certainly its schools—

can play a role. My new network of high schools, Vertex Partnership Academies, will embrace the FREE framework as a central strategy for individual decision-making with a stock ownership program for our student scholars. Our students will become actual business shareholders through Charles Schwab's Stock Slices program. In this program, anyone can own a "fractional share" of an S&P 500 company like Apple, Walmart, Google, or Amazon for just $5. Working with their parents, our school will seed each student a $50 stock portfolio made up of ten S&P 500 companies.·

Rather than just being consumers making calls on an iPhone or searching for information on Google, our students will understand what it means to be an owner of the company that produced the device or developed the search algorithms. Imagine how an early understanding of stock ownership, dividends, industry trends, and compounded growth can fuel financial literacy and a desire to be an entrepreneur later in life. Can it make a difference? Let me tell you about Alma.

One of the innovative ways schools I have led have helped students establish a future orientation was by seeding New York State College Savings Accounts for our students, starting in prekindergarten (PreK). Each year we would match parent contributions. Alma's parents told me the four-year-old's face lit up when she saw her name as the owner of a college savings account. It was one small step in her knowing that a better future awaited her. What would make the difference was not the hundreds of dollars added to her college savings account each year. Rather, it was the change in the nightly conversation at the dinner table. What college would she attend? How much should she study now to be prepared for the opportunity later? Her little brother wanted his own account, too. By making that investment, a future possibility became more probable. Alma and her parents knew it was within her grasp to be the first in her family to graduate from college.

Throughout the world of public education I occupy, social entrepreneurs abound who create new ways to stimulate opportunity for young people. Anand Kesavan is the Founder and CEO of Equitable Facilities Fund (EFF),[6] an innovative nonprofit social impact fund that empowers high-performing public charter schools to access low-cost, long-term financing to build or renovate school facilities. Since its inception in 2019 and with the support of the Walton Foundation, EFF has provided $585 million in low-cost loans to support more than one hundred public charter schools.[7] Seventy percent of students in schools that have received EFF financing are considered economically disadvantaged, and 94 percent of students in EFF schools academically outperform students in their local district. As an experienced investment banker who has turned his passion and expertise toward creating educational opportunity, Kesavan and his EFF team have helped Vertex Partnership Academies craft a recyclable loan fund that will help build a 96,000-square-foot permanent home.

And while some social entrepreneurs are helping to erect school buildings, others are helping to build the next generation of social entrepreneurs. One vibrant example is Ismael Hernandez, who grew up in a Communist household in Puerto Rico, his father being one of the founding members of its Socialist Party. Hernandez was taught by his father that America was the "enemy of humanity." In a video testimonial, Hernandez shared that "my environment growing up was one in which we hated America, we hated capitalism, we hated everything that makes America what it is today."[8] As a young adult, Hernandez moved north to attend the University of Southern Mississippi. He shared that "Right there in the Deep South, my lungs were filled with the air of freedom. For the first time in my life, the lived experience of freedom shattered my once-safe assumptions. America showed me that the individual matters. . . . I learned the vital connection between reward and accomplishment and that this connection is what leads to human flourishing and that we need to get busy rebuilding the shattered foundations of freedom in our country so that we can return to flourishing."[9]

Hernandez has now founded the Freedom and Virtue Institute, which offers K–12 schools the opportunity to launch Self-Reliance Clubs. These school-sponsored programs promote hard work, character development, creativity, and compassion, while *discouraging* laziness, extravagance, wastefulness, dependency, and entitlement. Club activities include tutoring younger students or peers, school beautification projects, gardening/farming, and recycling/sustainability initiatives. Hernandez says, "We help young people internalize the ideas of freedom as a value and that will flourish in them in lives dedicated to enterprise."[10]

With respect to encouraging new business formation, K–12 schools, colleges, philanthropic institutions, and companies should build young people's awareness of the career pathways and emerging forms of venture capital dedicated to changing the face of entrepreneurship. Models abound here as well. Harlem Capital Partners, an early-stage venture capital firm founded by two Harvard Business School graduates, is on a mission to invest in 1,000 minority and female founders over the next twenty years. Netflix has put $100 million into local financial institutions and organizations that "make a meaningful difference for the people and businesses in them, helping more families buy their first home or save for college, and more small businesses get started or grow." Tech billionaire and entrepreneur Robert F. Smith has made a $20 million contribution to Cornell University to recruit and support underrepresented students in science, technology, engineering, and math. He's also made a $50 million personal contribution to match his Fund II Foundation's $50 million donation to endow the nonprofit Student Freedom Initiative for mentoring, tutoring, targeted capac-

ity building, and access to paid internships for students at historically black colleges and universities.[11]

The entrepreneurial mind-set involves more than generating
financial wealth. There's a long legacy of social entrepreneurs who
have transformed our country for the better. In the early 1900s,
when faced with inferior educational options for black children
throughout the South, Tuskegee University founder Booker T.
Washington envisioned an idea to build a network of high-quality
schools. He partnered with Sears Roebuck CEO Julius Rosenwald.
Together they built some 5,000 schools, with Rosenwald match-
ing local contributions. The entrepreneurial Washington was
unconstrained by that day's Jim Crow discrimination. Nor was
Robert Woodson (author of this book's afterword), who for the past
forty years pioneered the approach to neighborhood enterprise, a
hyperlocal strategy to community revitalization that leverages the
strength of civil society leaders as anchors for change.[12]

Washington and Woodson both grasped what I have come to
understand as a serial, social entrepreneur myself: resiliency is the
character-based strength I have most relied on in leading organizations and teams in a range of sectors. Things will not always
go your way, but that doesn't matter. The odds may seem stacked
against you, but that doesn't matter. You may fail at first, but that
doesn't matter either. Instead, you matter. The choices you make
matter. Your agency matters.

As one of America's greatest social entrepreneurs and independent thinkers, Frederick Douglass, said in his 1859 "Self-Made
Men" speech,

> The lesson taught at this point by human experience is simply this,
> that the man who will get up will be helped up; and the man who
> will not get up will be allowed to stay down. This rule may appear
> somewhat harsh, but in its general application and operation it is

wise, just and beneficent. . . . Personal independence is a virtue and it is the soul out of which comes the sturdiest manhood. But there can be no independence without a large share of self-dependence, and this virtue cannot be bestowed. It must be developed from within.[13]

This statement is all the more powerful when you consider that Frederick Douglass, a former slave, uttered these empowering, entrepreneurial words years before the end of American slavery.

17

A New Age of Agency

"The year was 2081, and everybody was finally equal. They weren't only equal before God and the law. They were equal every which way. Nobody was smarter than anybody else. Nobody was better looking than anybody else. Nobody was stronger or quicker than anybody else. All this equality was due to the 211th, 212th, and 213th Amendments to the Constitution, and to the unceasing vigilance of agents of the United States Handicapper General."[1]

So begins the first paragraph of "Harrison Bergeron," Kurt Vonnegut's short story about a dystopian future. Harrison Bergeron is a strong, handsome, and intelligent fourteen-year-old who's landed in jail. What was his crime? He committed the sin of being strong, handsome, and intelligent! In prison, Bergeron is required to wear 300 pounds of scrap metal and wear a red rubber ball for a nose; he has to shave his eyebrows and his straight white teeth are covered with black snaggle-toothed caps. All this is to ensure that Bergeron achieves the same level of general mediocrity as everyone else, all of whose talents are also being forcibly flattened. The 1961 short story's "handicapping" ideology—from each according to one's ability, to each according to one's need—echoes the box removal and redistribution in the popular "Equality versus Equity" meme discussed in Chapter 5 (see Figure 5.1).

Vonnegut's "2081" is the extreme but logical conclusion of the social ideology of those clamoring today for equity as a form of social justice. Taking from individuals in some "privileged" class to give to others deemed less "privileged" is not how we create an opportunity society for a rising generation. We can do better—for everybody.

Let's imagine it *is* 2081 in the real world. It's more than a century after passage of landmark civil rights legislation prohibiting discrimination on the basis of race, color, religion, sex and national origin. It is more than 300 years after the Declaration of Independence declared that all men are created equal. What will our legacy be? I wrote this book so that the rising generation—those aged twenty-four and under—will have a decision-making framework to help them lead productive lives of their own choosing. My hope is that the United States will be in the middle of a sustained awakening in which continuously rising generations of people of all backgrounds have learned to embrace the ideals of family, religion, education, and entrepreneurship. That is how we will know that our work today has ushered in a new age of agency. Our young people and the institutions of civil society that surround and nurture them will have created a powerful social norm around FREE as a passageway into young adulthood:

> **F** is the healthy family you *form* by understanding the power of the Success Sequence, not necessarily the family you are *from*.
>
> **R** is the personal faith commitment you make to one of the world's great religions, whether it is following the four noble truths of Buddhism or the principles Jesus espoused in the Sermon of the Mount; it's also the support and encouragement you receive from faith-based institutions as you learn how to master your own destiny.

E is the education you earn—the learning you yourself
are responsible for—the knowledge and skills you
accrue that can never be taken away.

E is the entrepreneurial spirit you embrace to experience
the dignity and discipline of work as well as to create
opportunity and wealth for yourself and others who
seek to lead a FREE life.

If more young people adopted a FREE life that incorporated
the wisdom of the Success Sequence on when to start their own
family, *their* children and their children's children would more
likely be born into stable, married, two-parent households and to
break the sad cycle of despair we have seen for generations.

"Youth get sex education, but rarely do they get high quality
relationship education to help them navigate the world of romantic relationships, sexual decision-making and on determining the
timing for family formation," Marline Pearson, author of the Love
Notes curriculum, told me. "What's missing from the larger understanding of youth success is the role their intimate relationships
will play, for better or for worse. Not addressing this as seriously
as education and employment is to fail to recognize how troubled,
destructive and/or unstable intimate relationships and unintended
pregnancies can derail the progress a young person might otherwise make with regards to education, employment and parenting
(in the case of young parents)."

To envision what FREE can make possible, let's examine how
we can learn from past successes. As we saw in Figure 8.5, the
National Campaign to Reduce Teen Pregnancy experienced unpar-
alleled success in reducing teen pregnancies and births, even as
a new crisis of nonmarital births arose slightly up the age scale.
Figure 17.1 shows what the reduction in nonmarital births would
be for women aged twenty-four and under over the *next* thirty years

FIGURE 17.1   Nonmarital births to women aged 20–24 (the next 30 years).

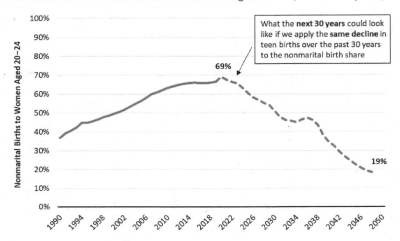

SOURCE: Centers for Disease Control and Prevention, National Vital Statistics Reports. https://medium.com/@CRA1G/the-evolution-of-an-accidental-meme-ddc4e139e0e4# .pqiclk8pl.

if the rate of decline over the *last* thirty years in teen pregnancies was applied to nonmarital births. We have done this before; we can do it again.

In raw numbers, considering such factors as fertility rates, number of women in each age group, and the projected nonmarital birth shares shown in the figure above, I have produced a very rough estimate of the additional number of births within marriage we could expect to see if we make the same progress on nonmarital births over the next three decades as we have on teen pregnancy over the past three decades. This ranges from a low estimate of 38 million children to a high of 59 million children. The numbers are striking! While these are very high-level estimates, they give a general sense of the number of children who would be born into more stable families.

And what would such a dramatic reduction in nonmarital births mean to these tens of millions of young adults and their children?

Consider that boys and girls raised in single-parent families are more than four times more likely to be poor than children raised by married parents.[2] Socially and emotionally, girls are 2–5 times more likely to end up pregnant in adolescence and boys are 2–3 times as likely to end up incarcerated before they turn 30 if they grow up in a non-intact family.[3] Children raised in cohabiting families are more than twice as likely to be suspended or expelled from high school compared to adolescents living with married parents.[4] Educationally, children raised in intact homes are more likely to graduate from college, compared to children from non-intact families.[5] Young adults from intact families also earn more money later in life and are more likely to realize the American Dream—to have more family income as adults than they did growing up—compared to their peers from unstable families.[6]

Put simply, the evidence supports an assertion that such an improvement in family stability would lead to dramatically better outcomes for kids and our nation as a whole! My wish to see this kind of change in young people's attitudes and behaviors is why I run public charter schools. It is also why I successfully ran for school board in my hometown on a platform of "equality of opportunity, individual dignity and common humanity"—core principles that will help our kids build agency, regardless of circumstance.

These are core principles that will equip the next generation with tools that will empower them to flourish in their own lives. Take it from a young boy, Leo, beginning his journey toward a FREE life.

"*We can do hard things. We can do hard things. We can do hard things . . .*" Those are the words of Leo, as he struggles to complete a rigorous reading assessment. They're also the mantra of his school, Archbishop Lyke Catholic Elementary in Cleveland, Ohio. Leo drew strength by repeatedly reciting his school mantra in a soft voice to himself. During the COVID-19 pandemic, Leo had been meeting with his principal, teacher, and mom to find ways to address his academic and behavioral challenges. Rather than some external intervention, they had encouraged Leo to *internalize* one of the school's core values—the belief that Leo and his classmates had within themselves the tools for self-renewal and self-betterment, especially in the midst of adversity. *We can do hard things.*

Leo was part of a school culture that nurtured and promoted an "overcomer's mind-set." This kind of culture didn't just happen. The school makes a deliberate effort to have young people absorb their own capacity to confront and overcome seemingly insurmountable obstacles. Christian Dallavis, an assistant superintendent of the Partnership Schools, the Catholic network that helped Archbishop Lyke develop a culture that fosters spiritual and academic growth, summed up the philosophy: "While we know that the human condition is one of brokenness . . . , Saint Ambrose tells us, 'We are taught to have faith, and not draw back from doing those things that [we fear] are above our human strength.'" Like many in K–12 education, I have committed my life to help children like Leo "not draw back" in times of challenge or strife. *We can do hard things. . . .*

It is a fundamental element of human nature to strive to excel and flourish and resist externally imposed limitations. And this brings us back to Harrison Bergeron and the false utopia of a society built on equity of result, rather than equality of opportunity. Bergeron ultimately escapes from prison. He tears off his scrap-iron handicaps, his red rubber-ball nose, and his black tooth caps. He emancipates himself from the shackles of equity. He then liberates a ballerina whose beauty and talent had also been handicapped. Together, they dance and defy the laws of gravity; together, they exercise the power of love and free will; and together, they experience agency for the first time.

FIGURE 17.2   Equality vs. Equity vs. FREE (1).

SOURCE: AEI graphic design team.

Perhaps they felt like I did when, as a twelve-year-old, I per-suaded my parents to let me stay and make my own way in my junior high school. That was my "coming of agency" moment. When is the moment you realize your agency and overcome the idea that you have to be a powerless victim?

In this book, I have defined agency as the force of one's free will, guided by moral discernment. My hope is that our young people experience agency by embracing the ideals of a FREE life. But they cannot do so on their own. They need our help and guid-ance. FREE institutions must embrace them. It is a reciprocal rela-tionship. Different supports will come from each institution in the FREE framework. Combined with their own actions, these sup-ports should offer each young person the equality of opportunity, individual dignity, and common humanity necessary to lead a self-determined life (see Figures 17.2 and 17.3).

It is Aristotle who is credited with the quote: "Our problem is not that we aim too high and miss. Our problem is that we aim too low and hit." You have within your grasp the ability to lead the life you want. If we are really able to usher in an age of agency, then children of all backgrounds will be able to aim high and be ready to help achieve the ambitious new goals being set for America's future.

Now it is your turn. Freedom unexercised may become freedom forfeited.[7] Do not throw away your shot. You can be the master of your own fate, the captain of your own soul.

Live.

Be FREE.

FIGURE 17.3 Equality vs. Equity vs. FREE (2).

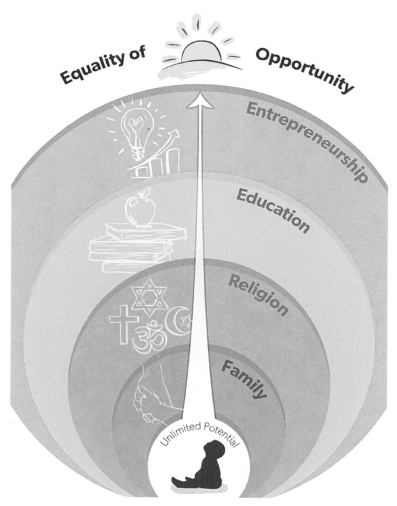

SOURCE: AEI graphic design team.

AFTERWORD

Robert L. Woodson, Sr.

I have spent my life working for upward mobility and neighbor-hood enterprise in American communities facing some of our greatest challenges, from crime and violence to poverty and edu-cational failure. And without hesitation, I echo my colleague Ian Rowe's assertion that a sense of agency is vital to progress. Nei-ther individuals nor communities improve themselves if they don't first believe that they can. Those who remind us incessantly of all the unfair obstacles in our paths should not flatter themselves that they are doing us any favors.

Unfortunately, denying the agency of the poor has been a hall-mark of people on both the right and the left. Where progressives see helpless victims who need to be rescued, too many on the right see aliens who need to be corralled and controlled. Neither side believes much in the capacity of lower-income individuals to exer-cise agency on their own behalf.

Autonomy—along with things like healthy relationships, a sense of meaning, and earned success—is widely acknowledged by psychologists to be an inborn human need. Robbing any young person of autonomy—whether by telling a low-income black child that life is so stacked against them that it is pointless to try or preventing an upper-income white child from making any of their own decisions so that they are paralyzed when out on their own—is cheating them out of an essential component of human flourishing.

I am particularly grateful that Ian addressed the irreplaceable role of mediating institutions—including institutions of faith—to shape the moral reasoning and behavioral norms of our young people. We do not cultivate life habits in a social vacuum. We absorb them from those around us. And it is beyond hypocritical for those who have been blessed enough to absorb good ones to undermine their development in anyone they are presuming to help.

I would particularly like to applaud Ian's focus on the rising generation and the affirmation of the essential place of religion in the lives of the less fortunate, an inconvenient truth in a secularizing age. Like many of the children Ian serves in his public charter schools, I have experienced the loss of immediate family members to both homicide and tragedy. I could never have survived these experiences without faith in God and the people of faith who surround me.

What should you do with what you've just read? After decades of working to revitalize our nation's most challenging neighborhoods, I will share one of the most important lessons I have learned: There is nothing more lethal than a good excuse for failure. When a person is exempted from any personal responsibility for control of their life, you deprive them of the privilege and opportunity to craft solutions to improve their own condition.

To cultivate a greater sense of agency, we must actually give young people opportunities to exercise agency. For those from lower-income backgrounds, this may require helping prepare them with the skills and habits they need to take advantage of those opportunities. For the affluent, we may have to step back and let them struggle at a few things so they learn by experience that their choices really do matter.

I have watched how this can work in a number of powerful ways. One of my grassroots leaders, Robin, teaches chess to young girls in Washington, DC. Through mastering this difficult game, the girls learn life skills from impulse control to strategic decision making, all in a nurturing, value-aligned community of their peers. Robin doesn't lecture them on agency; she gives them the opportunity to exercise their "agency muscles" in a protected setting, which they then put into practice in the real world.

But I cannot emphasize enough that the secret ingredient here is not chess. The girls could most likely learn similar skills playing golf or building robots. The secret ingredient is Robin: she grew up and still lives in their neighborhood. She listens to their hopes and dreams and understands their challenges. She has their trust.

Ian quoted Tocqueville's brilliant observation about America's special ability to repair our own faults. This reminded me of another program we supported, which, among other things, facilitated former juvenile offenders serving the elderly. These previously troubled young folks helped the elders in their community by running errands, doing chores, and keeping them company. They went from being predators to being needed and valued. The results were transformational for everyone involved.

The path from poverty to prosperity is not paved with grievance or bitterness but rather with hope and aspiration. Ultimately, no young person should be defined by the circumstances of their birth, nor mistakes they may have made early in their life—it is never too late to start afresh, or self-correct. To make the journey requires the opportunity to add value to someone else. That desire—and the will to act on it—is agency, ratified.

APPENDIX

Love Notes

Relationship Skills for Love, Life, and Work

An Evidence-Based Program

Marline E. Pearson, MA

Decide, Don't Slide!
Pathways and Sequences for Success

Overview

This lesson introduces an important concept: *Decide, Don't Slide!* Sliding (i.e., getting involved quickly with someone before knowing them very well) is one way people end up in relationships that don't work out. It carries the risk of landing in a place a person never planned to be. Sliding can lead to finding oneself in an unhealthy or abusive relationship, with an STI, or with an unintended birth. Indeed, sliding quickly into romantic or sexual involvements carries risks not only for a young person, but for a child as well.

The *Sliding vs. Deciding* concept is applied to forming healthy relationships and for sexual decision-making and planning.[1] This approach may help participants navigate their first—or next—relationship more wisely. It can also help those currently in relationships move from a *sliding* to a *deciding* mode by making decisions and taking steps.

Participants are encouraged to appreciate how important it is to decide and not slide when it comes to transitions that can be life altering, like sex, pregnancy, having a child, living together, or getting married. A decision-making framework for relationship transitions will help identify the kinds of things that can help a person make good decisions. The journal application *Making Decisions* (pp. 28–30) is particularly useful for participants to complete and share with a trusted adult.

The concept *Sliding vs. Deciding* is a safety strategy for navigating the terrain of attractions, relationships, and sex that is relevant to all teens. Regardless of gender identity or sexual orientation, youth can be vulnerable to pregnancy involvement and unintended parenthood. Findings have emerged across multiple settings and samples showing that adolescent girls who identify as bisexual, unsure, or lesbian, are more likely to report teen pregnancies than their cisgender heterosexual peers.[2] LGBTQ adults typically use reproductive technologies or adoption if they have a child, but all teenage LGBTQ pregnancies result from penis-vaginal sexual intercourse. How is this? Adolescence is a time of identity formation and exploration. Teens' decisions about sex and fertility are influenced by a host of environmental factors and relationships that may be protective or hostile. Youth who are members of sexual minority groups experience disproportionately high levels of hostile environmental factors.

The *Success Sequences—Pathways to Adulthood,* another important concept of *Love Notes,* will be integrated into the *Sliding vs. Deciding* discussion. A combination of certain milestones or achievements in young adult life can really matter for successful economic outcomes and family stability (if children are a part of one's vision for their future).[3] This requires planning and making clear decisions. These two concepts are introduced here after seven lessons on developing healthy selves and healthy relationships and before the program directly addresses sexual decision-making, presents sexual health information, and engages participants in personal planning for one's sexual choices.

Goals

1. Analyze the risks associated with sliding.
2. Learn a low-risk, deciding approach to handling attractions and developing relationships.
3. Review relationship concepts and skills from Lessons 1 through 7.
4. Identify decisions one can potentially make; identify what one needs to find out or do in order to help make those decisions.
5. Become acquainted with the *Success Sequences—Pathways to Adulthood.*

Success Sequences— Pathways to Adulthood

❖ **(PP)** *You have had the opportunity to think about relationship decisions and expectations.*

❖ *So, here's a couple of expectations that I want to ask about. These expectation questions apply to the **long term**—like your life ten years out or further, not now.*

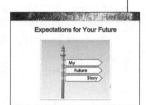

Expectations for Your Future

1. *When you think about your future adult life, how many expect or hope to have enough money to live on? To avoid poverty? To live a comfortable middle-class life? Pause for show of hands.*

2. *When you think about your future adult life, how many expect or desire to have children someday and provide them a stable family life—parents who stay together in a satisfying loving relationship? Pause for show of hands.*

Instructor Note: While you can expect everyone to say they want financial well-being for their futures, you will have a greater diversity with the second expectation question. Acknowledge the fact that while everyone wants to avoid poverty in adulthood, not everyone expects/desires to have children. Being a parent is not for everyone and that is okay. Acknowledge they can achieve a successful life with or without having children.

❖ *Thanks for sharing your expectations.*

• *Now I want to introduce you to some powerful pathways to avoid poverty and achieve a middle-class status and higher household income in adulthood.*

• *And, if in addition to your desire to avoid poverty and have a middle-class lifestyle, you also want to someday have children with a partner in a satisfying relationship and a stable family life, there are advantageous pathways for that as well.*

• *Do you have any ideas of what things a person can do to up their chances of achieving one or both of these expectations? Pause for brief responses.*

❖ **Well, there are four** *milestones in life that appear to be key factors associated with either* **increasing or decreasing** *one's chances of avoiding poverty, having a greater household income, and a middle-class status by one's 30s.*[4]

• *And they are also some of the main factors associated with either* **increasing or decreasing** *one's chances of family stability by one's 30s (2 parents in a stable and satisfying relationship).*[5]

• (PP) *They are:*
  o *Completing high school (and better yet add further education or training)*
  o *Full-time employment*
  o *Marriage*
  o *Children*

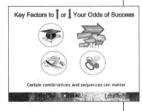

❖ (PP) *Three of these milestones (or factors) in particular, (1)* **high school completion,** *(2)* **full-time employment,** *and (3)* **marriage,** *are associated with increasing your chances of avoiding poverty and achieving middle-class status and higher household income. Adults who have completed these three are the most likely to achieve a middle-class lifestyle and avoid poverty by their 30s.*[6]

- *Does anyone have an idea of why marriage might matter here? Pause for responses before continuing.*

- *Marriage can mean the combining of two potential incomes and those combined earnings can build over the years.*

- *Cohabiting relationships, on average, are much more likely to break up, thus losing the advantage of combined earnings. (More on this in a bit.)*

❖ **(PP)** *As we know, not everyone expects or desires to have children or get married. Completing two of the milestones, (1) education and (2) employment (but no children, no marriage), makes it just about as likely to have good financial outcomes by one's 30s as the three above.*[7]

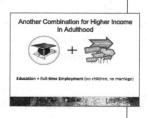

Another Combination for Higher Income in Adulthood

Education + Full-time Employment (no children, no marriage)

❖ *So, as you see, there are varied pathways to successful economic outcomes in adulthood. The sequence may not be as important as simply achieving a certain number and combination of milestones.*[8]

❖ **(PP)** *Now let's examine when the best time is to add children to the mix. Here, a particular combination of milestones and doing them in a particular sequence can make a significant difference.*

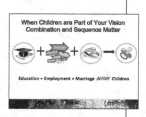

When Children are Part of Your Vision Combination and Sequence Matter

Education + Employment + Marriage *BEFORE* Children

- *For those who in addition to desiring economic well-being, also envision children in their future—and desire to do so with a partner in the context of a stable and satisfying relationship—the marriage factor matters, and the sequence of doing that before having a child makes a big difference.*

- *The **marriage milestone** has a consistent association with family stability by the time one is in their 30s.*[9]

- ***Instructor note:** Family stability is measured as (1) the presence of 2 adults in the home, (2) the number of residential partner transitions (i.e., none or few break-ups or divorces), and (3) relationship satisfaction between the parents.*

❖ *As you see, some combinations of milestones and the sequence (order) in which one achieves these, may be more **advantageous** than others.*

- *In particular, if **children** are part of one's vision, the sequence in which one does them can matter in terms of how challenging it may be to achieve a good economic future and family stability.*

- ***For example:** Having a child as a teen may make it difficult to finish high school. Caring for a child while finishing school is doable, but more challenging. And without an education, a person may be at a disadvantage in finding good-paying employment.*

- *And without a committed partner, a parent may be on their own financially. Neither parent may have the earnings to cover the expenses of a child, housing, etc.*

- *And even if one has achieved high school completion and is working at let's say 19 or 20 years of age, if they don't have a partner to share in child rearing, it is challenging on many fronts. Children take a lot of time, care, and money.*

  - *Whatever one's gender identity or sexual orientation, having a committed partner—a spouse—with whom to raise a child really helps financially, socially, and emotionally.*

❖ *It really makes a difference to have finished high school, and better yet, acquired additional education or training, to have a committed partner, and for at least one person to have a full-time job **before** having a child. That sequence offers advantages.*

❖ *(PP) Let's examine some more research that looked at thousands of 28- to 34-year-olds. Look at this chart.*[10]

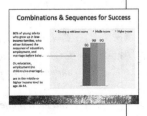

- *Focus on the left bar in the graph with the red arrows: **86%** (51% + 35%) of those who either achieved the combination and sequence of education, employment, and marriage **before** children, or who achieved education and employment, but no children/no marriage, are in the middle or higher income groups by 28-34 years of age.*[11] *(Instructor Note: In this research, the latter is referred to as "on track.")*

❖ *(PP) Even those born into **low-income** families who achieved the milestones of education, employment, and marriage before children OR, if they achieved the two milestones of education and employment—but no children, no marriage—all equally landed in the middle to higher income groups as adults.*[12]

- *See **dark blue bar on the left**: 80% of those who grew up low-income were in the middle to higher income groups by age 28–32. That's impressive.*

❖ *Key take-away points:*

- *If children **and** financial stability are part of your future expectations, waiting to have a child until you are settled* *with education and employment and married can make a big difference.*

- *And, if marriage and children are not your thing, achieving your education and full-time employment while avoiding getting pregnant or getting someone pregnant can make a big difference.*

❖ *Why do we include marriage as a milestone for those who desire children and financial stability, and not, let's say, just living together? A few points:*

1. *First, because the research shows these outcomes for marriage, not for cohabitation.*

2. *We know from research that cohabiting relationships are relatively unstable—there are more break-ups and re-partnerings. As more young adults enter into and end cohabiting relationships, a pattern of serial cohabitation has increased.[13]*

   - *Perhaps the **upside** to this is that young people may be learning to end cohabiting relationships that aren't working.*

   - *But the **downside** is that if the cohabiting relationship includes children (as 54% do), the relationship instability from serial cohabitation (one relationship, then another, and maybe another) can have negative consequences for children.*

     o *Of the 54% of cohabiting relationships that include children, 35% share at least one biological child and 19% include children from a previous relationship.[14]*

Let's Go Deeper than Money and Income

❖ **(PP)** *Having a child is a life-changing event. Making a clear decision—having clear intentions—about **when** you are ready to do that, under **what circumstances**, and **with whom** is really important.*

Having a Child is a Life-Changing Event

- *Having a **committed partner**—a **spouse**—with whom to raise a child really helps—financially, socially, and emotionally.*

❖ *Today, many births occur to teens and especially young adults in their 20s who have not previously decided they are committed to a future together and to starting a family.[15]*

- *71% of births to women under 24 years of age are to unmarried women.[16]*

- *Most of the pregnancies are unintended.[17]*

- *And many have not finished their **education** nor obtained **full-time employment**.[18]*

❖ *The majority of relationships of unmarried parents fall apart.[19]*

- *It's tough to raise a child alone, and especially when there are relationship troubles with the other parent (i.e., baby mama/baby daddy drama).*

- *It's tough to support a child if one hasn't finished one's schooling or secured a full-time job. It contributes to many challenges for both parents and child.*

❖ (PP) *While achieving the milestones that matter—with or without children—may look or sound simple, it is clearly easier for those born with privilege to finish high school, go to college, obtain additional education or training, find a good full-time job, and in the case of having children, marry before doing so.*

Achieving milestones can be challenging

- *For example, if you have parents who are in a healthy relationship and have college educations and higher incomes, live in a neighborhood with good schools, have a network of adults to help you, and parents to help pay for college, it really assists a young person in achieving these milestones.*

❖ *There are more hurdles for those without these advantages. For some young people, it's harder—a lot harder—to finish school and find employment, and even to wait on having a child.*

❖ *But, no matter how hard, for those who do commit to completing their education and training so they are better positioned for employment, there are real benefits.*

- *This is why it's so important to seek out sources of support, like a school counselor, a caring teacher, or a trusted adult who may be able to help you stay on track for graduation or obtain a high school equivalency. They may be able to link you up with programs in the community and help you apply for college.*

- *Also, talk to a career counselor at your local community college to learn more about vocational, technical, apprenticeship, and college-transfer programs. Ask about grants, scholarships, and financial aid.*

Instructor Note: It's important to offer these suggestions and to know the specific places in your community where the youth can access support.

Aside from the school counselors and community college offices, is there a Youth Build or other community-based or youth-development organizations in your community that you can recommend?

The Key Importance of Avoiding an Unintended Pregnancy

❖ *Completing high school, acquiring further education or training, and obtaining stable employment can all be challenging, for sure.*

❖ *Being determined—no matter what—to do so will increase the odds of your success.*

❖ *But here is one thing you can all do. And, that is to **avoid a pregnancy—that is in your control.****

❖ *Whether children are or are not part of your vision:*

- *Not part of your vision: Avoiding an unintended pregnancy while you work toward achieving your education/training and secure full-time employment will mean fewer barriers on your pathway to your future goals.*

- *Part of your vision: Avoiding a pregnancy until your life is more settled with your education/training, employment, **and a committed partner—a spouse—will also mean fewer challenges as you travel on the path toward your future goals.***

❖ *(PP) **A person can avoid a pregnancy several ways. You've got this!***

- *Decide not to have sex now—enjoy the benefits of leaving sex out of your teen relationships.*

Avoiding a pregnancy is possible

- Decide not to have sex now; avoid risky situations.
- Pace your involvements more slowly and make real decisions vs. sliding. Practice assertiveness skills. Or,
- Have a clear plan and agreement on condoms and contraception

But it takes a lot of **motivation**.

- *Avoid risky situations; pace your involvements more slowly. Make clear decisions, don't slide.*

- *Have a clear plan and agreement for condom use and other contraception if sexually active.*

❖ *Either way, it takes motivation—knowing why it really matters.*

- *You've got the facts on why avoiding an unintended or a poorly timed pregnancy can make a real difference.*

*Point out that not everyone has control. Some have been forced, trafficked, or coerced. See Lesson 7 for tips and support.

Expecting and Parenting Young Adults

❖ **(PP)** *Sometimes, despite a person's best intentions, including the possibility of contraception failure, a pregnancy can occur. For young parents, there are milestones and a sequence that can increase the odds of having the life you want:*

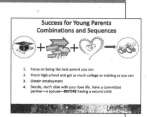

1. *Focus on being the best parent you can be. Reach out to a family resource center or public health department in your area for parenting classes and programs for health, nutritional, and financial assistance for young parents.*

2. *Finish high school and get as much college or training as you can to help you obtain better employment. Seek support from a caring teacher or school counselor who may be able to help you get back on track for graduation or obtain a high school equivalency diploma. See a career counselor at your local community college to learn more about vocational, technical, apprenticeship, and*

college-transfer programs. Ask about grants, scholarships, and financial aid.

3. *And most importantly: Decide, don't slide with your love life. Use the knowledge and skills you are gaining in Love Notes to make wise relationship choices. Avoid sliding into a second pregnancy.*

❖ *Focusing on parenting, education, and employment are key. And if additional children are part of your vision, WAIT until you are more settled and with a committed partner in a healthy relationship/ marriage.*

Instructor Note: Be familiar with the resources and supports in your community for young parents.

ACKNOWLEDGMENTS

If you like this book, you have Eula and Vincent Rowe to thank (or chastise, if you don't). The epiphany that I had with my parents at twelve years old—that my race was not going to limit my sense of what was possible—influenced me for the rest of my life to believe that any externally imposed limitation can be overcome by a self-actualized belief in *Agency*. Now this book seeks to pay that idea forward by revitalizing the four pillars of Family, Religion, Education, and Entrepreneurship (FREE).

To bring a book like this to fruition requires many hands to make light work. First and foremost, I thank my wife, Sylvia, my trusted confidante, thought partner, and the bedrock of our family. I write and speak frequently about the importance of family stability, and she no less frequently reminds me of the joy that family brings when I prioritize our own *over all else.* Thank you my love.

I am so proud and thankful that *Agency* has been published by Templeton Press, particularly given its mission to produce books that Sir John Templeton considered of ultimate concern to human flourishing. That is the entire essence behind *Agency* and why I was blessed to have a team that "got it." With the wonderful and insightful Susan Arellano at the helm, and the dynamic group of Dan Reilly, Dave Reinhard, Angelina Horst, and Trish Vergilio, advising and editing, I was in very good hands from the beginning.

Yuval Levin and Bob Woodson—thank you both for your respective foreword and afterword that so beautifully frame my thoughts.

To the entire team at American Enterprise Institute, thank you: Robert Doar, Ryan Streeter, Naomi Schaefer Riley, Nique Fajors, Rachel Manfredi, and most notably my research assistant, Peyton Roth, whose insight and wisdom of what it means to lead a meaningful, faith-based life far surpasses his years.

To the entire team at the Woodson Center and 1776 Unites who every day demonstrate "from the suites to the streets" what is possible when you empower local leaders to become agents of their own uplift.

To the many researchers and practitioners who have informed my thinking on the importance of family formation—Brad Wilcox, Wendy Wang, Ron Haskins, Isabel Sawhill, and Sarah Brown—thank you.

Finally, I must acknowledge the person who was an intellectual inspiration far before I had ever conceived of writing *Agency*. When I first read the *Content of Our Character* by Shelby Steele, I was a twenty-something professional in New York along with my friends trying to understand our way in the world, especially on matters of race. His words leapt off of the page. I had never read anyone with the clarity to not only name the complex challenges around race that mirrored the issues of self-doubt that so many of my peers seemed to face. But he also had the courage to articulate a path forward:

> The victim-focused black identity encourages the individual to feel that his advancement depends almost entirely on that of the group. Thus he loses sight not only of his own possibilities but of the inextricable connection between individual effort and individual advancement.... Hard work, education, individual initiative, stable family life, property ownership—these have always been the means by which ethnic groups have moved ahead in America.... What we need is a form of racial identity that energizes the individual by putting him in touch with both his possibilities and his responsibilities.[1]

While Shelby Steele's words were focused on race, the transformative theme of self-determination—of *Agency*—is universal for anyone wanting to avoid becoming a victim, regardless of their circumstance. It does not have to be this way. These "laws of advancement," as he called them, apply to everyone. Shelby's words inspired me then, and in that same spirit today, I hope to inspire young people, philanthropists, parents, educators, policy makers, religious leaders, and anyone who has the power to shape the destiny of a single child, to embrace the pillars of FREE to energize young Americans to be in touch both with their sense of "possibilities and their responsibilities."

As Marty Seligman says, "The human future is in our hands."

Let's go get it.

With gratitude,
Ian

NOTES

INTRODUCTION

Epigraph: Viktor E. Frankl, *Man's Search for Meaning* (Boston: Beacon Press, 2006).

1. "Martin Luther King Jr.—Acceptance Speech," *The Nobel Peace Prize 1964*, 2021, https://www.nobelprize.org/prizes/peace/1964/king /26142-martin-luther-king-jr-acceptance-speech-1964/.

2. Clay Routledge, "Existential Agency in America," Archbridge Institute, Oct. 28, 2021, https://www.archbridgeinstitute.org/2021/10/28 /existential-agency-in-america/.

3. UNICEF and Gallup, "The Changing Childhood Project," 2021, https://changingchildhood.unicef.org.

4. Routledge, "Existential Agency in America," 9.

5. See, for example, Horatio Alger, Jr., *Strive and Succeed or The Progress of Walter Conrad* (New York: Wentworth Press, 2019), and *Struggling Upward; Or, Luck Larkin's Luck* (reprint, Stilwell, KS: Digireads.com Publishing, 2008).

6. Angela Duckworth, *Grit: The Power of Passion and Perseverance* (New York: Scribner, 2016); and Carol S. Dweck, *Mindset: The New Psychology of Success* (New York: Random House, 2006).

7. Martin Luther King, Jr., "The Purpose of Education," *Maroon Tiger* (Jan.–Feb. 1947), online at https://kinginstitute.stanford.edu/king -papers/documents/purpose-education.

8. Urie Bronfenbrenner et al., *The State of Americans: This Generation and the Next* (New York: Free Press, 1996), viii.

9. Isabel V. Sawhill, *Generation Unbound: Drifting into Sex and Parenthood without Marriage* (Washington, DC: Brookings Institution Press), ix.

10. W. Bradford Wilcox and Wendy Wang, "The Millennial Success Sequence: Marriage, Kids, and the 'Success Sequence' among Young Adults," American Enterprise Institute, June 14, 2017, https://www.aei.org/research-products/working-paper/millennials-and-the-success-sequence-how-do-education-work-and-marriage-affect-poverty-and-financial-success-among-millennials/.

11. *New York Times*, "Transcript of Bush's Address to N.A.A.C.P.," July 20, 2006, https://www.nytimes.com/2006/07/20/washington/20text-bush.html.

12. Peter L. Berger and Richard John Neuhaus, *To Empower People: From State to Civil Society*, 2nd ed., ed. Michael Novak (Washington, DC: AEI Press, 1996), 148.

13. "A Driving Force throughout Human History, Agency Plays Key Role in Positive Psychology," description of Martin Seligman, keynote address, Evolution of Psychotherapy conference, Psych Congress Network, 2021, https://www.hmpgloballearningnetwork.com/site/pcn/article/driving-force-throughout-human-history-agency-plays-key-role-positive-psychology.

CHAPTER 1

Epigraph: Personal correpondence with Prabjhot Singh, email, November 21, 2021.

1. Cristin Strining, "I.S. Magnatech 2000," *InsideSchools*, Feb. 2009; updated by Pauline Zaldonis, Aug. 2013, https://insideschools.org/school/29Q231.

2. "Agency," *etymonline*, https://www.etymonline.com/word/agency, accessed June 2021.

3. "Martin Luther King Jr.: Facts," *The Nobel Peace Prize 1964*, 2021, https://www.nobelprize.org/prizes/peace/1964/king/facts/.

4. "Martin Luther King Jr.—Acceptance Speech," *The Nobel Peace Prize 1964*, 2021, https://www.nobelprize.org/prizes/peace/1964/king /26142-martin-luther-king-jr-acceptance-speech-1964/.

5. Kim I. Mills, "Positive Psychology in a Pandemic, with Martin Seligman," *Speaking of Psychology*, Jan. 2021, https://www.apa.org /research/action/speaking-of-psychology/positive-psychology.

6. Diary entry, Apr. 30, 1870, quoted in Ralph Barton Perry, *The Thought and Character of William James* (Cambridge: Harvard University Press, 1948) 1:323; see also *Letters of William James* (Washington: Atlantic Monthly Press, 1920), 1:147.

7. Albert Bandura, "Perceived Self-Efficacy in the Exercise of Human Agency," *Journal of Applied Sport Psychology* 2, no. 2 (1990): 128, online at https://www.jstor.org/stable/23764608.

8. Albert Bandura, "Toward a Psychology of Human Agency," *Perspectives on Psychological Science* 1, no. 2 (June 2006): 164–80, https:// journals.sagepub.com/stoken/default+domain/qFwnReCip8X BumvvAxrz/full.

9. Albert Bandura, *Social Foundations of Thought and Action: A Social Cognitive Theory* (Englewood Cliffs, NJ: Prentice Hall, 1986), 395.

10. Clay Routledge, "Existential Agency in America," *Archbridge Institute*, Oct. 2021, https://www.archbridgeinstitute.org/wp-content /uploads/2021/10/Existential-Agency-in-America_Routledge.pdf.

11. Goodreads, "C.G. Jung Quotes," accessed January 1, 2022, https:// www.goodreads.com/quotes/50795-i-am-not-what-happened-to -me-i-am-what.

CHAPTER 2

1. Neil Bhutta, Andrew C. Chang, Lisa J. Dettling, and Joanne W. Hsu, "Disparities in Wealth by Race and Ethnicity in the 2019 Survey of Consumer Finances," *FEDS Notes*, Board of Governors of the Federal

Reserve System, Division of Research and Statistics, Sept. 28, 2020, https://doi.org/10.17016/2380-7172.2797.

2. Bhutta et al.'s concept of wealth is equivalent to the net worth concept defined in the "Changes in U.S. Family Finances from 2016 to 2019: Evidence from the Survey of Consumer Finances (PDF)," *Federal Reserve Bulletin* 106(5). See the appendix to the *Bulletin* article for more details on components of wealth and net worth. Except for received inheritances, dollar values are adjusted to 2019 dollars using the "current methods" version of the consumer price index for all urban consumers (CPI-U-RS), which is available for every year since 1977. Received inheritances are adjusted to 2019 dollars using the consumer price index for all urban consumers (CPI-U) to account for inheritances received prior to 1977.

3. Bhutta et al., "Disparities in Wealth by Race and Ethnicity."

4. Dedrick Asante-Muhammad, Chuck Collins, Darrick Hamilton, and Josh Hoxie, "Ten Solutions to Bridge the Racial Wealth Divide," *Inequality.org*, Apr. 15, 2019, https://inequality.org/great-divide/ten -solutions-bridge-racial-wealth-divide/.

5. William Darity, Jr., Darrick Hamilton, Mark Paul, Alan Aja, Anne Price, Antonio Moore, and Caterina Chiopris, *What We Get Wrong about Closing the Racial Wealth Gap*, Duke University, Samuel DuBois Cook Center on Social Equity and Insight Center for Community Economic Development, Apr. 2018, 4, https://socialequity .duke.edu/wp-content/uploads/2019/10/what-we-get-wrong.pdf.

6. Claire Cain Miller, Emily Badger, Noelle Hurd, Ibram X. Kendi, Nathaniel Hendren, and Raj Chetty, "'When I See Racial Disparities, I See Racism': Discussing Race, Gender and Mobility," *New York Times*, Reader Center, March 27, 2018, https://www.nytimes.com /interactive/2018/03/27/upshot/reader-questions-about-race -gender-and-mobility.html.

7. Nikole Hannah-Jones, "What Is Owed," *New York Times Magazine*, June 30, 2020, https://www.nytimes.com/interactive/2020/06/24 /magazine/reparations-slavery.html.

8. *The Oprah Conversation*, episodes 1–2, "Uncomfortable Conversations with a Black Man," created by Oprah Winfrey, Apple TV+, aired July 31, 2020, https://www.imdb.com/title/tt12900056/.

9. Manhattan Institute, "Barriers to Black Progress: Structural, Cultural, or Both?," conference address, Feb. 11, 2019, online at https://www.youtube.com/watch?v=rzOApVTfT48.

10. Ian Rowe, "Creating an Opportunity Society and Upward Mobility for People of All Races," Statement before the Joint Economic Committee on "Examining the Racial Wealth Gap in the United States," May 12, 2021, https://www.jec.senate.gov/public/_cache/files/3d27 6158-3186-4552-8209-2f66dad7852b/ian-rowe-final-testimony-may -12-us-congress-joint-economic-committee.pdf.

11. Bettina L. Love, "How Schools Are 'Spirit Murdering' Black and Brown Students," *Education Week*, May 23, 2019, https://www .edweek.org/leadership/opinion-how-schools-are-spirit-murder ing-black-and-brown-students/2019/05.

12. Ben Wilterdink, "The Denigration of Personal Agency as Self-Fulfilling Prophecy," Archbridge Institute, September 25, 2020, https://medium.com/archbridge-notes/the-denigration-of-per sonal-agency-as-self-fulfilling-prophecy-4afe5f7b6f55.

13. Claire Cain Miller and Alicia Parlapiano, "Where Are Young People Most Optimistic? In Poorer Nations," *New York Times*, Nov. 23, 2021, https://www.nytimes.com/2021/11/17/upshot/global-survey -optimism.html.

14. Edutopia.org, biography, Carol Dweck, accessed December 30, 2021, https://www.edutopia.org/profile/carol-dweck.

15. HBR Editors, "How Companies Can Profit from a 'Growth Mindset,'" Nov. 2014, online at https://hbr.org/2014/11/how-companies -can-profit-from-a-growth-mindset.

16. Jill Barshay, "Research Scholars to Air Problems with Using 'Grit' at School," *Hechinger Report*, Mar. 11, 2019, https://hechinger report.org/research-scholars-to-air-problems-with-using-grit-at -school/.

17. Carol Dweck, "The Power of Believing That You Can Improve," TEDxNorrkoping, Nov. 2014, https://www.ted.com/talks/carol _dweck_the_power_of_believing_that_you_can_improve?language =en; and Angela Lee Duckworth, "Grit: The Power of Passion and Perseverance," TED Talks Education, Apr. 2013, https://www.ted .com/talks/angela_lee_duckworth_grit_the_power_of_passion_and _perseverance?language=en.

18. Carol S. Dweck, "Brainology," Independent School, Winter 2008, https://www.nais.org/magazine/independent-school/winter-2008 /brainology/.

19. Angela Duckworth, *Grit: The Power of Passion and Perseverance* (New York: Scribner, 2016), 42.

20. Duckworth, *Grit*, 51.

21. Jal Mehta, "The Problem with Grit" (Opinion), *Education Week*, Apr. 27, 2015, https://www.edweek.org/education/opinion-the-prob lem-with-grit/2015/04.

22. Diane Ravitch, "'Grit' and 'Resilience' Are Buzzwords That Blame the Victim for Not Pulling Him/Herself by Bootstraps," *Diane Ravitch's Blog*, Nov. 25, 2019, https://dianeravitch.net/2019/11/25 /grit-and-resilience-are-buzzwords-that-blame-the-victim-for-not -pulling-him-herself-by-bootstraps/.

23. Peter L. Berger and Richard John Neuhaus, *To Empower People: From State to Civil Society*, 2nd ed., ed. Michael Novak (Washing-ton, DC: AEI Press, 1996).

CHAPTER 3

Epigraph: William M. Klimon, "Mediating Institutions," *Religion & Lib-erty* 2, no. 3 (Jul. 20, 2010), https://www.acton.org/pub/religion-liberty /volume-2-number-3/mediating-institutions.

1. Peter L. Berger and Richard John Neuhaus, *To Empower People: From State to Civil Society*, 2nd ed., ed. Michael Novak (Washing-ton, DC: AEI, 1996), 148.

2. Raj Chetty, Nathaniel Hendren, Patrick Kline, and Emmanuel Saez, "Where Is the Land of Opportunity? The Geography of Intergenerational Mobility in the U.S.," Executive Summary, *Opportunity-Insights.org*, Jan. 2014, https://opportunityinsights.org/wp-content /uploads/2018/03/Geography-Executive-Summary-and-Memo -January-2014-1.pdf.

3. Chetty et al., "Where Is the Land of Opportunity?"

4. Wilfred M. McClay, "Mediating Institutions," review of Richard John Neuhaus and Peter Berger, *To Empower People, FirstThings .com*, Apr. 2009, https://www.firstthings.com/article/2009/04/002 -mediating-institutions.

5. *Hearings Before the Committee on Ways and Means, House of Representatives*, 91st Cong. 1837–1838 (Nov. 6, 1969) (statement of Urie Bronfenbrenner).

6. Urie Bronfenbrenner, *The Ecology of Human Development: Experiments by Nature and Design* (Cambridge, MA: Harvard University Press, 1979), 3.

7. Urie Bronfenbrenner, "Toward an Experimental Ecology of Human Development," *American Psychology Magazine*, Jul. 1977, 514.

8. Todd R. Risley and Betty Hart, *Meaningful Differences in the Everyday Experience of Young American Children* (Baltimore: Paul H. Brooks Publishing Co., 1995).

9. Samantha Marsh, Rosie Dobson, and Ralph Maddison, "The Relationship between Household Chaos and Child, Parent, and Family Outcomes: A Systematic Scoping Review," *BMC Public Health* 20, no. 513 (2020).

10. *Hearings Before the Committee on Ways and Means.*

11. National Commission on Neighborhoods, *People Building Neighborhoods: Final Report to the President and the Congress of the United States* (Washington, DC: National Commission on Neighborhoods, 1979), 276.

12. Commission on Race and Ethnic Disparities, *Independent Report: Foreword, Introduction, and Full Recommendations*, Apr. 28, 2021, https://www.gov.uk/government/publications/the-report-of-the -commission-on-race-and-ethnic-disparities/foreword-introduc tion-and-full-recommendations.

CHAPTER 4

1. Lyrics at https://www.blumenthalarts.org/assets/doc/Hamilton -Lyrics-ACT-I1-e82b4f261a.pdf.
2. "The 1619 Project," *New York Times magazine*, Aug. 14, 2014, https:// www.nytimes.com/interactive/2019/08/14/magazine/1619-ame rica-slavery.html.
3. Robert J. Kunikoff, "An Eye-Opening Project about Slavery," Opin- ion: Letters, *New York Times*, August 21, 2019, https://www.nytimes .com/2019/08/21/opinion/letters/slavery-new-york-times-project .html.
4. California Newsreel with the Association of American Colleges and Universities, "Race Literacy Quiz," from the PBS documentary *Race: The Power of an Illusion*, *newsreel.org*, 2003, http://www.whatsrace .org/images/racequiz.pdf.
5. Ian Rowe, "Testimony: From Persecution to Prosperity," Ameri- can Enterprise Institute, March 11, 2021, https://www.aei.org /research-products/testimony/testimony-from-persecution-to -prosperity/.
6. "NAEP Report Card: 2019 NAEP Reading Assessment," National Center for Education Statistics, Accessed August, 2021, at https:// www.nationsreportcard.gov/highlights/reading/2019/.
7. National Park Service, "Dr. Martin Luther King on the Eman- cipation Proclamation," Sept. 12, 1962, transcript at *NPS.gov*, Apr. 10, 2015, https://www.nps.gov/anti/learn/historyculture/mlk -ep.htm.

8. Alexis de Tocqueville, *Democracy in America*, trans., ed., and with an intro. by Harvey C. Mansfield and Delba Winthrop (Chicago: University of Chicago Press, 2000) I:iiix.
9. Hendrik Hertzberg and Henry Louis Gates, Jr., "Comment," in "The African-American Century," special issue, *New Yorker,* Apr. 21, 1996, https://www.newyorker.com/magazine/1996/04/29/the-african-american-century.
10. "Transcript: Barack Obama's Speech on Race," *NPR.org,* Mar. 18, 2008, https://www.npr.org/templates/story/story.php?storyId=88478467.

CHAPTER 5

1. Craig, "The Evolution of an Accidental Meme," *Craig* (blog), Apr. 14, 2016, https://medium.com/@CRA1G/the-evolution-of-an-accidental-meme-ddc4e139e0e4#.pqiclk8pl.
2. "Equity vs. Equality: What's the Difference?," George Washington University, Milken Institute School of Public Health, Nov. 5, 2020, https://onlinepublichealth.gwu.edu/resources/equity-vs-equality/.
3. Disruptive Equity Education Project, https://digdeepforequity.org/.
4. Karl Marx, *Critique of the Gotha Programme* (Rockville, MD: Wildside Press, 2008), 27.
5. The Schott Foundation, "Black Lives Matter: The Schott 50 State Report on Black Males and Public Education," 2015, http://blackboysreport.org/.
6. Brian Solka, "Racial Equity in Education: Seven Key Points," USC Rossier School of Education, 2021, https://rossier.usc.edu/racial-equity-in-education-seven-key-points/.
7. Laura Gesualdi-Gilmore, "'DEEPLY INSULTING' African American museum accused of 'racism' over whiteness chart linking hard work and nuclear family to white culture," The U.S. Sun, July 16, 2020, https://www.the-sun.com/news/1149007/african-american-museum-whiteness-chart-protestant-values/.

8. Christopher F. Rufo, "Radicals in the Classroom," City Journal, January 5, 2021, https://www.city-journal.org/radicalism-in-san-diego-schools.

9. ThePoliticalHat, "Building Anti-Racist & Restorative School Communities," San Diego Unified School District "Freedom Summer 2020" Board Workshop, July 21, 2020, https://www.scribd.com/document/480833428/Building-Anti-Racist-Restorative-School-Communities.

10. ThePoliticalHat, "Building Anti-Racist & Restorative School Communities."

11. Author's calculations based on Sandra L. Hofferth, Sarah M. Flood, Matthew Sobek, and Daniel Backman, "American Time Use Survey Data Extract Builder: Version 2.8 [dataset]," University of Maryland and IPUMS, 2020.

12. ThePoliticalHat, "Building Anti-Racist & Restorative School Communities."

13. ThePoliticalHat, "Building Anti-Racist & Restorative School Communities."

14. Shannon Handy, "San Diego Unified Revamps Grading System after Minority Students Disproportionately Impacted," CBS8, October 21, 2020, https://www.cbs8.com/article/news/education/learning-curve/san-diego-unified-changes-grading-system-after-minority-students-disproportionately-impacted/509-04bf22ea-51df-428a-84c5-82ccc63f36ec.

15. "San Diego Unified School District Changes Grading Policy," Oct. 15, 2020, https://www.nbcsandiego.com/news/local/sdusd-changes-grading-policy/2425362/.

16. Conor Friedersdorf, "The Narrative Is, 'You Can't Get Ahead,'" The Atlantic, April 3, 2021, https://www.theatlantic.com/ideas/archive/2021/04/black-lives-matter-curriculum-has-unintended-lesson/618501/.

17. U.S Department of Education, "A Nation at Risk," April 1983, https://www2.ed.gov/pubs/NatAtRisk/risk.html.

18. The Nation's Report Card, "See How U.S. Students Performed in Reading at Grades 4 and 8," accessed August 2021, https://www.nationsreportcard.gov/highlights/reading/2019/.

19. National Center for Education Statistics, NAEP Data Explorer, accessed August 2021, https://nces.ed.gov/nationsreportcard/data/.

20. U.S Department of Education, "A Nation at Risk," April 1983, https://www2.ed.gov/pubs/NatAtRisk/risk.html.

21. KIPP, "Results," Accessed December 31, 2021, https://www.kipp.org/results/national/#question-1:-who-are-our-students.

22. KIPP, "KIPP Commitment to Excellence (Sample)," http://www.kipp.org/wp-content/uploads/2016/09/KIPP_Commitment_to_Excellence_Sample.pdf.

23. Jay Mathews, *Work Hard. Be Nice.* (Chapel Hill, NC: Algonquin Books, 2009).

24. "Richard Barth's Weekly Thoughts: Turning Words into Action," https://www.kipp.org/news/weekly-thoughts-turning-words-into-action/

25. Tykeena Watson, "Learning a Life Lesson: Work Hard. Be Nice," Jul. 6, 2012, *KIPP:Blog*, https://blog.kipp.org/teamandfamily/learning-a-life-lesson-work-hard-be-nice/.

26. Dave Levin, "Why KIPP Has Retired 'Work Hard. Be Nice,'" *Wall Street Journal*, July 10, 2020, https://www.wsj.com/articles/why-kipp-has-retired-work-hard-be-nice-11594418618.

27. Levin, "Why KIPP Has Retired 'Work Hard. Be Nice.'"

28. Christopher F. Rufo, "'Antiracism' Comes to the Heartland," *City Journal*, January 19, 2021, https://www.city-journal.org/antiracism-comes-to-the-heartland.

29. Dom Giordano, "'Privilege Walks' Reek of Entitlement," *Philadelphia Inquirer*, January 20, 2016, https://www.inquirer.com/philly

/opinion/20160120__Privilege_walks__reek_of_entitlement .html.

30. Christopherrufo.com, "Critical Race Theory Briefing Book," accessed January 3, 2022, https://christopherrufo.com/crt-briefing-book/.

CHAPTER 6

1. Christopher Cerf, former superintendent of public schools in Newark, New Jersey, found in Ian Rowe, "The Parable of the River: Bedtime reading for the education reform (A.K.A. "repair") community," Fordham Institute, February 21, 2018, https://fordhaminstitute.org /national/commentary/parable-river-bedtime-reading-education -reform-aka-repair-community.

2. Citizen's Committee for Children, "Keeping Track 2015: Our Newest Databook on Child Well-Being in NYC," April 23, 2015, https:// cccnewyork.org/keeping-track-2015-our-newest-databook-on -child-well-being-in-nyc/.

3. Stephen Rex Brown and Ben Chapman, "EXCLUSIVE: 90 city schools failed to pass a single black or Hispanic student on state tests, study shows," New York Daily News, September 2, 2014, https://www.nydailynews.com/new-york/education/exclusive-achi evement-gap-worsens-black-hispanic-students-article-1.1924366.

4. Marc Santora, "Rolling DNA Labs Address the Ultimate Question: 'Who's Your Daddy?,'" *New York Times*, November 8, 2016, https:// www.nytimes.com/2016/11/09/nyregion/rolling-dna-labs-address -the-ultimate-question-whos-your-daddy.html.

5. Jared Rosenthal, "New Docu-Reality TV Series—Who's Your Daddy Truck," Health Street, February 6, 2014, https://www.health-street .net/vh1-swab-stories/new-docu-reality-tv-series-whos-your-daddy -truck/.

6. IMDB, "Swab Stories," accessed August 2021, https://www.imdb .com/title/tt3973254/.

7. IMDb, "30 Something Grandma," accessed August 2021, https://www.imdb.com/title/tt6291796/.

8. IMDb, "16 and Pregnant," accessed August 2021, https://www.imdb.com/title/tt1454730/; and IMDb, "Teen Mom OG," accessed August 2021, https://www.imdb.com/title/tt1566154/.

9. Citizen's Committee for Children, "Keeping Track 2015: Our Newest Databook on Child Well-being in NYC."

10. James S. Coleman et al., "Equality of Educational Opportunity," U.S. Department of Health, Education, and Welfare, Office of Education, National Center for Education Statistics, July 2, 1966, http://files.eric.ed.gov/fulltext/ED012275.pdf.

11. Coleman et al., "Equality of Educational Opportunity."

12. Heather C. Hill, "The Coleman Report, 50 Years On: What Do We Know about the Role of Schools in Academic Inequality?," *ANNALS of the American Academy of Political Science* 64, no. 1 (2017): 9–26.

13. Heather C. Hill, "50 Years Ago, One Report Introduced Americans to the Black-White Achievement Gap: Here's What We've Learned Since," *Chalkbeat*, July 13, 2016, http://www.chalkbeat.org/posts/us/2016/07/13/50-years-ago-the-coleman-report-revealed-the-black-white-achievement-gap-in-america-heres-what-weve-learned-since/.

14. New York State, Department of Health, "Table 7: Live Births by Mother's Age and Resident County New York State—2016," July 2018, https://www.health.ny.gov/statistics/vital_statistics/2016/table07.htm.

15. Elizabeth Wildsmith, Jennifer Manlove, and Elizabeth Cook, "Dramatic Increase in the Proportion of Births Outside of Marriage in the United States from 1990 to 2016," *Child Trends*, August 8, 2018, https://www.childtrends.org/publications/dramatic-increase-in-percentage-of-births-outside-marriage-among-whites-hispanics-and-women-with-higher-education-levels.

16. P. R. Amato, "The Impact of Family Formation Change on the Cognitive, Social, and Emotional Well-Being of the Next Generation," *The Future of Children* 15, no. 2 (2006): 75–96; S. S. McLanahan and I. Sawhill, "Marriage and Child Wellbeing Revisited: Introducing the Issue," *The Future of Children* 25, no. 2 (2015): 3–9; M. S. Kearney and P. B. Levine, "The Economics of Non-Marital Childbearing and the 'Marriage Premium for Children,'" National Bureau for Economic Research, Working Paper no. 23230, March 2017; R. K. Raley, M. L. Frisco, and E. Wildsmith, "Maternal Cohabitation and Educational Success," *Sociology of Education* 78, no. 2 (2005): 144–164; Kathryn Harker, "Family Structure Pathways and Academic Disadvantage among Adolescents in Stepfamilies," *Sociological Inquiry* 77, no. 3 (2007): 383–424; Suet-Ling Pong, "Family Structure, School Context, and Eighth-Grade Math and Reading Achievement," *Journal of Marriage and Family* 59, no. 3 (1997): 734–746; Bryan Neighbors, Rex Forehand, and Lisa Armistead, "Is Parental Divorce a Critical Stressor for Young Adolescents? Grade Point Average as a Case in Point," *Adolescence* 27, no. 107 (1992): 639–646.

CHAPTER 7

1. Barak Obama, "Remarks by the President On Strengthening the Economy for the Middle Class," February 15, 2013, White House, Office of the Press Secretary, https://obamawhitehouse.archives.gov/the-press-office/2013/02/15/remarks-president-strengthening-economy-middle-class.
2. Maria Gavrilovic, "Obama's Father's Day Message," CBS News, June 15, 2008, https://www.cbsnews.com/news/obamas-fathers-day-message/.
3. Cate Cahan et al., "Every Other Hour," WBEZ 91.5, Chicago, 2017, http://interactive.wbez.org/everyotherhour/#about-61638.

4. Cook County Department of Public Health Epidemiology Unit, "Birth 2000," 2000, https://www.cookcountypublichealth .org/wp-content/uploads/2018/12/2000_Birth_All_Sections .pdf.

5. Kay S. Hymowitz, "Boy Trouble," *City Journal*, Autumn 2013, https://www.city-journal.org/html/boy-trouble-13615.html; Melvin Konner, "The Link between Detached Dads and Risk-Taking Girls," *Wall Street Journal*, June 2, 2017, https://www.wsj.com/articles/the -link-between-distant-dads-and-risk-taking-girls-1496414606; and Cate Cahan et al., "Every Other Hour."

6. Cynthia C. Harper and Sara S. McLanahan, "Father Absence and Youth Incarceration," Center for Research on Child Wellbeing, Working Paper No. 99-03, 2004, https://www.fatherhood.gov/sites /default/files/resource_files/e000000172_0.pdf.

7. Robert Putnam, "Closing the Opportunity Gap Initiative: Finding Solutions for Our Kids," William T. Grant Foundation, August 16, 2017, http://wtgrantfoundation.org/closing-opportunity-gap-initia tive-finding-solutions-kids.

8. Daniel Geary, "The Moynihan Report: An Annotated Edition," *The Atlantic*, September 14, 2015, https://www.theatlantic.com/politics /archive/2015/09/the-moynihan-report-an-annotated-edition /404632/.

9. Dale Alquist, "Remembering G. K. Chesterton," *Chronicles Magazine*, March 2021, https://www.chroniclesmagazine.org/remem bering-g--k--chesterton/_1/.

10. Clarence Page, "Left Speechless?," *Chicago Tribune*, July 20, 2008, https://www.chicagotribune.com/news/ct-xpm-2008-07-20-080 7190337-story.html.

11. Ta-Nehisi Coates, "The Case for Reparations," *The Atlantic*, June 2014, https://www.theatlantic.com/magazine/archive/2014/06/the -case-for-reparations/361631/.

12. Ian Rowe, "The diminishing significance of racism and poverty in education reform," The Fordham Institute, February 28, 2017, https://edexcellence.net/articles/whos-your-daddy-a-question-for-education-reformers.

13. Black Lives Matter, "BLACK LIVES MATTER . . . . What We Believe," Training Document, accessed September 2021, https://uca.edu/training/files/2020/09/black-Lives-Matter-Handout.pdf.

14. Centers for Disease Control and Prevention, National Center for Health Statistics, "Table 1-17. Number and Percent of Births to Unmarried Women, by Race and Hispanic Origin: United States, 1940-99," accessed November 2021, https://www.cdc.gov/nchs/data/statab/t991x17.pdf; and Joyce A. Martin et al., "Births: Final Data for 2019," National Vital Statistics Reports 70, no. 2 (2021): 1–51, https://www.cdc.gov/nchs/data/nvsr/nvsr70/nvsr70-02-508.pdf.

15. United States Department of Health and Human Services (US DHHS), Centers for Disease Control and Prevention (CDC), National Center for Health Statistics (NCHS), Division of Vital Statistics, Natality public-use data, on CDC WONDER Online Database.

16. Power to Decide, "Why it Matters," accessed September 2021, https://powertodecide.org/what-we-do/information/why-it-matters.

17. Ian Rowe, "From '16 and Pregnant' to 'Teen Mom' to '30 Something Grandma,'" Fordham Institute, January 25, 2017, https://edexcellence.net/articles/from-16-and-pregnant-to-teen-mom-to-30-something-grandma.

18. Ian Rowe, "Speaking Truth to Power—A Response to Bill Gates Mystifying Omission of Family Fragmentation," LinkedIn, November 4, 2017, https://www.linkedin.com/pulse/speaking-truth-power-response-bill-gates-mystifying-ian-rowe/.

19. Nicole Sussner Rodgers, "A New Chapter," Family Story, October 23, 2018, https://familystoryproject.org/a-new-chapter/.

20. Personal correspondence with Nicole Sussner Rodgers, email, November 2, 2017.

21. Personal correspondence with Nicole Sussner Rodgers, email, December 16, 2021.

22. Personal correspondence, email, January 2, 2017.

23. Ron Haskins, "Three Simple Rules Poor Teens Should Follow to Join the Middle Class," March 13, 2013, https://www.brookings.edu /opinions/three-simple-rules-poor-teens-should-follow-to-join-the -middle-class/.

24. Ian Rowe, "The Diminishing Significance of Racism and Poverty in Education Reform."

25. Personal correspondence with Mona Davids, email, January 3, 2019.

CHAPTER 8

1. Dick Morris, *Behind the Oval Office* (New York: Random House, 1997), 80.

2. William J. Clinton, "1995 State of the Union Address," January 24, 1995, accessed at C-SPAN, https://www.c-span.org/video/?62882-1 /president-bill-clintons-1995-state-union-address.

3. John A. Meyers, "A Letter from the Publisher," *Time* magazine, December 9, 1985, http://content.time.com/time/magazine/article /0,9171,1074823,00.html.

4. Claudia Wallis, "Children Having Children," *Time* magazine, December 9, 1985, http://content.time.com/time/subscriber/article /0,33009,1074861-1,00.html.

5. Quote confirmed through personal correspondence with Rick Santorum, email, January 3, 2022.

6. Teen Pregnancy Prevention and Parental Responsibility Act, H.R. 1115, 104th Congress (1995–1996).

7. Domestic Policy Council, Carol Rasco, and Meetings, Trips, Events Series, "Teen Pregnancy Meeting October 5, 1995 [1]," *Clinton*

Digital Library, accessed January 3, 2022, https://clinton.presidentiallibraries.us/items/show/20608.

8. https://www.rwjf.org/en/library/research/2009/02/national-campaign-helps-reduce-the-rate-of-teen-pregnancy-by-one.html.

9. The National Campaign to Prevent Teen Pregnancy, "Parent Power: What Parents Need to Know and Do to Help Prevent Teen Pregnancy," February 1996, https://www.michigan.gov/documents/mdch/Parent_Power_-_What_Parents_Need_to_Know_and_Do_to_help_Prev_296509_7.pdf.

10. Personal correspondence with Sarah Brown, Zoom interview, April 23, 2021.

11. William J. Clinton, "1995 State of the Union Address," January 24, 1995, accessed at C-SPAN, https://www.c-span.org/video/?62882-1/president-bill-clintons-1995-state-union-address.

12. Susan G. Parker, "National Campaign Helps Reduce the Rate of Teen Pregnancy by One-Third in 10 Years," Robert Wood Johnson Foundation, February 9, 2009, https://www.rwjf.org/en/library/research/2009/02/national-campaign-helps-reduce-the-rate-of-teen-pregnancy-by-one.html.

13. *Public Papers of the Presidents of the United States: William J. Clinton* (Washington, DC: U.S. Government Printing Office, 1995), Book 1, March 20, 1995, 374–376.

14. IMDb, "Birth 101," *Murphy Brown*, season 4, episode 26, aired May 18, 1992, https://www.imdb.com/title/tt0653734/.

15. Dan Quayle, "Address to the Commonwealth Club of California," May 19, 1992, http://www.vicepresidentdanquayle.com/speeches_StandingFirm_CCC_3.html#:~:text=Ultimately%20however%2C%20marriage%20is%20a,must%20be%20unequivocal%20about%20this.

16. *New York Times*, cover page, May 21, 1992, https://timesmachine.nytimes.com/timesmachine/1992/05/21/issue.html.

17. Jacey Fortin, "That Time 'Murphy Brown' and Dan Quayle Topped the Front Page," *New York Times*, January 26, 2018, https://www .nytimes.com/2018/01/26/arts/television/murphy-brown-dan-quay le.html.

18. Kay S. Hymowitz, "The Black Family: 40 Years of Lies," *City Journal*, Summer 2005, https://www.city-journal.org/html/black-family -40-years-lies-12872.html.

19. Gretchen Livingston and Deja Thomas, "Why Is the Teen Birth Rate Falling?," PEW Research Center, August 2, 2019, https://www .pewresearch.org/fact-tank/2019/08/02/why-is-the-teen-birth-rate -falling/ft_19-08-02_teenbirths_us-teen-birth-rate-fallen-over -time/.

20. NurseryRhymes.org, "K-I-S-S-I-N-G," lyrics, accessed January 1, 2022, https://www.nurseryrhymes.org/k-i-s-s-i-n-g.html.

21. William Julius Wilson, *The Truly Disadvantaged* (Chicago: University of Chicago Press, 1987).

22. Charles Murray, *Losing Ground: American Social Policy, 1950–1980* (New York: Basic Books, 1984).

23. George A. Akerlof and Janet L. Yellen, "New Mothers, Not Married: Technology Shock, the Demise of Shotgun Marriage, and the Increase in Out-of-Wedlock Births," Brookings Institution, September 1, 1996, https://www.brookings.edu/articles/new-mothers-not -married-technology-shock-the-demise-of-shotgun-marriage-and -the-increase-in-out-of-wedlock-births/.

24. https://powertodecide.org/news/we-are-power-decide.

25. Robert Doar et al., "Opportunity, Responsibility, and Security: A Consensus Plan for Reducing Poverty and Restoring the American Dream," American Enterprise Institute and Brookings Institution, December 3, 2015, https://www.aei.org/wp-content/uploads/2015/12 /opportunity_responsibility_security_doar_strain_120315_FINAL .pdf; Robert Putnam, "Closing the Opportunity Gap Initiative:

Finding Solutions for Our Kids," William T. Grant Foundation, August 17, 2016, http://wtgrantfoundation.org/closing-opportunity-gap-initiative-finding-solutions-kids.

26. Isabel V. Sawhill, "Beyond Marriage," *New York Times*, September 13, 2014, https://www.nytimes.com/2014/09/14/opinion/sunday/beyond-marriage.html.

27. Isabel V. Sawhill, "Beyond Marriage."

28. Personal correspondence with Sarah Brown, email, April 17, 2021.

CHAPTER 9

1. Richard Zoglin, "Sitcom Politics," *Time* magazine, September 21, 1992, http://content.time.com/time/subscriber/article/0,33009,976534,00.html.

2. *New York Times*, cover page, May 21, 1992, https://timesmachine.nytimes.com/timesmachine/1992/05/21/issue.html.

3. Barbara Dafoe Whitehead, "Dan Quayle Was Right," *Atlantic*, Apr. 1993.

4. Isabel V. Sawhill, "Twenty Years Later, It Turns Out Dan Quayle Was Right about Murphy Brown and Unmarried Moms," *Washington Post*, May 25, 2012, https://www.washingtonpost.com/opinions/20-years-later-it-turns-out-dan-quayle-was-right-about-murphy-brown-and-unmarried-moms/2012/05/25/gJQAsNCJqU_story.html.

5. Sawhill, "Twenty Years Later, It Turns Out Dan Quayle Was Right about Murphy Brown and Unmarried Moms."

6. Isabel V. Sawhill, *Generation Unbound: Drifting into Sex and Parenthood without Marriage* (Washington: Brookings Institution Press, 2014), X.

7. Robert Doar et al., "Opportunity, Responsibility, Security: A Consensus Plan for Reducing Poverty and Restoring the American Dream," American Enterprise Institute and Brookings Institution,

December 3, 2015, https://www.aei.org/research-products/report
/opportunity-responsibility-and-security/.

8. Vincent J. Felitti et al., "Relationship of Childhood Abuse and Household Dysfunction to Many of the Leading Causes of Death in
Adults," *American Journal of Preventative Medicine* 14, no. 4 (1998):
245–258, https://www.ajpmonline.org/article/S0749-3797(98)00017
-8/fulltext.

9. https://firstthings.org/the-effects-of-childhood-trauma/.

10. David Frum, "Why Is the Abortion Rate Falling?," *Atlantic*, December 1, 2014, https://www.theatlantic.com/politics/archive/2014/12
/why-is-the-abortion-rate-falling/383300/.

CHAPTER 10

1. Michelle Castillo, "New York's Teen Pregnancy PSAs," CBS News,
March 4, 2013, https://www.cbsnews.com/pictures/new-yorks-teen
-pregnancy-psas/.

2. Michael Bloomberg "Mayor Bloomberg, Deputy Mayor Gibbs And
Human Resources Administration Commissioner Doar Announce
New Campaign To Further Reduce Teen Pregnancy," press release,
NYC.gov, March 3, 2013, https://www1.nyc.gov/office-of-the-mayor
/news/082-13/mayor-bloomberg-deputy-mayor-gibbs-human
-resources-administration-commissioner-doar-announce.

3. Michael Bloomberg "Mayor Bloomberg, Deputy Mayor Gibbs And
Human Resources Administration Commissioner Doar Announce
New Campaign To Further Reduce Teen Pregnancy."

4. Innovations in NYC Health and Human Services Policy—Teen Pregnancy Prevention, https://www1.nyc.gov/assets/opportunity/pdf
/policybriefs/teen-pregnancy-brief.pdf.

5. Ron Haskins and Isabel V. Sawhill, *Creating an Opportunity Society*
(Washington, DC: Brookings Institution Press, 2009).

6. Brian Goesling, Hande Inanc, and Angela Rachidi, *Success Sequence:
A Synthesis of the Literature*, OPRE Report 2020–41 (Washington,

DC: U.S. Department of Health and Human Services, Administration for Children and Families, Office of Planning, Research, and Evaluation, 2020).

7. Johns Hopkins School of Education, "Should Schools Promote the Success Sequence? Why or Why Not?," October 2018, https://edpolicy.education.jhu.edu/should-schools-promote-the-success-sequence-why-or-why-not/.

8. "The Millennial Success Sequence: Marriage, Kids, and the 'Success Sequence' among Young Adults," Working Paper: Poverty, American Enterprise Institute, June 14, 2017, https://www.aei.org/research-products/working-paper/millennials-and-the-success-sequence-how-do-education-work-and-marriage-affect-poverty-and-finan cial-success-among-millennials/.

9. Matt Bruenig, "The Success Sequence Is about Cultural Beefs Not Poverty," Matt Bruenig Dot Com, July 31, 2017, https://mattbruenig .com/2017/07/31/the-success-sequence-is-about-cultural-beefs-not -poverty/.

10. Richard V. Reeves, Edward Rodrigue, and Alex Gold, "Following the Success Sequence? Success Is More Likely If You're White," Brookings Social Mobility Papers No. 12, Brookings Institution, August 6, 2015, http://www.brookings.edu/blogs/social-mobility-memos /posts/2015/08/06-following-success-sequence-race-reeves.

11. Michael D. Tanner, "The Success Sequence—and What It Leaves Out," *Cato Unbound*, May 9, 2018, https://www.cato-unbound.org /2018/05/09/michael-d-tanner/success-sequence-what-it-leaves -out.

12. Philip N. Cohen, "The Failure of the Success Sequence," *CATO Unbound—A Journal of Debate*, May 16, 2018, https://www.cato -unbound.org/2018/05/16/philip-n-cohen/failure-success-seq uence.

13. Cohen, "The Failure of the Success Sequence."

14. Glenn Loury, "Black Kids Are Not Being Developed to Their Full Human Potential," *YouTube*, Nov. 26, 2020, https://www.youtube .com/watch?v=MNXs658B5gA.

15. Bruenig, "The Success Sequence Is about Cultural Beefs."

16. Patrick T. Brown, "The 'Success Sequence' Is about More Than Economic Outcomes," *Jacobite*, Sept. 9, 2017, https://jacobitemag.com /2017/09/09/the-success-sequence-is-not-just-about-economic-out comes/.

17. Bryan Caplan, "What Does the Success Sequence Mean?," Econ Lib, February 22, 2021, https://www.econlib.org/the-meaning-of-the -success-sequence/.

18. Haskins and Sawhill, *Creating an Opportunity Society*.

19. Ron Haskins, "Education and the Success Sequence," in *Education for Upward Mobility*, ed. Michael J. Petrilli (Rowman and Littlefield, 2015), 6.

20. Wendy Wang, "'The Sequence' Is the Secret to Success," *Wall Street Journal Opinion*, Mar. 27, 2018.

21. Bryan Caplan, "What Does the Success Sequence Mean?"

22. "After the Ballots Are Counted: Conspiracies, Political Violence, and American Exceptionalism: Findings from the January 2021 American Perspectives Survey, Survey Center on American Life, Feb.11, 2021, https://www.americansurveycenter.org/american-perspec tives-survey/; Nat Malkus, "Uncommonly Popular: Public Support for Teaching the Success Sequence in School," American Enterprise Institute, Dec. 2021.

CHAPTER 11

1. Nicholas Zill, "How Family Transitions Affect Students' Achievement," *Family Studies*, October 29, 2015, 1, https://ifstudies.org /ifs-admin/resources/how-family-transitions-affect-students-achieve ment-family-studiesfamily-studies-1.pdf.

2. Bill Gates, "Our Education Efforts Are Evolving," *Gates Notes: The Blog of Bill Gates*, Oct. 19, 2017, https://www.gatesnotes.com /Education/Council-of-Great-City-Schools.

3. Bill Gates, "Council of the Great City Schools," speech, Bill & Melinda Gates Foundation, Oct. 19, 2017, https://www.gatesfoun dation.org/ideas/speeches/2017/10/bill-gates-council-of-the-great -city-schools.

4. Bill and Melinda Gates, "Why We Swing for the Fences," 2020 Annual Letter, *Gates Notes: The Blog of Bill Gates*, Feb. 10, 2020, https://www.gatesnotes.com/2020-Annual-Letter.

5. Paul R. Amato, "The Impact of Family Formation Change on the Cognitive, Social, and Emotional Well-Being of the Next Generation," *Future of Children* 15, no. 2 (fall 2005): 75–96, doi: 10.1353/ foc.2005.0012.

6. Rachel DeSantis and Charlotte Triggs, "'Combo of Things' Led to Bill & Melinda Gates' Divorce, But 'Nobody' Wants 'More Scrutiny,'" *People Magazine Exclusive*, May 7, 2021.

CHAPTER 12

1. Amanda Barroso, "With a Potential 'Baby Bust' on the Horizon, Key Facts about Fertility in the U.S. before the Pandemic," PEW Research Center, May 7, 2021, https://www.pewresearch.org/fact-tank/2021 /05/07/with-a-potential-baby-bust-on-the-horizon-key-facts-abou t-fertility-in-the-u-s-before-the-pandemic/

2. Arthur C. Brooks, "America's New Culture War: Free Enterprise vs. Government Control," *Washington Post*, May 23, 2010, https://www .washingtonpost.com/wp-dyn/content/article/2010/05/21/AR20 10052101854.html.

3. Viktor E. Frankl, *Man's Search for Meaning* (Boston: Beacon Press, 1959), 71.

CHAPTER 13

Epigraph: Wilfred McClay, "Free Societies as Schools of the Soul: Fragmented Families and Splintered Classes," Center of the American Experiment Symposium, Oct. 2012, https://files.americanexperiment.org/wp-content/uploads/2017/03/12.10-Frag.-Families-Splintered-Classes-Symp.pdf.

1. Jill Lepore, "The Meaning of Life: What Milton Bradley Started," *New Yorker*, May 14, 2007, https://www.newyorker.com/magazine/2007/05/21/the-meaning-of-life.

2. This media file is in the public domain in the United States and can be accessed at http://chnm.gmu.edu/exploring/19thcentury/checkeredgame/assignment.php.

3. Milton Bradley, *The Checkered Game of Life* (Springfield, MA: Milton Bradley Company, 1866), Liman Collection of American Board Games and Table Games, Henry Luce III Center for the Study of American Culture, New-York Historical Society.

4. Jill Lepore, "The Meaning of Life—Jill Lepore—Harvard Thinks Big, *YouTube*, Mar. 14, 2012, https://www.youtube.com/watch?v=YspXDn7z_6s.

5. The Game of Life: Twists and Turns (Pawtucket, RI: Hasbro, 2007).

6. Lepore, "The Meaning of Life."

7. Wendy Wang and W. Bradford Wilcox, "The Millennial Success Sequence: Marriage, Kids, and the 'Success Sequence' among Young Adults," Working Paper: Poverty Studies, American Enterprise Institute, June 14, 2017, https://www.aei.org/research-products/working-paper/millennials-and-the-success-sequence-how-do-education-work-and-marriage-affect-poverty-and-financial-success-among-millennials/.

8. J. Daugherty and C. Copen, "Trends in Attitudes about Marriage, Childbearing, and Sexual Behavior: United States, 2002, 2006–2010, and 2011–2013," *National Health Statistics Reports* (Hyattsville,

MD: National Center for Health Statistics), no 92 (2016), https://www.cdc.gov/nchs/data/nhsr/nhsr092.pdf.

9. A participant in the Family Stability Working Group, Brad Wilcox, has proposed a national campaign to promote the success sequence. See B. Wilcox and R. Lerman, "For Richer, For Poorer: How Family Structures Economic Success in America," American Enterprise Institute, 2014.

10. For example, Isabel Sawhill refers to "5 inconvenient truths that young adults need to know," including: "1) the likelihood of pregnancy using a condom alone for 5 years is 63%. Use the pill—or even better—an IUD; 2) An early unplanned birth affects a child's success later in life; 3) Cohabitation is not a substitute for marriage; 4) Later marriages are more stable than early ones, so waiting is a good idea; 5) Children are expensive—expect to spend about $500,000 to $1 million per child. This social marketing campaign could also focus on the most effective means of contraception for interested women." See I. Sawhill and J. Venator, "Proposal Three: Reducing Unintended Pregnancies for Low-Income Women," in *Policies to Address Poverty in America*, ed. M. Kearney and B. Harris (Washington, DC: Brookings Institution Press, 2014).

11. Isabel V. Sawhill and Robert D. Putnam, "Promoting Stable Families and Effective Parents," in Closing the Opportunity Gap, The Saguaro Seminar, 2016, https://pathforyou.org/wp-content/uploads/2019/10/Closing-the-Opportunity-Gap-2016.pdf.

12. Robert Doar et al., "Opportunity, Responsibility, and Security: A Consensus Plan for Reducing Poverty and Restoring the American Dream," American Enterprise Institute and Brookings Institution, December 3, 2015, https://www.brookings.edu/wp-content/uploads/2016/07/full-report.pdf.

13. Thomas Adam, "The Role of Mass Media Campaigns in Preventing Unintended Pregnancy," *Journal of Media and Communication Studies* 6, no. 1 (2014): 23–27.

14. Isabel V. Sawhill and Robert D. Putnam, "Promoting Stable Families and Effective Parents."

15. W. Bradford Wilcox, Spencer James, and Wendy Wang, "Declining Divorce in Jacksonville: Did the Culture of Freedom Initiative Make a Difference?," Philanthropy Roundtable and the Institute for Family Studies, October 17, 2019, https://www.philanthropyroundtable .org/docs/default-source/briefings/final_cof_nov.pdf?sfvrsn=10 afa840_1.

16. "The Nation's Report Card," accessed August 15, 2019, https://www .nationsreportcard.gov/.

17. "The NAEP Law," National Assessment of Educational Progress Authorization Act, P.L. 107-279, Jan. 8, 2002, National Assessment Governing Board, https://www.nagb.gov/about-naep/the-naep-law .html.

18. W. Bradford Wilcox, Chris Gersten, and Jerry Regier, "Marriage Penalties in Means-Tested Tax and Transfer Programs: Issues and Options," Office of Family Assistance, Administration for Children and Families, US Department of Health and Human Services, January 20, 2020, https://www.aei.org/research-products/report/mar riage-penalties-in-means-tested-tax-and-transfer-programs-issues -and-options/.

19. Douglas J. Besharov and Neil Gilbert, "Marriage Penalties in the Modern Social Welfare State," RStreet Institute, September 2015, https://www.rstreet.org/wp-content/uploads/2015/08/RSTREET 40.pdf.

20. U.S. Department of Health and Human Services, Centers for Disease Control and Prevention, "CDC Winnable Battles Final Report," November 2016, https://www.cdc.gov/winnablebattles/report/docs /winnable-battles-final-report.pdf.

CHAPTER 14

Epilogue: "Washington's Farewell Address to the People of the United States," September 19, 1796, transcript found at US Senate, https://www.senate.gov/artandhistory/history/resources/pdf/Washingtons_Farewell_Address.pdf.

1. New York State, "Raise the Age: Improving the Way New York's Justice System Treats Young People," accessed September 2021, https://www.ny.gov/programs/raise-age-0.
2. W. Bradford Wilcox, "The Happiest Wives: The J-Curve in Women's Marital Quality," Institute for Family Studies, May 30, 2019, https://ifstudies.org/blog/the-happiest-wives-the-j-curve-in-womens-marital-quality.
3. National Marriage Project, "The State of Our Unions 2004: The Social Health of Marriage in America," Rutgers, The State University of New Jersey, June 2004, http://www.stateofourunions.org/pdfs/SOOU2004.pdf.
4. "Apostolic Pilgrimage to Bangladesh, Singapore, Fiji Islands, New Zealand, Australia and Seychelles: Homily of John Paul II," Perth (Australia), Nov. 30, 1986, https://www.vatican.va/content/john-paul-ii/en/homilies/1986/documents/hf_jp-ii_hom_19861130_perth-australia.html.
5. Joey Marshall, "Are Religious People Happier, Healthier?: Our New Global Study Explores This Question," Pew Research Center, Jan. 31, 2019, https://www.pewresearch.org/fact-tank/2019/01/31/are-religious-people-happier-healthier-our-new-global-study-explores-this-question/.
6. Ellen Childs, "Religious Attendance and Happiness: Examining Gaps in the Current Literature—A Research Note," *Journal for the Scientific Study of Religion*, Wiley Online Library, Sept. 1, 2010, https://onlinelibrary.wiley.com/doi/full/10.1111/j.1468-5906.2010.01528.x.

7. Mandy Robbins, Leslie J. Francis, and Bethan Edwards, "Prayer, Personality and Happiness: A Study among Undergraduate Students in Wales," *Mental Health, Religion & Culture* 11, no. 1 (2008): 93–99.

8. M. Green and M. Elliott, "Religion, Health, and Psychological Well-Being," *Journal of Religion and Health* 49, no. 2 (June 2010): 149–163.

9. Christopher Alan Lewis and Sharon Mary Cruise, "Religion and Happiness: Consensus, Contradictions, Comments and Concerns," *Mental Health, Religion & Culture* 9, no. 3 (2006): 213–225.

10. S. J. Jang, "Religiosity, Crime, and Drug Use among Juvenile Offenders: A Test of Reciprocal Relationships over Time," *International Journal of Offender Therapy and Comparative Criminology* 62, no. 14 (2018): 4445–4464.

11. Melvina Sumter, Frank Wood, Ingrid Whitaker, and Dianne Berger-Hill, "Religion and Crime Studies: Assessing What Has Been Learned," *Religions* 9, no. 6 (2018): 193.

12. Jang, "Religiosity, Crime, and Drug Use among Juvenile Offenders."

13. Anna Gunther, "Younger Generations Are Lonelier and Social Media Doesn't Help, Survey Finds," CBS News, Jan. 23, 2020, https://www.cbsnews.com/news/younger-generations-are-lonelier-and-social-media-doesnt-help-survey-finds-2020-01-23/.

14. Walton Family Foundation, "Opening Doors to Opportunity— Generation Z and Millennials Speak," October 2020 Research Report, https://8ce82b94a8c4fdc3ea6d-b1d233e3bc3cb10858bea65 ff05e18f2.ssl.cf2.rackcdn.com/b1/02/ddcbc1d6434d91e8494f007 0fa96/echelon-insights-walton-family-foundation-generation-z-mille nnials-and-opportunity-report-october-2020-10-6-20.pdf.

15. Pew Research Center, "In U.S., Decline of Christianity Continues at Rapid Pace," *PewForum.org.*, Oct. 17, 2019, https://www.pewfo rum.org/2019/10/17/in-u-s-decline-of-christianity-continues-at-rapid -pace/.

16. Jeffrey N. Jones, "U.S. Church Membership Down Sharply in Past Two Decades," Gallup, Apr. 18, 2019, https://news.gallup.com/poll /248837/church-membership-down-sharply-past-two-decades .aspx.

17. Matthew Kaemingk and James K. A. Smith, *Christian Hospitality and Muslim Immigration in an Age of Fear* (Grand Rapids, MI: Wm. B. Eerdmans Publishing Company, 2018). https://www.google.com /books/edition/Christian_Hospitality_and_Muslim_Immigra/S8 hEDwAAQBAJ?hl=en&gbpv=1&dq=abraham%2Bkuype r%2Bultimate%2Bpoint%2Bof%2Bloyalty&pg=PT152&amp ;printsec=frontcover.

18. "G. K. Chesterton 1874–1936: English Essayist, Novelist, and Poet," in Susan Ratcliffe, *Oxford Essential Quotations* (Oxford: Oxford University Press, 2016), https://www.oxfordreference.com/view /10.1093/acref/9780191826719.001.0001/q-oro-ed4-00002890.

19. John McWhorter, *Woke Racism: How a New Religion Has Betrayed Black America* (New York: Portfolio / Penguin, 2021).

20. W. Bradford Wilcox, Wendy R. Wang, and Ronald B. Mincy, "Black Men Making It in America: The Engines of Economic Success for Black Men in America," American Enterprise Institute and Institute for Family Studies, 2018, https://www.aei.org/wp-content/up loads/2018/06/BlackMenMakingItInAmerica-Final_062218.pdf? x91208.

21. "Can We Strengthen Marriage? Lessons from the Culture of Freedom Initiative in Jacksonville, Florida," event, American Enterprise Institute, Washington, DC, October 18, 2019, https://www.aei.org /events/can-we-strengthen-marriage-lessons-from-the-communio -initiative-in-jacksonville-florida/.

22. Seton Education Partners, "Why We're Here: A New Way Forward after the Collapse of Urban Catholic Education," accessed August 2021, https://www.setonpartners.org/who-we-are/why-were-here/.

23. Seton Education Partners, "12 Ways Seton Cultivates Virtue," accessed August 2021, https://www.setonpartners.org/stories/12-ways-seton-cultivates-virtue/.

24. Seton Education Partners, "Our Impact: Numbers Tell the Story of Our Impact," accessed August 2021, https://www.setonpartners.org/what-we-do/impact/.

25. Glenn C. Loury, "Hope in the Unseen: On Being a Christian and an Economist," Address to Powell Center for Economic Literacy, Richmond, Va., June 2005, online at https://www.brown.edu/Departments/Economics/Faculty/Glenn_Loury/louryhomepage/cvandbio/Richmond%20Speech.pdf.

CHAPTER 15

Epigraph: Frederick Douglass, Speech given at the 1894 dedication of the Manassas Industrial School for Colored Youth, September 3, 1894, accessed at Library of Congress, "The Frederick Douglass Papers," http://memory.loc.gov/cgi-bin/ampage?collId=mfd&fileName=49/49002/49002page.db&recNum=0&itemLink=/ammem/doughtml/dougFolder9.html&linkText=7.

1. United States Supreme Court, *Students for Fair Admissions, Inc., v. Presidents and Fellows of Harvard College*, Petition for Writ of Certiorari, Feb. 25, 2021, https://www.supremecourt.gov/DocketPDF/20/20-1199/169941/20210225095525027_Harvard%20Cert%20Petn%20Feb%2025.pdf.

2. Martin Luther King Jr., "The Purpose of Education," Maroon Tiger, January–February, 1947, https://kinginstitute.stanford.edu/king-papers/documents/purpose-education.

3. Selim Algar and Carl Campanile, "The Charter School Cap Is Making Life Harder for This NYC Parent," *New York Post*, April 17, 2019, https://nypost.com/2019/04/17/the-charter-school-cap-is-making-life-harder-for-this-nyc-parent/.

4. NY Post Editorial Board, "Minorities, Poor NYers Say 'Lift the Charter Cap,'" *New York Post*, June 20, 2021, https://nypost.com/2021 /06/20/minorities-poor-nyers-say-lift-the-charter-cap/.

5. National Alliance for Public Charter Schools, "Letter to DNC Platform Committee," 2020, https://www.publiccharters.org/sites /default/files/documents/2020-07/CMO Letter to DNC Platform Committee 2020.pdf.

6. Lindsey M. Burke, "Grand Reforms in the Grand Canyon State: Education Savings Accounts Bring Civil Society Life to Arizona," RStreet Institute, 2019, https://www.rstreet.org/wp-content/uploads/2019 /11/CSEW-Series-3-Burke.pdf.

7. Education Commission of the States, "Vouchers: Voucher Amount," accessed November 2021, https://reports.ecs.org/comparisons /vouchers-06.

8. Ed Choice, "Minnesota: Education Deduction," accessed November 2021, https://www.edchoice.org/school-choice/programs/min nesota-education-deduction/.

9. David S. D'Amato, "School Choice Is the Only Way to Save U.S. Education," Forbes, December 8, 2016, www.forbes.com/sites /realspin/2016/12/08/school-choice-is-the-only-way-to-save-u-s -education/amp/.

10. Lindsey Burke et al., "The Culture of American K–12 Education: A National Survey of Parents and School Board Members," Heritage Foundation, January 11, 2021, https://www.heritage.org/education /report/the-culture-american-k-12-education-national-survey -parents-and-school-board.

11. Wendy Wang and W. Bradford Wilcox, "The Millennial Success Sequence: Marriage, Kids, and the 'Success Sequence' among Young Adults," Working Paper: Policy Studies, American Enterprise Institute, June 14, 2017, https://www.aei.org/research-products/working -paper/millennials-and-the-success-sequence-how-do-education

-work-and-marriage-affect-poverty-and-financial-success-among -millennials/.

12. Marline E. Pearson, "Love Notes 3.0: Relationship Skills for Love, Life, and Work," Dibble Institute, February 19, 2020, https://www .dibbleinstitute.org/wp-new/wp-content/uploads/2020/02/LN -3.0-Sample-Lesson-2.19.20.pdf.

13. M. R. Cunningham, M. A. van Zyl, and K. W. Borders, "Evaluation of Love Notes and Reducing the Risk in Louisville, Kentucky," Final Evaluation Report to the University of Louisville Research Foundation, Louisville, KY, 2016, https://www.ncbi.nlm.nih.gov/pmc /articles/PMC5049476/.

14. Eric A. Hanushek et al., "The Achievement Gap Fails to Close," *Education Next* 19, no. 3 (Fall 2021).

15. "The Nation's Report Card," accessed August 15, 2019, https://www .nationsreportcard.gov/.

16. Natalie Wexler, "Elementary Education Has Gone Terribly Wrong," *The Atlantic*, August 2019, https://www.theatlantic.com/magazi ne/archive/2019/08/the-radical-case-for-teaching-kids-stuff/59 2765/.

17. Natalie Wexler, *The Knowledge Gap: The Hidden Cause of America's Broken Education System—and How to Fix It* (New York: Penguin Random House, 2019), 131.

18. Natalie Wexler, "Why American Students Haven't Gotten Better at Reading in 20 Years," *The Atlantic*, April 3, 2018, https://www.the atlantic.com/magazine/archive/2019/08/the-radical-case-for-teach ing-kids-stuff/592765/.

19. Hanushek et al., "The Achievement Gap Fails to Close."

20. Natalie Wexler, "Why American Students Haven't Gotten Better at Reading in 20 Years."

21. Reconstruction, "About Us," accessed November 2021, https:// reconstruction.us/about.

22. 1776 Unites, "1776 Unites Curriculum: Empowering, Historically Accurate Lessons for Students of All Backgrounds," accessed September 2021, https://1776unites.com/our-work/curriculum/.

23. United States Supreme Court, *Students for Fair Admissions, Inc., v. Presidents and Fellows of Harvard College*, Petition for Writ of Certiorari, Feb. 25, 2021, https://www.supremecourt.gov/Docket-PDF/20/20-1199/169941/20210225095525027_Harvard%20Cert%20Petn%20Feb%2025.pdf.

24. Issa Kohler-Haussman, "What's the Point of Parity? Harvard, Groupness, and the Equal Protection Clause," *Northwestern University Law Review*, May 8, 2020, https://northwesternlawreview.org/articles/whats-the-point-of-parity-harvard-groupness-and-the-equal-protection-clause/.

25. United States Supreme Court, *Grutter v. Bollinger*, 539 U. S. 306 (2003), https://www.law.cornell.edu/supct/html/02-241.ZS.html.

26. United States Supreme Court, Expert Report of Peter S. Arcidiacono, *Students for Fair Admissions, Inc., v. Presidents and Fellows of Harvard College*, June 15, 2018, https://samv91khoyt2i553a2t1s05i-wpengine.netdna-ssl.com/wp-content/uploads/2018/06/Doc-415-1-Arcidiacono-Expert-Report.pdf.

27. Howard Gold, "The Harsh Truth about Black Enrollment at America's Elite Colleges," Market Watch, June 25, 2020, https://www.marketwatch.com/story/the-harsh-truth-about-black-enrollment-at-americas-elite-colleges-2020-06-25.

28. Jesse J. Tauriac and Joan H. Liem, "Exploring the Divergent Academic Outcomes of U.S.Origin and Immigrant-Origin Black Undergraduates," *Journal of Diversity in Higher Education* 5, no. 4 (2012): 1–21.

29. John U. Ogbu, "Immigrant and Involuntary Minorities in Comparative Perspective." In *Minority Status and Schooling*, ed. Margaret A. Gibson and John Ogbu (New York: Garland, 1991), 3–33; John Ogbu, *Black American Students in an Affluent Suburb: A Study of Aca-*

demic Disengagement (Mahwah, NJ: Erlbaum, 2003); and John U. Ogbu and Herbert D. Simons, "Voluntary and Involuntary Minorities: A Cultural-Ecological Theory of Social Performance with Some Implications for Education," *Anthropology and Education Quarterly* 29, no. 2 (1998): 155–188.

30. US Department of Education, "A Nation at Risk," April 1983, https://www2.ed.gov/pubs/NatAtRisk/risk.html.

CHAPTER 16

Epigraph: Freedom and Virtue Institute, "FVI Ismael BG Vid," YouTube, March 1, 2016, https://www.youtube.com/watch?v=TFjx4N10hS0.

1. James Truslow Adams, *The Epic of America* (New York: Routledge, 2017), 214–215.
2. UNICEF and Gallup, "The Changing Childhood Project," 2021, https://changingchildhood.unicef.org.
3. Iresearchnet.com, "What Is Learned Helplessness?," accessed November 2021, http://psychology.iresearchnet.com/developmental-psychology/social-development/what-is-learned-helplessness/.
4. Steven F. Maier and Martin E. P. Seligman, "Learned Helplessness at Fifty: Insights from Neuroscience," *Psychological Review* 123, no. 4 (2016): 349–367, pp. 27.
5. Ian Rowe, "Creating an Opportunity Society and Upward Mobility for People of All Races," Statement before the Joint Economic Committee on "Examining the Racial Wealth Gap in the United States," May 12, 2021, https://www.jec.senate.gov/public/_cache/files/3d276158-3186-4552-8209-2f66dad7852b/ian-rowe-final-testimony-may-12-us-congress-joint-economic-committee.pdf.
6. Equitable Facilities Fund, "Our Board of Directors," accessed January 2022, https://eqfund.org/about/board/.
7. Equitable Facilities Fund, "Equitable Facilities Fund Commits $500 Million to Public Charter Schools Led by People of Color,"

December 9, 2021, https://www.prnewswire.com/news-releases /equitable-facilities-fund-commits-500-million-to-public-charter -schools-led-by-people-of-color-301441331.html?tc=eml_cleartime.

8. Freedom and Virtue Institute, "FVI Ismael BG Vid," YouTube, March 1, 2016, https://www.youtube.com/watch?v=TFjx4N10hS0.

9. Freedom and Virtue Institute, "Our Founder," accessed January 2, 2022, https://www.fvinstitute.org/our-founder/.

10. Freedom and Virtue Institute, "FVI Ismael BG Vid," YouTube, March 1, 2016, https://www.youtube.com/watch?v=TFjx4N10hS0.

11. Robertfsmith.com, "How Cornell Tech and Robert F. Smith Are Empowering Women," October 6, 2020, https://robertsmith.com /supporting-women-in-stem-how-cornell-tech-and-robert-f-smith -are-empowering-women/; and Robertfsmith.com, "Student Freedom Initiative Will Provide Millions for HBCUs and Black Students in STEM This Fall," August 20, 2021, https://robertsmith.com/student -freedom-initiative-will-provide-millions-for-hbcus-and-black-stu dents-in-stem-this-fall/.

12. Stephanie Deutsch, *You Need a Schoolhouse: Booker T. Washington, Julius Rosenwald, and the Building of Schools for the Segregated South* (Evanston, IL: Northwestern University Press, 2011); and The Woodson Center, "About Us," accessed December 2021, https:// woodsoncenter.org/about-us/.

13. Frederick Douglass, "Self Made Men," Speech, 1872, http://www .leeannhunter.com/english/wp-content/uploads/2015/01/Doug lass_SelfMadeMan1872.pdf.

CHAPTER 17

1. Margaret Chase Smith (1897–1995), Republican Senator from Maine, quoted in *NEA Journal: The Journal of the National Education Association*, Vol. 41 (1952), https://www.eriesd.org/cms/lib /PA01001942/Centricity/Domain/2098/Harrison%20Bergeron%20 Text.pdf.

2. Child Trends, "Children in Poverty: Indicators of Child and Youth Well-Being" (2016). Retrieved from https://www.childtrends.org /indicators/children-in-poverty; and R. Haskins, "The Family Is Here to Stay—or Not," *The Future of Children* 25, no. 2 (2015): 129–153.

3. B. J. Ellis, J. E. Bates, K. A. Dodge, D. M. Fergusson, L. J. Horwood, G. S. Pettit, and L. Woodward, "Does Father Absence Place Daughters at Special Risk for Early Sexual Activity and Teenage Pregnancy?," *Child Development* 74, no. 3 (2003): 801–821; P. R. Amato, "The Impact of Family Formation Change on the Cognitive, Social, and Emotional Well-Being of the Next Generation," *The Future of Children* 15, no. 2 (2005): 75–96; and C. C. Harper, and S. S. McLanahan, "Father Absence and Youth Incarceration," *Journal of Research on Adolescence* 14, no. 3 (2004): 369–397.

4. W. D. Manning and K. A. Lamb, "Adolescent Well-Being in Cohabiting, Married, and Single-Parent Families," *Journal of Marriage and Family* 65, no. 4 (2003): 876–893.

5. M. S. Kearney and P. B. Levine, "The Economics of Non-Marital Childbearing and the Marriage Premium for Children," National Bureau for Economic Research, Working Paper #23230, 2017; and R. K. Raley, M. L. Frisco, and E. Wildsmith, "Maternal Cohabitation and Educational Success," *Sociology of Education* 78, no. 2 (2005): 144–164.

6. R. Lerman and W. B. Wilcox, *For Richer, for Poorer: How Family Structures Economic Success in America* (Washington, DC: American Enterprise Institute/Institute for Family Studies, 2014); and T. DeLeire and L. Lopoo, *Family Structure and the Economic Mobility of Children* (Washington, DC: Pew Charitable Trusts, 2010).

APPENDIX

Notes for the appendix are in their original format.

1. Sliding versus deciding is a concept adapted for teens from the original work of Scott Stanley, Galena Kline Rhoades, and Howard

Markman. This concept has become important in scholarly discussions on cohabitation and the inertia effect. See Stanley, S. M., Rhoades, G. K., & Markman, H. J. (2006). Sliding versus deciding: Inertia and the premarital cohabitation effect. *Family Relations,* 55(4), 499–509. https://doi.org/10.1111/j.1741- 3729.2006.00418.x. Also, see Pearson, M. E., Stanley, S. M., & Rhoades, G. K. (n.d.). *Within my reach.* PREPInc. https://prepinc. com/collections/within-my-reach.

2. Everett, B. G., Turner, B., Hughes, T. L., Veldhuis, C. B., Paschen-Wolff, M., & Phillips, G. (2019). Sexual orientation disparities in pregnancy risk behaviors and pregnancy among sexually active teenage girls: Updates from the youth risk behavior survey. *LGBT Health,* 6(7), 342–349. https://doi.org/10.1089/ lgbt.2018.0206.

   Charlton, B. M., Roberts, A. L., Rosario, M., Katz-Wise, S. L., Calzo, J. P., Spiegelman, D., & Austin, S. B. (2018). Teen pregnancy risk factors among young women of diverse sexual orientations. *Pediatrics,* 141(4). https:// doi.org/10.1542/peds.2017-2278.

   Goldberg, S. K., Reese, B. M., & Halpern, C. T. (2016). Teen pregnancy among sexual minority women: Results from the National longitudinal study of adolescent to adult health. *Journal of Adolescent Health,* 59(4), 429–437. https://doi.org/10.1016/j.jadohealth.2016.05.009.

   Lindley, L. L., & Walsemann, K. M. (2015). Sexual orientation and risk of pregnancy among New York City high-school students. *American Journal of Public Health,* 105(7), 1379–1386. https:// doi. org/10.2105/ajph.2015.302553.

   Poteat, V.P., Russell, S. T., & Dewaele, A. (2019). Sexual health risk behavior disparities among male and female adolescents using identity and behavior indicators of sexual orientation. *Archives of Sexual Behavior,* 48(4), 1087–1097. https:// doi.org/10.1007/s10508 -017-1082-6.

Hughto, J. M., Biello, K. B., Reisner, S. L., Perez-Brumer, A., Heflin, K. J., & Mimiaga, M. J. (2016). Health risk behaviors in a representative sample of bisexual and heterosexual female high school students in Massachusetts. *Journal of School Health, 86*(1), 61–71. https://doi. org/10.1111/josh.12353.

Ybarra, M. L., Rosario, M., Saewyc, E., & Goodenow, C. (2016). Sexual behaviors and partner characteristics by sexual identity among adolescent girls. *Journal of Adolescent Health, 58*(3), 310–316. https:// doi.org/10.1016/j.jadohealth.2015.11.001.

See also Centers for Disease Control *Youth Risk Behavior Survey 2019* on sexual risk factors by reported identity. And particularly: Kann, L., Olsen, E. O., McManus, T., Harris, W. A., Shanklin, S. L., Flint, K. H., Queen, B., Lowry, R., Chyen, D., Whittle, L., Thornton, J., Lim, C., Yamakawa, Y., Brener, N., & Zaza, S. (2016). Sexual identity, sex of sexual contacts, and health-related behaviors among students in grades 9–12—United States and selected sites, 2015. *MMWR. Surveillance Summaries, 65*(9), 1–202. https:// doi.org/10.15585/mmwr. ss6509a1.

3. Haskins, R., & Sawhill, I. V. (2009). *Creating an opportunity society.* Brookings Institution Press. Data for their analysis drawn from CPS (Current Population Survey) Annual Social and Economic Supplement.

Wang, W., & Wilcox, W. B. (2017). The millennial success sequence: Marriage, kids, and the success sequence of young adults. *National Longitudinal Survey of Youth (NLSY)*. Data drawn from the National Longitudinal Survey of Youth (NLSY) to study the success sequence among the current generation of adults age 28–34.

4. Inanc, H., Spitzer, A., & Goesling, B. (2021). *Administration for Children & Families (OPRE Report 2021-148): "Assessing Benefits of Success Sequence for Economic Self-Sufficiency and Family Stability."* Washington, D.C: Targeted News Service. https://www.acf.hhs.gov

/opre/report/assessing-benefits-success-sequence-economic-self-s ufficiency-and-family-stability.

5. Ibid.
6. Ibid.
7. Ibid. See Figure 3 in report.
8. Ibid.
9. In the evaluation by OPRE, family stability was measured by *(1) the presence of 2 adults in the home, (2) the number of residential partner transitions, and (3) relationship satisfaction between the parents.*
10. Wang, W., & Wilcox, W. B. (2017). The millennial success sequence: Marriage, kids, and the success sequence of young adults. *National Longitudinal Survey of Youth (NLSY).* Data drawn from the National Longitudinal Survey of Youth (NLSY) to study the success sequence among the current generation of adults age 28–34.
11. Using longitudinal data from the National Longitudinal Survey of Youth allowed Wang and Wilcox to better capture the order of certain life events—for example, whether marriage occurred before or after childbearing along with the other key milestones of education and employment. And it could capture those who completed the first two milestones of their success sequence model (education and employment) but did not have children and were not married. Wang and Wilcox refer to this as "on track" in their report.
12. Wang, W., & Wilcox. W. B. (2017).
13. Hemez, P., & Manning, W. D. (2017). Over twenty-five years of change in cohabitation experience in the U.S., 1987- 2013. *Family Profiles, FP-17-02.* Bowling Green, OH: National Center for Family & Marriage Research. http://www.bgsu. edu/ncfmr/resources/data /family-profiles/hemez-manning-25-years-change-cohabitation -fp-17-02.html.

> Lamidi, E. O., Manning, W. D., & Brown, S. L. (2019). Change in the Stability of First Premarital Cohabitation Among Women in

the United States, 1983-2013. *Demography, 56*(2), 427–450. https:// doi. org/10.1007/s13524-019-00765-7.

Eickmeyer, K. J. (2019). Cohort Trends in Union Dissolution During Young Adulthood. *Journal of Marriage and the Family, 81*(3), 760–770. https://doi. org/10.1111/jomf.12552.

Eickmeyer, K. J., & Manning, W. D. (2018). Serial Cohabitation in Young Adulthood: Baby Boomers to Millennials. *Journal of Marriage and Family, 80*(4), 826-840. https://doi.org/10.1111/jomf.12495.

14. Horowitz, J. M., Graf, N., & Livingston, G. (2019, November). *Marriage and cohabitation in the U.S.* Pew Research Center's Social & Demographic Trends Project. See table on page 20.

15. Martin, J. A. (2021, March 23). Births: Final Data for 2019. *National Vital Statistics Reports 70, no. 2.* https://www.cdc.gov/ nchs/data /nvsr/nvsr70nvsr70-02-508.pdf.

16. Author's calculations from National Vital Statistics Report. (2021, March 23). Nonmarital birth share for women 24 and under, 2019, was overall 71.4%. (White: 61.0%, Non-Hispanic Black: 90.9%, Hispanic: 73.9%, Asian 43.4%.)

17. Guttmacher Institute. (2019, January). *Unintended Pregnancy in the United States.* https://www.guttmacher.org/ews-release/2016/us-un intended-regnancy-rate-falls-30-year-low-declines-seen-almost-all -groups.

Sawhill, I.V. (2014). *Generation unbound: Drifting into sex and parenthood without marriage.* Brookings Institution Press.

18. For a breakdown according to age, education, and race, see: Child Trends. (2018, August 8). *Dramatic increase in the proportion of births outside of marriage.*

Sawhill, I. V. (2014). *Generation unbound: Drifting into sex and parenthood without marriage.* Brookings Institution Press.

19. Fomby, P., & Osborne, C. (2016). Family instability, multipartner fertility, and behavior in middle childhood. *Journal of Marriage and Family, 79*(1), 75–93. https:// doi.org/10.1111/jomf.12349.

McLanahan, S., & Beck, A. N. (2010). Parental relationships in fragile families. *The Future of Children, 20*(2), 17–37. https://doi.org /10.1353/foc.2010.0007.

See Reeves, R. V., & Kraus, E. (2015). Cohabiting parents differ from married ones in three big ways. *The Future of Children, 25*(2), 17–37. See section on stability/longevity.

ACKNOWLEDGMENTS

1. https://www.commentary.org/articles/shelby-steele/on-being-black -and-middle-class/.

ABOUT THE AUTHOR

Ian V. Rowe is a senior fellow at the American Enterprise Institute, where he focuses on education and upward mobility, family formation, and adoption. Mr. Rowe is the cofounder and CEO of Vertex Partnership Academies, a new network of character-based, International Baccalaureate public charter high schools opening in the Bronx in 2022 and is the chairman of the board for Spence-Chapin, a nonprofit adoption services organization that provides adoption and adoption support services. Rowe is a senior visiting fellow at the Woodson Center and a writer for the 1776 Unites Campaign. He is a trustee at the Thomas B. Fordham Institute and a senior advisor for the Foundation Against Intolerance & Racism (FAIR For All), Parents Defending Education, and the National Summer School Initiative (NSSI).

Mr. Rowe is widely published and quoted in the popular press, including the *Wall Street Journal, USA Today, C-SPAN*, the *New York Post*, the *Washington Examiner, Education Week*, and *Education Next*. In addition to serving ten years as CEO of Public Prep, a nonprofit network of public charter schools based in the South Bronx and Lower East Side of Manhattan, he was deputy director of postsecondary success at the Bill & Melinda Gates Foundation. Rowe won two public service Emmys while serving as the senior vice president of strategic partnerships and public affairs at MTV. He was the director of strategy and performance measurement at the USA Freedom Corps office in the White House and cofounder and president of Third Millennium Media. In its early days, Mr. Rowe was also a senior staff member for Teach For America.

After receiving a high school diploma in electrical engineering from Brooklyn Technical High School, he earned a Bachelor of Science degree in Computer Science Engineering from Cornell University's College of Engineering. He earned an MBA from Harvard Business School, where he was the first black editor-in-chief of the *Harbus*, the Harvard Business School newspaper. Serving as an elected school board member, he resides in Pelham, New York, with his wife and two children.